Making This Better

Making This Better

Rosie Joseph

To order additional copies of this book, contact:
Xlibris
800-056-3182
www.Xlibrispublishing.co.uk
Orders@Xlibrispublishing.co.uk
797817

CONTENTS

APRIL 2007 - 'THE WAR'

MAY 2007

JUNE 2007

MY JOURNAL –A TEST OF TIME

2008

ROSIE'S JOURNAL FINDING MYSELF

2009

2010

2011

2012

'**Hope** – A belief that a desire will come to fulfilment
To want something to happen or to come true......

DEDICATION

This book is dedicated to all those who have supported us on our journey, and in the process of sharing our story. A special thanks to my sister for her honesty and understanding; we would not be here today if it were not for you and the advice you gave.

To my husband also, this was a brave thing to do and I love you for it.

This is a book to help those whose lives have
been blown apart by infidelity.

When my husband had an affair it was as if a bomb had been dropped
on our life together and blown it apart, it would never be the same
again. I came to call that part of my life 'The War'

I thought that to stay with my husband was all I ever wanted in
life, but then I found that I would struggle every day; fighting my own
mind. So I kept a journal and as a result I found myself. In this book
I share my journal that I kept all those years ago, true to what I wrote
then. I then reflect on how I feel about those entries now, all these
years later, after I have learned so much.

This is my story of how I survived my husband's infidelity and
how we survived as a couple: stronger and real.

If you have found yourself in the bleak place where I was once then
I hope this book helps you to grow stronger and survive whatever path
you take.

Out of respect to some of the people who were caught up in the
aftermath of our 'War' I have used a pseudonym, and all names and
places have been changed.

But I can assure you that the journal entries and the story is just
as it happened, just in a different place to where it happened with
different names.

Rosie

".........People need someone to look up to
I never found anyone who fulfil my needs
A lonely place to be
So I learned to depend on me

**The greatest love of all – George Benson
Written by Linda Creed, Michael Masser •**

CHAPTER 1

1998 - Finding each other

I first met Danny when my mum was gravely ill. I was in a nightclub with my friend who had persuaded me to go out to take my mind off things. We bumped into Danny with his friends, and my friend introduced us. As the night wore on Danny had come over to chat to us; he kept kneeling on the floor and singing to me but I was just ignoring him. When he asked for my number I was hesitant because I didn't even know if I fancied him at the time; but I gave him my number, telling him he could only call me on one particular night; I knew that he was keen when that was exactly what he did.

As we chatted on the phone I explained that I was a single parent and that my mum had cancer and was gravely ill; Danny seemed to understand and was really easy to talk to, so I agreed to go out with him. Although I wasn't sure about the attraction I needed a distraction from all of the pain and sadness that I was going through at the time. But when the day of the date arrived Danny didn't phone when he said he would. I was a bit surprised and pissed off; I'd thought that he was really keen.

A year later virtually to the day I met Danny again in the same nightclub; it seemed as if it was destined because I was out with the same friend. He came over to me, very apologetic that he had not called, and asked if we could start again. As we chatted I explained that my mum had died the year before and he seemed so embarrassed that he had let me down.

This time I did find him attractive and we spent the whole night together kissing. But being stubborn I refused to give him my number again. Undeterred Danny called my friend for my number and rang me the next day and we arranged to go on a date. On the day of the date Danny called 'just to check' that I still wanted to go. I found that really sweet, that he liked me that much he was worried I wouldn't go.

We went to a pub near to where I lived and during the date I asked Danny why he had not called the year before; he said that he felt I had too much going on to take him on as well, and that he was not sure if I really fancied him or not. It surprised me that he had obviously picked up that vibe from me; and I liked that. He made me laugh all night and came back to my house for coffee, and yes, he stayed. But now, looking back we did not make love because he was too nervous about disappointing me.

From our first date I felt that Danny would never let me down. I needed someone who would be there for me and support me. I was sick of trying to support myself and Ethan; sick of all of the crap that had happened in my life and here was a kind, caring man, who obviously really liked me.

I had always been so careful who I introduced to Ethan, but I knew that this time I wanted to introduce Danny to him; it all just felt right. Ethan loved Danny's fun loving ways and the fact that he liked computer games; Danny and I became inseparable, with him staying most nights and going to work from my house, we had quickly moulded into a family unit. After six weeks Danny moved into my home and we were engaged four months later. I can remember how Danny had said "All I want is for you to be my wife, I love you so much."

And I loved him too, so much....

CHAPTER 2

1999 - Wedding Days

On the night before our wedding Danny was leaving to stay at his brother's house. As he walked away from our house he turned to me and said "You will turn up won't you?" I laughed at him; I loved him so much why would I not turn up?

The next day as I walked towards Danny at the registry office he would not look at me, he was so nervous. "Do you want to marry Rosie?" asked the Registrar. Danny laughed and said "Yes". "Then hold her hand!" said the Registrar; and everyone laughed.

I loved Danny so much, but I knew that he had been insecure in the past and had experienced some difficult times. It was a standing joke amongst his friends that things always went wrong for Danny, so much so that they called him 'Lucky Danny'. At the wedding reception I was asked to do a speech I said how much I loved Danny and believed in him; that I knew he was called 'Lucky Danny' but I also knew that he would never let me down.

I was so happy: here was a kind wonderful man who worshipped Ethan and I; and loved the family life that he had found.

I treasured a picture of us both that someone had taken at our wedding without our knowledge; it was so natural. Danny had his arm around my shoulders as he chatted to someone and both of us looked so happy.

Little did I know that the picture would be one of the many casualties of 'The War'.

CHAPTER 3

1999 - 2003 - Building our Idyllic life

After marrying we worked hard to buy a house of our own. Danny changed his career and went to work for a railway company; and I went back to work with a local healthcare provider. The house we bought needed major renovation but that did not deter us and we worked hard in the evening and at weekends, turning it into something beautiful.

We were happy and would have wonderful evenings with our friends and neighbours but the area that we lived in was just outside London and it was changing, so we decided that we should chase the dream and move to a house by the sea.

Due our close proximity to London we gained a large profit from the sale of our home enabling us to buy a beautiful Edwardian house with a balcony, huge fireplaces, original sash windows, and a tiled path leading up to it; add to that it was in an avenue that led down to the sea and it was quite simply, perfect.

Danny was offered a job with a small railway company in our new area, and despite my promotions at work I was able to transfer my role to Hastings. We thought we had it made; Danny could work with a new company in Hastings, and would not have to commute back to his old job; and I could work part time with a new role in a company close to where we lived.

I remember clearly how on moving day, after the removal men had left, we stood in the kitchen with a celebratory drink and Danny burst into tears. He couldn't believe his life now: married to me, with a family of his own and a beautiful house in a leafy avenue that led down to the beach.

But the job with the new railway company fell through. Although Danny was bitterly disappointed he was happy to commute and only wanted me to work part-time to give me time to take care of him and Ethan. I was happy to work part-time, but not long after our move a full-time job came up, a good job as an Executive Assistant within a large organisation, and I wanted to take it. Danny didn't want me to go back to work full-time; he wanted to look after me; he wanted me to need him. But I persuaded him that we needed the money and it would be beneficial for us all and I took the job.

By this time everything had fallen into place, we had the beautiful house, were both earning good money and we were so in love. My life was perfect.

CHAPTER 4

2003 -2006 - Trouble was brewing

Over time we got to know more and more people: We would spend time with our neighbours and friends Jess and Matt at their beach hut. Often sitting on the beach until past midnight, chatting and watching the moon reflect on the sea;

By now I had returned to work part-time because Danny had wanted me to see to the renovations of the house whilst he commuted to work and worked overtime to enable us to do what we wanted to do. I was happy to let Danny support me, I loved that he wanted to provide for both Ethan and I and I loved him for it.

I would work for half a day four days a week and then come home and work hard on the house, painting nearly every room and managing the installation of a new bathroom and kitchen We both loved our house and loved what we had achieved.

We found it to be a friendly community, and made friends with all our neighbours, often going out with a couple who lived in our street; although they argued a lot and I found her to be quite competitive with other women, including me. She would flirt with Danny, inviting him to go outside for cigarettes with her; but I wasn't worried because I knew that Danny loved me so much, I was safe, and we were safe.

Despite all of my apprehensions I thought that she seemed unhappy and so I befriended her, often inviting them out with us, or over to our house.

In the July of 2006 they had a party where there had been lots of alcohol available. I had been in the kitchen and when I walked into the garden I could see 'her' pulling Danny onto the dancefloor that 'had been set up in the garden. I was shocked that Danny was going with 'her' and I marched up to them and pulled him away. I said that I was not comfortable with them dancing together; but Danny just laughed and said that "there was nothing to it."

I was starting to think that 'she' and Danny were too friendly. I was angry with Danny because we had talked about 'her' behaviour towards him only that morning, and how I was starting to feel uncomfortable with it all; but even then Danny had just laughed it off. When I found him agreeing to dance with her it hurt me that he seemed to have no care for my feelings. Alarm bells were ringing, and I wasn't listening. But I trusted Danny and so I thought that I was being stupid doubting him.

For our wedding anniversary that year, Danny bought me a red glass heart, the card with it said to take care of it because it held his love for me.

Little did I know how fragile that love really was.

CHAPTER 5

March 2007 - Gaslighting

It was a Saturday night and Danny was on a night shift. I was watching the television in the living room half asleep when Ethan came in and said "Mum, there's a weird message on our phone"

I listened to the message and I could hear my blood start to pound in my ears as the robotic voice said "Been thinking about you all day today, can't stop. I can't wait to be with you, I want you so much."

I sat up, Ethan was looking at me as he said "What does it mean mum?"

I lied and said "Probably the wrong number." But after he left the room I redialled and listened again. Then I checked the number, it was 'her' number. I called Danny:, "Why is 'she' sending text messages to our landline that say that 'she' wants you?" I asked.

I could hear the panic in Danny's voice. "What? I don't know! What does it say?"

"I told you to be careful of her; I told you she could cause us damage." I said. "Is there something going on between you?"

But Danny just said "No darling, there is nothing going on. I don't know why 'she' sent a message to our house. I have said before that I think we should stop having anything to do with them."

I thought back to how Danny had suggested that we stop spending time with them, but then 'she' would come over for something and Danny would change his mind.

Ten minutes later my phone rang: it was 'her' "I'm so sorry; I think I sent a text to your landline number by mistake. It was meant to go to this man that I have been seeing. Please don't tell my partner as I have been doing it behind his back, please don't tell him will you?" 'She' said.

My gut told me not to believe 'her' so I was cool to 'her' and told 'her' to "just forget it" But later that night 'she' knocked at the door, 'she' was pissed and kept saying how 'sorry' 'she' was. I told 'her' to just go home; but I didn't sleep that night.

When Danny got home the next morning I was up waiting for him. I said how I had warned him that 'she' was unhappy and dangerous to be around. We both agreed that we didn't want to spend time with them anymore. We sat at the breakfast bar in our beautiful kitchen and Danny stroked my hand and looked me in the eyes and said "Seriously darling, do you really think that I am going to risk all that we have for someone like 'her'? I would never risk losing you I love you so much."

I believed him, I wanted to.

The following week 'she' invited us to their house for a meal to celebrate my birthday from the previous January; because they had not been available to come out for the celebrations, and to say how sorry 'she' was for the text 'she' had sent.

Danny said it would look rude if we did not go.

As per usual 'she' kept topping up my glass with wine, I never managed to finish a glass before 'she' poured some more. As the evening wore on 'she' and Danny went outside for a cigarette, as they always did, and I saw 'her' reach out and stroke him, it was how 'she' touched him, and I knew! I knew!!

I lost my temper and accused them of having an affair but they cried me down, telling me I was imagining it. 'Her' partner just stood there watching, he did not seem bothered and I thought that it must be me.

Danny took me home, told me I was imagining things, that I had acted like an idiot and then returned their house without me.

I was in my pyjamas, wandering around the house like a mad woman, muttering to myself that they were trying to make a fool of me. I clearly remember shouting at the poor dog, "They think I am some sort of stupid cunt, but I know"

Eventually I went back to their house; because I was in my pyjamas and dressing gown I must have looked like an insane woman as I walked down the road; I was convinced that I was going to catch them out.

But when I burst through the door all three of them were sitting there having coffee. 'she' was holding court, as 'she' had all evening, saying how 'she' had lost weight, how 'she' measured us all to see who was the shortest: me!

But I looked like even more of a fool, standing there in my nightclothes, and it just reinforced the idea that I was imagining it.

But now I know: I should have gone with my gut!!

CHAPTER 6

April 2007 - 'The War' is declared

A Monday in April 2007

It was Easter Monday and an unusually hot day for the time of year, so we decided to invite some friends to a BBQ, including 'them'; and our old friends Susan and Malcolm who had recently moved to our area.

Danny and I had been shopping to buy food and drink for the BBQ. I loved being able to do this with him because he was so often at work. As we walked around the supermarket I slipped my hand up the back of his shirt and stroked the small patch of hair that he had at the bottom of his back. It was something that I did so often, we always held hands and stroked each other. I was so happy.

By early evening the BBQ was well under way and we were all having a great time: lots of alcohol had been consumed and people were dancing in the kitchen. I was exhausted from all of the preparation and just a little bit pissed, so I went into our snug off of the kitchen and sat down and as I did so 'her' partner approached me.

"You know that they have been texting each other don't you?" He said "That there is something going on behind our backs."

I assumed that he had seen the text message 'she' had sent to our house so I looked at him and said, "That's not true. Danny loves me too much to put our relationship at risk."

He smiled as he proceeded to tell me how he had been monitoring 'her' phone without 'her' knowledge and that 'she' and Danny had been messaging each other for some time.

He told me that he had told Danny that he knew and that he had confronted them both upstairs in my house only hours earlier, and told them that he was going to tell me. He seemed to take joy in telling me that Danny didn't care and had told him to go ahead and tell me. He pointed out to me that only that afternoon 'she' and Danny had been kissing in the pantry and he had caught them; that he and Danny had argued about it; he emphasised how much 'she' and Danny had been making a fool of me in my own home.

Through the open doorway I could see Danny looking at us, with everyone dancing and singing around him; and he was oblivious to anything other than what was going on with me and what I was being told. The look on his face was one of pure pain. You could see he was thinking 'That's it! I've lost her! She knows!' I knew then that what I was being told was true.

I couldn't believe it; I wanted Danny to come in and tell me I was being told lies; but I knew at that point that that even if he had I would not believe him. I realised at that moment that I had denied what was happening; I had lied to myself, I felt like a stupid bitch for fooling myself. I could hear the blood rushing in my ears, hear 'her' laughing in the kitchen; it was like everything was in slow motion and I wanted to fucking kill 'her'.

All hell broke loose: I went into the kitchen and screamed at Danny, screamed at 'her' and told 'her' partner to get out. Everybody just stopped and looked at me and when Susan asked what was going on; I shouted how Danny had been seeing 'her' behind my back.

I stumbled up to the balcony, the beautiful balcony that had made me fall in love with our house; our forever home. I couldn't believe that my life was crumbling around me. I thought that Danny would come up to me but 'she' came up instead, to say that I had to understand that they were just 'friends', that they supported each other, that they had just been talking to each other, and how I must accept that.

I told her to 'get off the balcony and leave me alone' and that if 'she' didn't I was going to 'push 'her' off the fucking balcony'. I swear to God, I would have.

Downstairs the music had been turned off and there was a stunned silence. I could hear my friend Susan ask Danny if it was true, and I could hear Danny crying. I couldn't bear it, I just felt as if I was in a dream and I had to get out of the house. I ran down the stairs and out of the door, but it was my dear friend Susan who ran after me, not Danny. I was sobbing uncontrollably and kept asking Susan how he could have done this to me. We walked to the end of the road with me babbling about how it couldn't be true, about how Danny loved his life too much.

Susan didn't know what to do with me, and was trying to persuade me to go back to the house when Danny walked down the road towards us: he too was sobbing, and I knew from his reaction that it was true. Danny was with Susan's husband Malcolm, who just looked shell-shocked and didn't know what to say.

I lunged at Danny and just screamed at him, saying how I couldn't believe he had done this, had ruined everything we had, everything we had worked so hard for; and I ran back to the house. I was convinced that Danny would come after me, tell me that it would all be alright, and say how sorry he was.

But he didn't come back…

CHAPTER 7

October 2006 - Remembering

(Lying to Myself, Gas lighting)

By the October of 2006 I had started to grow uneasy about Danny and 'her'. They seemed to be having more and more smoking time outside, leaving me with 'her' partner. 'She' seemed to be more and more competitive towards me; 'she' lost weight and was always dressed up in something new. I had put on weight and weighed well over fifteen stone, and I had started to feel insecure about my looks.

We had decided to have a big Halloween party; but on the day of the party Danny and I had a serious talk about 'her' behaviour and how 'she' was making me feel. I asked Danny to be careful of 'her', explained that I thought 'she' was trying to cause trouble between us; felt as if 'she' was trying to ridicule me. I explained that when he spent so much time with 'her' outside she relished in it and would smirk at me when 'she' came back in. Danny just laughed and said that I had nothing to worry about.

For the party Danny bought me a new dress to wear and a pair of black leather calf length boots; so that I could dress up as a glamorous witch. But on the night of the party she arrived dressed as a black cat, wearing shorts and cat ears. Although I knew that I was prettier than her I felt so unattractive; I just knew that her outfit was for the benefit of Danny.

As the party wore on I couldn't find Danny anywhere. I eventually found him sitting on the sofa and 'she' was sitting on his lap. I went fucking mad and pulled her off. (When I look back now I wished I had punched her as well) I told Danny that if I ever found out that he was cheating on me I would do it back to him tenfold, and I would always have my revenge; warning him that if he had so much as kissed 'her' I would do the same and more.

I stormed out of the party thinking that Danny would come after me because I had been so upset. But he didn't my friend Nel came after me and in the pit of my stomach I knew that we needed to get out of our relationship with 'them.'

CHAPTER 8

April 2007 - The early hours….

I couldn't believe Danny didn't come back. Malcolm told me that he had tried to persuade him but that Danny was too afraid to face me. Malcolm said that as he had been talking to Danny 'she' had walked past them and Danny had followed 'her'.

I was in a state of disbelief! How could Danny, the man who loved me so much, not come back to comfort me?

I couldn't stay in the house; I had to find him, I had to make him come home so we could talk. I went down to the seafront to see if I could see him. I didn't believe for one minute that Danny would have gone with 'her' and had convinced myself that he would have been so distraught, because he loved me so much, that he might have tried to commit suicide thinking he had lost me. I really thought that he had thrown himself in the sea because he was so upset!

It was the early hours of the morning and pitch black down on the beach but I didn't care if I was in danger, or alone in the dark; I had to get Danny back.

I ran up and down the beach screaming out his name, but there was no sign of him. So I ran along the seafront into town still calling out his name: I didn't care if I woke anyone up, didn't care if they would be angry with me, didn't care about anything other than trying to make my life go back to normal. I was crying and sobbing, uncontrollably at times, but there was nobody to see me, the streets were deserted and Danny was nowhere to be seen.

I must have looked like a mad woman, walking up and down the seafront calling for Danny; I just didn't believe he would throw it all away.

I called his mobile a hundred times but it just went to voicemail. I begged him to come home, told him we could work it out; but he never answered, and he never called me back.

I went to bed, and lay there waiting to hear Danny's key in the lock. I couldn't sleep and by five in the morning I was so afraid that he had done something stupid I called the police. When they arrived I could see the pity on their faces: here was this overweight woman, with a bloated tear stained face, whose husband had clearly been playing away behind her back. One of the policemen looked at me with sadness in his eyes (they must have seen it so many times before) and said that there was nothing they could do; they believed that Danny had chosen to leave and that they didn't think he was missing.

APRIL 2007 - 'THE WAR'

CHAPTER 9

'The War' - Day 1 – Being Strong

A Tuesday in April 2007

I didn't sleep all night I lay in bed and then got up and just walked between living room and kitchen, I just couldn't sit still. I looked out at the debris from the BBQ: sausages and burgers burnt to crisp, paper napkins strewn across the garden, half full bottles of wine and glasses with drinks left in them and I was afraid to go out there.

I was going mad not knowing where Danny was, or knowing if he was with 'her'. I could not understand how my life had gone from holding hands with my husband yesterday morning to him being with someone else by today. I still didn't believe he was with 'her', surely he would have known that there would be no chance of reconciliation if he was; and surely he would not have thrown that away. Surely he wouldn't?

I needed to make sense of it but didn't know who I could turn to, the people that Danny and I had relied on since moving to the coast four years before had been each other; and now he wasn't here.

I went to my friend Della's house and just broke down. She hugged me and said that she would go out in her car and look for Danny; she couldn't believe that Danny had been seeing 'her', didn't believe that he would go with 'her'. She said 'she' was no comparison to me; that surely Danny knew that.

Della drove all around the town but couldn't find Danny. I could see that she just didn't know what to do to help me. I think the pain that I felt at that time was so palpable that others could actually feel it.

I went back to my house in turmoil; I had no idea what to say to Ethan who seemed to be swinging between anger and denial at what Danny had done. So I did the only thing I could do and I started to load the dishwasher: it was a simple, normal thing to do in the world of madness I had now been thrown into.

At ten o clock Danny called me from 'her' mobile. He said that he didn't have his mobile with him, and I hadn't heard it ringing when I called him because it had been on silent. It was then that I realised that it had been on silent for weeks if not months now: It was always on silent: to ensure that I didn't know when 'she' had been texting him.

I couldn't believe that Danny was with 'her'. I asked him what he was doing, was he with 'her'? A stupid question given he had called from 'her' phone, but I just didn't want to believe it what was clearly true. Danny said that he was with 'her' and that he was coming to pick up his stuff. My heart came into my mouth; I could feel it beating so hard that I thought it would burst: Why was he coming to pick up his stuff? I asked him what did he mean, and Danny said that he was leaving with 'her'.

I was dumbstruck! I didn't know what to say it was as if the world was in slow motion. I could not process what Danny had just said; the blood was rushing in my ears, drowning out any other noise, then he put the phone down.

When Danny came to the house he knocked on the door and didn't use his key. When I opened the door he would not look at me and was cold towards me; not the loving man that I had just spent the last nine years of my life with.

I was crying and asked Danny why he was going with 'her'? How long had it been going on? Had he sex with 'her'? Did he have sex with 'her' last night? Where had they stayed? Had they been together? Danny wouldn't answer me other than to say that he had not had sex with 'her'. I wanted to believe him; I needed to believe him; because at that moment I couldn't bear to think about the alternative.

In my mind if they had not had sex I could forgive him, we could survive, we could get through this, and I could put it behind me. So I begged and pleaded with him to stay, but he wouldn't listen; he started to cry as he said that because of what he had done he knew that I would do it back to him, that I had told him that at the Halloween party; that he would not be able to bear me being with someone else; that he was so afraid of that. I just looked at him in disbelief: he was telling me that he was going to leave because he couldn't bear the thought of me doing to him what he had done to me!

I was so fucking angry that I just flew at him and punched the shit out of him; I just kept punching and punching and Danny just let me, until I couldn't punch him anymore. I stood there out of breath and sobbing and he just walked away and went upstairs to collect his things. I heard him moving about packing as I just sat there. What could I do, he wouldn't listen to me?

When Danny came down the stairs he told me that he was meeting 'her' in the park and leaving with 'her'. I asked him why? He said because it was best to go with her than stay with me waiting for me to get my revenge.

In desperation I rang Danny's mum in the hope that she would help me and talk some sense into him; she asked him to think about what he was doing, although Danny was crying he just kept saying that he had to leave that he couldn't stay.

I was begging him, promising him that I wouldn't make him pay, and promising him anything. But suddenly I heard myself: I was begging somebody who had just spent the night with another woman to stay with me. Someone who had been making a fool of me for God knows how long. I suddenly stopped; I wasn't going to do this; I was worth more than this, I wasn't going to beg.

Danny made his way to the door and stopped and looked at me. I said "just go; I am not begging you to stay" and I walked away from him and up the stairs. I really thought at that point he would stay; that he would come after me and say it was all a terrible mistake; so I couldn't believe it when I heard the door close and his car start up and pull away. I just sat on the bed with this suffocating silence around me. What the fuck had happened? How did we go from being so happy to this? How could it be the end; of something I had believed to be so beautiful?

As I sat there something within me told me to get it together, I had to survive for Ethan and I. It was as if a fire had been lit, and, little did I know then, I was getting back the person that I used to be before my mum died, or that the fire inside me would never be put out again.

I called my friend Toni in Cornwall; she had always been there for me when I needed her; she couldn't believe what I told her, said that she would come straight away, drive through the night if she had to and be with me the next day.

Ethan rang my sister Louise who I hadn't spoken to for six years; despite that she was immediately there for me, told me to go to her in Essex; but I knew that there was something I had to do first: I had a shower and washed my hair and made sure I looked my best, but this time it was for me. I checked our bank account on line and could see that Danny had already drawn out his daily limit of two hundred pounds and I was so angry: he didn't give a shit about us, and now he was taking our fucking money! I knew that for Ethan and me to survive I needed to fight back and the only way we would do that was for me to stay strong and to move fast.

I went to the bank in town and opened my own bank account; I then went home and transferred all our savings that we had saved for our holiday from our savings account into my bank account, along with all of the money from our joint current account. Danny had only been paid the Friday before so virtually all of his salary was in the joint account and I now had it all. This meant that they were well and truly fucked because Danny had no control over my account because it was just in my name which meant that they had no access to any more of our money.

After that I called the bank's general line and told them that we had split up and could they freeze the joint account. Ethan and I needed money to survive and it wasn't going to happen on a part time secretary's salary. That was it done, I had left them with nothing other than each other, and I hoped they were happy!

How I kept it together whilst I sat in that bank I don't know. I never let it show that anything was wrong, or that I was upset in any way. I knew what I had to do, and that kept me going. But I wasn't finished: I called Danny's car insurance and told them that he didn't live at our address anymore; which meant that Danny's car insurance was null and void because they cancelled it immediately. I hoped that they had a fucking accident.

My friend Sherri from work called and said that all of the girls in the office were worried about me, what could she do? I was just crying and talking gibberish so she said that she would come to my house that evening. I asked if she could come the next day as my sister had told me to go to her for the night.

I went upstairs to our bedroom, our beautiful bedroom, with its original fireplace and tongue and groove walls, the sun was streaming in through the windows and it looked so pretty; and then I looked at the bed where only two nights before I had lain in with Danny. I felt as if I was in a nightmare that I was going to wake up from if I tried hard enough.

I went out onto the balcony and looked down at the empty space where Danny's car had been parked, and reality hit me like a wave: he really was gone. I changed the bedding; I couldn't bear to lie in a bed where Danny had lay with me, all the time making a fool of me. The tears brimmed over and I couldn't stop them, I sobbed and sobbed; great big howling sobs. I felt as if I was in a parallel universe, hoped against hope that it was not real.

There was a knock at the door: it was 'her' partner who said that he had put a trace on their phones and he knew that they had been to the shopping outlet nearby and that they were somewhere in a seaside town just up the coast. After he left I just sat there in a state of shock because shopping was one of 'her' favourite pastimes, 'she' loved the shopping centre near to us, went there at least twice a week; and now 'she' was there with my husband. My husband was shopping with another woman, how could that be?

Ethan went to his friend's house; I don't think that he could bear to be in the house, it felt so sad; there was a stunned silence in the air. I could feel the strength throbbing through my veins; actually hear it pounding in my ears. I knew that I had to survive, so I got into my car and drove to Essex to be with my sister, and the tears ran down my face as I drove down the motorway. I didn't care who saw me as I sat in the queue for the River crossing, I knew that people were staring at me, let them stare; my fucking heart was broken.

When I got to my sister Louise's house the first thing she did was hug me with tears in her eyes, despite the fact that we had not spoken for so long; I just sobbed in her arms.

Danny's sister called my mobile and when I answered she was crying and saying that she couldn't believe Danny had done this to me; that she would call me the next day, come down to see me to make sure that I was alright. I was grateful that she had called, hoped that if Danny saw how upset she was it might make him see sense.

Louise asked me to go through what had happened; to tell her about our life over the last six years. She said that she was surprised that Danny had left me, because she always thought that it would be me who would leave Danny. But when I explained to her that I had worked part-time whilst Danny worked every hour he could; that in the past two months he had worked for eighteen days without a break: all different shifts, sometimes finishing work at six in the morning, coming home, going to bed, and then going back to work at ten at night, she looked at me and said "Who are you, Princess Fucking Tippy Toes? You need to get off your arse and go back to work full-time! No wonder 'she' was able to use things against you."

I knew at that moment that she was right.

Louise and her husband Tom gave me some wine and some 'paracetamol' for the pounding headache that had developed. I knew it had been caused by the floods of tears that I had cried since the night before and took the tablet gratefully. But in fact they had given me something to knock me out and help me sleep because I hadn't slept in nearly forty eight hours. Louise knew that I was going to need all my strength to get through this fight.

At one o clock in the morning I could hear my mobile phone bleeping, alerting me that there had been a missed call from an unknown number. I thought how it had to be Danny because I couldn't forget the look on his face when he knew I had found out. I just knew that despite the way he was behaving he was heartbroken; I can honestly say that I could feel his pain; but I couldn't face calling his mobile only for him to ignore it; I couldn't face that humiliation again. I told myself that I wanted to believe it was Danny but to face reality, he had left me and he had made it clear that he didn't love me, so I just let it go.

CHAPTER 10

'The War' - Day 2 - The Purge

After the missed call I had lain awake the rest of the night; I couldn't sleep: every time I closed my eyes I could see Danny and 'Her' having sex, kissing, naked together and it jolted me awake as if someone had slapped me.

By seven in the morning I knew that I had to face my reality so I woke my sister Louise and told her that I needed to go home. Poor Louise she was so tired after listening to me the night before: ranting like a mad woman, and here I was early the next morning ranting again. I had no concept of time or consideration for others, I was heartbroken and that was consuming me by the minute.

I had to go home, I had to face it: the garden, the house, all left exactly as it had been from two nights ago. I was terrified because I was going back to an empty house; a house where Danny was never going to be with me again. I left my sister with tears in her eyes; she didn't know what she could do for me to make it better, because there was nothing she could do. As I left she told me I was worth more than Danny, and I knew that she was right.

As I drove home I started to get angry, really angry at how they had made such a fool of me for so long; but mainly at how I had fucking let them. So by the time I arrived at the house I knew that I had to remove all remnants of Danny from it. As I pulled into the kerb outside the house I just sat in the car with an awful feeling of dread,

I was afraid to go into our beautiful loved house that was now so sad and empty.

I called Danny's sister to see if she had been able to talk any sense into him, in the hope that she would be able to tell me that she had and that Danny was coming home. But when she answered the phone she was very cool, in fact quite off; saying that she didn't want to talk to me because, after all, Danny was her brother and her loyalties should be with him. Just like that she didn't want to know me anymore! I just didn't understand any of it, how it could all change so quickly, or why his sister seemed to think Danny was doing the right thing. I couldn't understand why nobody from Danny's family had tried to make contact with me to see if I, or more importantly Ethan, was alright. I had been with Danny for nine years and now none of them seemed to give a shit that he had left, or about what he had done. It was at that point I started to wonder if I had been living a lie for the last nine years. It was really was just surreal.

My lovely neighbours Jess and Matt came out to me because they could see me crying in the car, and they knew that I was being watched. Jess put her arms around me and hugged me and I explained that I was terrified of going into the house, the empty house that only days before had been full of laughter and happiness. Jess told me she would come with me and as we went in I explained that I had to get every single item of Danny out of our house: everything that belonged to him that would trigger a memory of him. I had been living a lie, it had all been crap, I couldn't bear to look at the memories, couldn't bear to look at pictures and mementos that would taunt me, and remind me of what a load of shit my life had actually been.

There was one particular photo of Danny and Ethan that I loved: Ethan had his arms around Danny looking over his shoulders. We were so happy then, on holiday in Menorca, having a wonderful time. I just couldn't understand where that loving, kind, gentle man had gone. I couldn't bear to look at that photo ever again. I never did it got lost in aftermath of 'The War'.

So everything went: photos, jewellery, a tiny small silver heart Danny had bought me to hang from my silver bangle; the glass heart that he had bought me for our anniversary, the one that had, supposedly, held his love for me (what a load of shit that was!) All of it went into black bin liners. Danny's pants, his clothes, in fact every single thing that reminded me of our life together; and the bags were carried over to Della's house across the road and just thrown onto her driveway. Della had agreed to have it in her garden because she could see how distressed I was. I even took Danny's bike over and dumped it on the drive unceremoniously. Luckily Della's husband put it in the garage after I left, before it was stolen, because little did I know that I would need it in the future.

After we had finished Jess commented that when you walked into the house it was as if Danny had never existed. I didn't care if all the precious things we had together were stolen or smashed to pieces; I didn't care what would be lost. We were lost.

I asked Susan if Malcom would come and put a new lock on the door. There was no way that I was giving them the opportunity to just walk in the house and take things. Danny had left so he could fuck off if he thought he was just going to come back when he wanted to. Poor Malcom, he was Danny's friend, but he still came and changed the locks for me and put a security chain on the door.

My friend, my beautiful friend Toni arrived after driving the four hundred miles from Cornwall since early morning; she had brought with her a cheque for me to put in my bank to help me 'until things got sorted out'. It was a gesture that will remain with me for the rest of my life: that sometimes people just do things because they're kind, and not for any other reason. This gave me leverage; it helped my frenetic mind, it was a life saver at that time; and I felt good knowing that I had left Danny and her' without a penny to their name.

Ethan decided to go to his girlfriend's house in Essex. I understood why; he couldn't bear to see his mum, who was always so strong and had always kept it all together, even in the years when she was a single parent, in such a mess. It was frightening for him. He kept asking me if I was going to be alright, that we were going to be alright.

Remembering the way that I was then I can understand why Ethan thought that things might all go wrong.

My friend Sherrie from work arrived that evening and I could see she was shocked to see me as I was: A mad woman, going from intermittently swearing and calling Danny all the bastards (or worse) under the sun, to sobbing uncontrollably.

I had still not gone into the garden, it looked abandoned: as if everyone was eating and drinking one moment and then had got up and just left; which is exactly what had happened. The garden represented me and my life: abandoned.

I could literally not go out there; I was so afraid of the memories it held, with the remnants of that day all around me, taunting me; reminders of the day that I realised what a fucking fool they had made of me. There was stuff that belonged to 'them' everywhere: a heater, some chairs, plates, my friends just took it and dumped it in their garden. Everything else just got thrown away, including china plates, Danny's beloved BBQ tools, everything. I just didn't care. I wanted it gone along with the memories.

When I told my friends that 'her' partner had been to see me and had told me that he had put a tracker on their phone they told me to distance myself from him, to not listen to what he was saying because it wouldn't do me any good; I knew that they were right.

I weighed myself; I had lost six pounds in two days.

CHAPTER 11

'The War' – Day 3 - Shit Creek

A Thursday in April 2007

My poor friend Toni was up all night with me. I was sitting on the end of her bed, reliving what had happened over and over again: questioning things. I thought right back to our holidays the year before, when we had gone to their house for a drink and 'she' had come downstairs in new pyjamas, and how Danny had commented on them. How did Danny know that they were new? Nothing made sense and my mind was just trying to find a reason, any reason to answer my biggest question: why?

Toni suggested that I text Danny because she, along with all of our other friends, couldn't believe this was happening. To them it was clear that Danny had loved me so much that something must have happened to cause this. We had so much to sort out, not only about our relationship, but about the house and bills, our whole life in fact; and I needed to talk to him about what we would do.

I felt sick as I text Danny the next morning because I just didn't know this man anymore, and I was terrified that he would ignore me. I asked him to please answer my text and call me as we needed to talk about the house. I was shaking after I sent it because I was so afraid that if he contacted me he would tell me that he was still staying with 'her'. I hoped in my heart of hearts that if the missed call had been from Danny he was having second thoughts.

Little did I know it would be worse than I could have imagined.

Danny called me within five minutes and when I answered the phone he was cold and hard towards me. I could hear 'her' in the background and when Danny spoke to 'her' he sounded happy and upbeat as he relayed to 'her' what I was saying; I knew that 'she' was telling him what to say back to me. I just felt sick to my stomach that 'she' was now the person who was advising Danny against me!

I asked him if he was happy and he said that yes he was, 'very happy'. I just sat there on the outside step of our house listening to this man who I didn't know, in fact wondered if I had ever known him at all. How could he be happy when he had caused so much destruction?

Danny then asked me what I was going to do about the house; he said that I didn't earn enough money to keep it so what was I going to do. I said that I was going to keep the house and he snorted with derision and said "How will you keep it on what you earn? You won't be able to afford to!" I heard 'her' laugh in the background as he said it and Danny started to laugh too.

My heart was well and truly broken as I sat there listening to this man who I believed would never let me down, laugh at me with 'her'. I realised then that the plan was to get poor, fat Rosie out of the house and take everything from her because she only worked part time and would not be able to survive.

At that moment in time I hated Danny with all my heart. My eyes filled up with tears, but I would not cry, I would not let them know that I was broken; not this time.

Little did Danny know that his behaviour was like putting a match to a pilot flame: it re-ignited strength in me that I had not had since my mum had died. I told Danny that "I" was keeping the house; and that in a few months' time when he had "fuck all", and was up shit creek without a paddle, in a bedsit with nothing but a small T.V.", he would remember this conversation and how wrong he was. Then I hung up.

This time the only thing I could feel burning inside of me was anger, and I needed that to win, because I was fucked if that cunt was going to take everything from me. That was it! It was a battle and I was going to fucking beat them. All of them!

I felt better; the old Rosie was coming back.

My sister Louise called me and we talked about things that had happened leading up to the war, and the fact that Danny had brought the house up in the conversation. Louise said that it was clear that 'she' wanted my life: Danny, the house I had worked so hard on, and the money from Danny's job. Louise then said "She's' run off with the wrong one, because you are the driving force and she should have run off with you if 'she' wanted what you had."

What a fool, 'she' had picked on the wrong one this time!

> Took all the strength I had not to fall apart
> Trying hard to mend the pieces of my broken heart
> And I spent so many nights feeling sorry for myself
> I used to cry, but now I hold my head up high....

Performed by Chantey Savage Written by Mick Mars, Nikki Sixx

CHAPTER 12

'The War' – Day 4 - Battle Commences

Friday in April 2007

Toni took me to the Doctor; she was so worried about me: I couldn't sleep, every time I closed my eyes I pictured Danny together with 'her' naked and kissing; it was driving me insane. But it was when I called Danny's mum, despite the fact that it was two in the morning, that my friend knew I needed help. Danny's mum had been very cool towards me and said that she had not seen or heard from Danny; I was so upset, but Toni said it was probably because I had called her in the middle of the night and woken her.

I remember the Doctor being so kind when I told her what had happened between Danny and I: coming out from behind her desk to sit with me and hold my hand. I saw her close her eyes in disbelief because only two weeks before Danny had come to an appointment with me when I had been suffering from a recurrent chest infection. Danny had been worried I had cancer. Even the Doctor said that it didn't make sense: why he would do that if he was planning to leave me.

Toni told her that I was not sleeping at all and she advised me that the tablets she could prescribe would only help me get to sleep and wouldn't enable me to stay asleep. I never ever took those tablets: I was afraid to go to sleep and see Danny and 'her' having sex. I couldn't bear the thought that I might be trapped in that dream and not able to get out. I also knew that the tablets were only ever going to be a short term fix; that the only way to get through this was to face the realities.

When I got home I called our mortgage broker Grant, who had always had a soft spot for me. Even he was shocked and couldn't believe that Danny had left me; he said that he always thought that Danny was lucky to have me; that Danny had made a terrible mistake because he thought if anyone was going to leave the relationship it would have been me. It seemed to be a recurrent theme that people thought that it would be me who would leave Danny and not the other way around.

I told Grant about the conversation I had with Danny and how he didn't think that I would be able to buy him out; and I told him that I believed that 'she' wanted to take the house from me, and how they had both laughed at me. Grant said that he would make sure that I would be able to buy the house and that I would be able to prove Danny wrong. By the end of the day I had a mortgage proposal emailed to me.

My boss May called; she was so worried about me, as were all my friends and colleagues. I couldn't think about going back to work; I felt as if I was plugged into the electricity and all I could feel was a permanent hum in my chest where my heart was; it was as if it was beating at a hundred beats a minute, drilling its way out of my ribcage.

I went over things again and again: weird scenarios, because I truly didn't know the man that I had spent the last nine years of my life with. I even questioned if Danny was gay, and told Toni that I could never allow myself to be naked in front of Danny again.

In the afternoon 'her' partner came over and told me that they were in Essex, and that they were staying with Danny's mum. I was stunned; it meant that when I had called Danny's mum the night before they had actually been there then, and Danny's mum had lied to me: told me that she had not seen or heard from him when in fact they were in her fucking house.

I couldn't understand why Danny's family were being like they were; none of the life I had over the last nine years made any sense. It was clear that Danny's family had not liked me; in fact were welcoming her with open arms. I was distraught; I could imagine them all laughing at me.

Toni was going to have to return to Cornwall the next day and I was dreading being in the house alone and Toni was worried about leaving me there alone. So I called another friend and asked her if she would come to stay with me, because I was so afraid of the quiet: I felt as if it would drown me.

CHAPTER 13

'The War'- Day 5 - Friends or Foe?

A Saturday in April 2007

I had bought a stepper just two days before Danny had left me: mainly because 'she' had made me feel so uncomfortable with the way that I looked. Looking back I knew in my heart of hearts (although I had ignored it at the time) that 'she' was making a play for my husband, and I didn't feel as if I could compete.

Once 'The War' broke out I started to use the stepper at least once a day, sometimes twice if I needed to clear my head. It gave me control of my emotions, as well as my body: it was a symbol of re-gaining control of my life. The exercise was like a fix, which was something that I needed because I was finding that no matter how much alcohol I drunk I firmly stayed stone cold sober.

I found it difficult to listen to most of the music I had in my collection because every album, every song, reminded me of Danny. Along with my marriage my ability to find solace in the songs I loved had been destroyed. The only ones I could play were ones I had bought the weekend before 'The War': Carlos Santana, and Billy Joel. At the time Danny had ridiculed me for liking them; had said that he didn't like them. Because of this they had no memories of Danny attached to them and I would play them both over and over again.

Toni left to return to Cornwall with tears in her eyes because she didn't want to leave me. I knew that everyone was struggling to see

Rosie (my nickname for those who loved me) in such a bad way; I was always so strong, and now I was in tatters on the floor. But I was coming back.

I was terrified of being in the house alone, it was as if I could hear the happy times like recordings coming out of the wall, and then bouncing off the other walls all over the house. I could also hear the echoes of the fated BBQ. There were memories of Danny and me everywhere: when he used to sing to me in our snug, when he sat at the breakfast bar and just lied to my face when she had rung our home. I couldn't bear it. So I cleaned the house to try and fill my mind, whilst I waited for my new 'baby sitter' to arrive. I had Carlos Santana blaring out of my stereo on full volume. Despite it being April the weather was unseasonably hot and sunny so I opened the balcony door so that the entire road could hear. Fuck them all I was not going to be beaten!

I found a pair of Danny's underpants in the drawer, a pair I had missed in 'The purge', and I threw them off the balcony into the road; there was something rewarding in the thought of cars running over them. I made a decision that I was never going to pick them up; they could lay there forever with me running over them in my car, every fucking day. I seriously thought about throwing my wedding ring with them, but something stopped me. I had taken it and my engagement ring off and put them in the drawer but something made me want to keep them, perhaps if only to give to Ethan one day.

Della came over and said that she had seen Danny outside our house that morning; looking up at the balcony at the same time I had Carlos Santana blaring out at full volume. I was glad that it looked as if I didn't care; glad that he was looking at a beautiful house that he once lived in, a house that he was never, ever going to get back.

'Her' partner came over to tell me that 'she' and Danny were in the town, and that he just thought that I should know. In parting he also told me that I should know that Danny's sister had brought them to town so that 'she' could visit 'her' little boy; that Danny's sister had lent 'her' some clothes because 'she' had none of her own. The fact that Danny's sister was lending her clothes just hurt even more. I just didn't understand, but I was starting to get the picture: that I wasn't really part of Danny's family, and I questioned whether I ever had been.

My whole life had turned upside down and I just couldn't fathom why; I was truly lost.

CHAPTER 14

'The War' – Day 6 - The Fear

A Sunday in April 2007

My friend left early, in fact I never saw her again. She had told me how she thought that Danny was not good enough for me when I married him; how she always thought that he was a loser. This really surprised me, because she had never said anything before. It was becoming apparent that all the things that I thought existed: that my friends liked Danny, that his family liked me, had perhaps not existed at all and more and more I felt as if I had been living a lie.

Louise and Tom came to help me with the old washing machine that I needed to disconnect in preparation for my new one to be delivered. Danny's pants were still lying in the road where I had thrown them the day before; there was something symbolic in knowing that cars were running over them it implied that they were as worthless as Danny. Louise looked at the pants and asked me if they were Danny's. When I said yes she told me I should pick them up but I refused. I didn't give a fuck at that point, and they could lay there forever until they rotted.

Perhaps due to overuse the stepper had stopped working properly and I had to take it back to the shopping outlet near to us which was something I was dreading because that is where 'she' and Danny had gone on the day Danny had left, when they had gone shopping with our money, apparently without a care in the world.

I was so afraid of going there my sister had to come with me. I think that she seriously thought hard about letting me do the driving, but realised how important it was that I did. My heart was in my mouth and I thought that I was going to throw up just driving past the main centre, I couldn't look at it, because they had been there, having a lovely time and here I was destroyed.

Ethan came back that night, Louise had asked him to because she had not wanted to leave me alone in the house; and I was grateful for that. I can remember so clearly that Ethan slept in my bed that night in the hope that it would help me sleep.

I weighed myself that night; I had lost a stone in weight.

CHAPTER 15

'The War' – Day 7 - The battle of wits

A Monday in April 2007

I was still having babysitters with me every day; on the Monday my friend Nel arrived with her little girl to spend the day. Whilst everyone knew how important it was not to leave me alone I could see that for some it was difficult to be with me and see the state that I was in. Nel especially was finding it difficult because she knew that she could not take my pain away. Nothing could.

The washing machine was being delivered and it just seemed so weird that when I had bought that machine my husband still lived with me and now he wasn't here, I was here alone, being babysat by people who loved me and were worried about me, because of the damage that had been done by my husband; the one person that I thought would never let me down.

As the delivery men carried the machine in I could see the look on their faces, which seemed to veer from sympathetic (as if they knew that my husband had left me) to terrified in case they were tarred with the 'all men are bastards' brush. They could obviously see that something had happened to me: probably because my face was permanently swollen and tear stained. As if to show how sorry they were they offered to install the machine for me, even though I had not paid for that service; another act of kindness out of so many during this time.

That morning I had searched the internet and found that I could have a telephone consultation with a solicitor for a nominal fee; I needed to know what I could get and how much I could screw Danny and 'her' over. I needed to find out the facts regarding any kind of maintenance I could receive and whether Danny could make me sell the house.

The solicitor advised that Danny couldn't make me sell the house because Ethan was under eighteen years of age; and because Danny was the main earner in the household, and I only worked part time in order to support him in his career, I was entitled to spousal maintenance whilst my son was still below the age of eighteen. In addition I could take half of Danny's pension as well. I then knew that I had all of the information that I needed to fuck up 'her' plans to take everything from me; in fact I had everything I needed to fuck them both up completely.

As if in complete contrast to the hell that was my life it was a lovely sunny day and Nel persuaded me to go to the beach. It was something I was afraid to do because it bought back so many memories of Danny and I lying there together all day; and of the time when Danny had said to me that he would be lost without me, that I was 'his life.' How could I go to the beach knowing it was all crap? But I knew that I had to face it sometime so I went.

The irony was not lost on me as I sat on that beach, with the blue skies and the sun beating down on me, the infinity of the sea in front of me, and the wind blowing through my hair. Everything was so beautiful and my life was shit! I felt numb; this was someone else's world, it wasn't mine. I didn't know where I belonged anymore.

As I sat there Grant called to say that the mortgage was on course and that I would be able to buy Danny out of the house; I called my sister Louise from the beach and asked her to call Danny and tell him I was in a position to buy him out of the house. I asked her to tell him that I would pay five thousand pounds only and that if he didn't agree to it I would take him to court to gain spousal maintenance and access to his pension. I was getting to that point that I didn't want to speak to Danny anymore; I just wanted to move forward. To be honest I was exhausted; I had not been eating or sleeping but exercising like a maniac and it was finally dulling my brain to the pain, and making me feel as if I didn't give a shit anymore.

Despite receiving calls from Grant when I got back to the house I had a missed call from Danny, and also a text. I had not heard my phone ring or seen the text until I got home. It was as if someone or something greater than any of us didn't want me to speak to him.

The text from Danny said "I am worried about you; what are you going to do about the bills?" I didn't answer.

Louise called and said that she had spoken to Danny and that he had seemed really shocked that I was in a position to buy him out, and shocked that I was even considering it. She said that he sounded lost, and really upset. I was furious: Fucking upset! What right did he have to be upset? None!

I was so angry that Danny had the audacity to feel or even sound hurt after he had laughed at me when he was with 'her'; laughed with 'her' about me. It spurred the fighter in me and I called Danny, only this time he answered the phone. He sounded as if he had been crying. I asked him if he "was enjoying his new life?" and he said that he was. I pointed out that he didn't sound as if he was. I told him that I had spoken to a solicitor and with that Danny asked me if I was going to divorce him, because he didn't want me to. I told him that I had no plans to divorce him at the time; I just needed to sort out our finances and the house. With that Danny said that he was sorry for what he had done, sorry for hurting me and that he had never meant to hurt me.

So why didn't he come back? Why didn't he want me to divorce him? Nothing made any sense.

I could feel the anger towards him bursting like bubbles in my chest, my heart was pounding to such a degree I could hear it in my ears, feel the blood rushing through my veins. I was angry with him for sounding upset, angry with him for saying that he was enjoying his new life, angry with him for contacting me if he was so happy. I told him that I hated him and hung up.

But something was not adding up: Danny was telling me that he was happy with 'her', was in love with 'her', and in the next breath asking me not to start divorce proceedings. I thought about how Danny had not bothered to contact me once in the last week, other than when I told him he would be 'up shit creek without a paddle'. Yet here he was a week later making contact and had said, for the first time, that he was worried about me. I knew then that things were starting to unravel between them, I knew in my heart of hearts that Danny loved me.

Her partner came over to tell me that they were still in London with Danny's family, and that 'she' had told him that they were in love. I started to feel as if a game was being played: 'she' was telling him knowing that he would tell me; and that he was telling me in the hope that I would never have Danny back.

Although I knew I should be distancing myself from what I was being told it was as if I had to know what was going on, even though it was driving me insane. But what I did realise was that neither of 'them' appeared to know that Danny had been in contact with me. Perhaps, Danny was playing a game as well, a game to help him and I.

CHAPTER 16

'The War' – Day 8 - Laying plans for Divorce

A Tuesday in April 2007

For the first time since Danny had left I was in the house alone so I went to Susan's house and her sister Jo, who worked in a solicitor's office was there. I told them about the conversation Danny and I had the day before and Jo advised me to see a solicitor and start divorce proceedings, otherwise Danny would be entitled to half the house even if I bought him out.

I really didn't want to divorce Danny, but it made sense. I had to move forward with the circumstances as they were, not live in hope that Danny might come back one day, because as each day progressed I didn't know if I wanted him anyway. So Jo arranged for me to go and see someone in her firm because they provided legal aid, and I had no money to pay for a divorce.

I still needed an initial payment to start proceedings; so I got Danny's bike back from Della's house and I took the bike that Danny had bought himself, to the bike shop at the end of the road and sold it for eighty pounds. With the money from this in hand I made the appointment with the solicitor to commence divorce proceedings. How ironic! Danny had paid for me to start the divorce proceedings that he didn't want!

I had to cancel the holiday we had booked for the end of June. I found that really hard: thinking back to the year before; to what had been a wonderful holiday, we had been so happy had such a lovely time which is why we had booked to go again. But I then thought of all the times that Danny had been on the balcony with his phone, supposedly on the pretext of having a cigarette; and I wondered if even then the holiday was just crap and he was lying to me.

Despite the emotional turmoil I was in I was able to sort out our finances and the mess of our life, because it helped take my mind off my pain and made me feel as if I was in control of something. But once I stopped doing admin things I couldn't sit still, or stay in my house, and despite stepping three times a day it was making no difference to my nervous state. I was not getting any better, I was still crying all of the time, and couldn't be still because my mind was, quite simply whirring all the time.

I went over to Della's house and sat in her kitchen crying. Her neighbour came in, a lovely man, and asked me why I looked so sad which made me cry again. Della explained to him what had happened, and he just looked at me so kindly and said "Don't cry." It just seemed so unreal that all of these people were offering so much kindness to me and the person I had spent the last nine years of my life with was acting like a cunt.

The radio was on and I remember a song by Justin Timberlake, 'What goes around comes around', playing over and over again on the radio; I thought how apt it was because one day everything was going to come back on Danny.

Everyone that I saw was so shocked at what had happened; they just kept saying that it didn't add up. I felt like I was trapped on a television show, or in a film, because this was my life and it was happening but no-body else seemed able to believe it!

My next door neighbour and good friend Jessie came round to say that a crowd of them were going to a 'soul' night at a nearby town on the Saturday night and that she would buy me a ticket if I wanted to go. I knew that she wanted me to get out, to take my mind off it, so I reluctantly agreed. We had to dress up in seventies gear so it would help to distract me: another kind deed.

That evening my friend Petra knocked at the door. She used to be friends with 'her' and when I opened the door she was already crying. As she came in to the hallway all she kept saying was how sorry she was, how she couldn't believe it, didn't believe it when she was told at the school gates by 'her' that Danny had left me and was living with 'her'. All Petra could say was "Why did he leave you? You're so beautiful, so much better than 'her'?" She was so upset that I found myself comforting her.

Ethan had gone out with his friends and girlfriend so I had to go somewhere that evening, I visited some friends who we had lost touch with. Despite the fact that I had not seen them in over two years when they opened the door and I burst into tears they embraced me and welcomed me in.

When I got home I was alone so I got back on the stepper and after I weighed myself: I'd lost sixteen pounds.

> Should've known better when you came around
> That you were gonna make me cry
> It's breaking my heart to watch you run around
> Cos I know that you're living a lie

What Goes Around – Justin Timberlake
Written by Nathaniel Hills, Justin Timberlake, Timothy Mosley

CHAPTER 17

'The War' – Day 9 - The Bomb

A Wednesday in April 2007

The mortgage was moving at a pace now and I was pulling together the paperwork for all of the loans that we had because they had to be paid off as part of the buying out process. I was shocked at how much debt we actually had, and I was determined that I wasn't paying them all off on my own; so I sent a text to Danny to advise him that my initial buy-out offer would be less due to the amount of loans outstanding; as a result Danny then rang me!

As soon as I heard his voice I just felt so much anger towards him for what he had done, what he was putting us all through, how he had turned our life upside down for a woman who had made a play for nearly every other person's husband that we knew. So why did it have to be my husband who had fell for it?

I asked Danny if he was still happy with 'her', and he laughed at me, and said that yes he was happy with 'her', that in fact he did love 'her'. It felt as if someone was stabbing me in the chest, but this time I didn't cry.

I asked him why? Why was he doing this when we had been so happy? He said that he had started to fall out of love me the year before and that it had been coming for a long time: that I had been too needy, always wanting him to show how much he loved me, and it had begun to grate on him.

I'd had enough! As Danny was talking to me he called me Rosie, so I told him not to call me Rosie because only people who were my friends and who I loved were allowed to call me Rosie. I reminded him that he was not my friend and certainly not someone I loved, so he was never to call me fucking Rosie again!

I was more determined than ever and told him he would get as little as possible out of the house, reminded him of our wedding speeches, when all his friends who knew him called him 'Lucky Danny': implying that really he was just a loser. I reminded him of how I didn't believe he was a loser at that time; that I had believed in him; but how now I believed that they were right: That he was a fucking loser! That even my sister had said about what had happened and about how the people who had really known him (because clearly I didn't) had been right and that he could "fuck off!" I hung up, my resolve to proceed with the divorce and for him to end up with nothing hardened. Then I started to cry; and wondered to myself how I got to this place in such a short space of time.

When I went to visit some friends later that night the oil light came on in the car and Susan's husband Malcom sorted it out for me: another kindness.

After I got home Della's neighbour, the man who had seen me crying in her house came over. He had been to France that day and he had brought me a big bag of fresh prawns from Calais and some French bread and wine. When I thanked him he told me that Della had told him that I wasn't eating and that perhaps the prawns would tempt me to eat; yet another kindness.

After he left I started to cry. I couldn't eat because food just felt like cardboard in my mouth. But I knew that Ethan was worried about me and he asked me to try some; I managed one prawn and three mouthfuls of potato. I drank the wine though!

I mention the kindness of other people because it was something that kept me going in what were some of my darkest hours; and also because it highlighted to me just how badly Danny was treating me and that all added up gave me strength.

CHAPTER 18 – APRIL 2007

'The War' – Day 10 - Divorce

A Thursday in April 2007

It was the day I had to attend the solicitors. I put on a dress that I had always loved and not been able to get into for some time. It was still unseasonably hot for April, and it hit me that it was far too nice a day to be attending solicitors to start divorce proceedings.

I can honestly say that I drove there in a blur, a state of shock at what I was going to do. Grant called me as I was going into the solicitor's and asked me if I was okay. Bless him, he cared more about me than the man I had been with for nine years.

There I was, sitting in the Solicitors waiting room with other women of all different ages wondering what the hell I doing there. This time last year Danny and I were on holiday in Mallorca, we had such a lovely time, as we always used to do; we laughed constantly throughout the holiday. So how was I, only a year later, sat in a solicitor's office getting ready to start divorce proceedings against Danny?

I think the solicitor knew that I was still in a state of shock; my eyes were brimming with tears and I was shaking; he asked if I was sure that I wanted to do this. I told him I was sure. I instructed him to start proceedings against Danny citing adultery. I explained that I did not know where Danny was; although I was aware he was with his family in London; and I asked him to send it to Danny's sister's address: She appeared to think that the sun shone out of Danny's arse, let her give the divorce petition to him.

When I came out of the office Grant rang me again to check that I was okay. Whilst I was talking to him I realised for the first time in a long time, that I was getting admiring glances from men; it was a small thing that meant so much at a time when you feel like crap. It made me realise just how much 'she' and Danny had played cruel mind games with me, like a dripping tap over the months: making me feel unattractive and awful. And that although I was devastated I was looking better than I had in years, I was thinner and fitter and I was finally getting back to being 'me'.

On the way home to Sussex I was caught up in a traffic jam at the river crossing and I noticed that some men in a van were looking at me. I wasn't interested in them, but the fact that they were looking at me made me feel good; and I again realised that I was no longer the insecure person that I had been for the past few months, maybe even the last year. Despite all the things that 'she' and Danny had done I was no longer in the shadow of someone else; I had found myself again and I knew that I was, and always would be, better than 'her'.

When I got home I stopped in town and bought myself two new CD's and one of them was the Justin Timberlake album: 'Future sex, love sounds'. I bought it for the song 'What goes around comes around'. I knew that where Danny was concerned it so was going to come around and bite him on the arse.

That song became my anthem during this time, because I knew that what it said would come true.

CHAPTER 19

'The War' – Day 11 - Weeping for the Lost

A Friday in April 2007

I was still not sleeping. Every time I closed my eyes I could see Danny and 'her' together, naked and kissing. I was awake throughout the night so I got up at five o'clock and did the ironing. I knew that I had to keep my mind occupied and I had read that doing things was a mechanism to allow you to feel as if you were in control. I so needed to feel in control at that time; because in reality I was still so out of control. I tried to look at the positive at least I was getting the ironing done!!

My boss May called, as she had every day since 'The War' had broken out; she was seriously concerned about me and wanted to make sure that I was alright. She suggested I go into work to see the girls in the office because they were also all worried about me. The thought of going into work frightened me: all those pitying looks and hushed whispers, but I knew that those people really cared for me and that I had to move forward so I agreed to go in to see them all.

Driving into work I had music blaring out: 'Hit 'em up style' by Blu Cantrell. I needed anything to try and fill my mind, and I cried all the way there. When I got to work and walked into the office all of the girls came and hugged me; told me that they were there for me, that I was worth more than what had happened. All of them were shocked at the amount of weight I had lost and I knew that May was especially worried because I was now nearly two stone thinner.

No-one could understand why Danny had done what he had done, when it was clear that he loved me so much. I knew that they were trying to help me when they told me that, but it didn't help because I couldn't understand it either; and if it were true, and he had loved me that much, then that would mean that all that love had just been wasted and thrown away. They were all so caring that I decided to go back to work the following Monday. I had to start to make a new sense of normality.

When I got home I sat in the car for about five minutes gaining the courage to go into my own home that was now just a shell: there was no love, no happiness, and all of the memories that were oozing out of every wall were tainted. As I walked on the bare floorboards, the floorboards that I had lovingly sanded and varnished, I could hear the echo of my own footsteps, a constant reminder that I was alone. The house felt so sad you could almost hear it sigh.

Within five minutes of arriving home 'her' partner knocked on the door to tell me that 'she' had contacted him and told him that 'she' and Danny were going to rent a house together in a town nearby; and that they had a tenancy agreement in place. I asked him why he was telling me; explained to him that this was exactly what 'she' wanted him to do, that 'she' wanted him to tell me because that would increase the chances that I would never have Danny back. I told him that I didn't want to know anymore and asked him to leave.

I was so shocked. That was it then, Danny wasn't coming back! Danny was setting up home with someone else and I couldn't believe it: he was setting up a home with 'her'. How did I go from holding hands with that man two weeks before, to him moving to a new home with a new woman?

I couldn't stay in the house; it was a Friday night, a night we would have spent together If Danny had still been at home. He would have just finished a night shift and we would have had a rare weekend together. I had to get out, so I went down to a pub where I knew the landlady well. I didn't care about the fact that I was going into a pub on my own; I saw it as a rite of passage: I was on my own and I needed to get used to it, and get used to doing things on my own; I saw going to the pub alone as a fear to face.

Being a Friday evening the pub was full of men celebrating finishing work for the week. I knew that it looked as if I had been crying for a fortnight, because I had, but I didn't care. I sat at the bar and bought myself a wine. Some of the men in the pub lived in our road, and it was as if they all rallied round me because they knew what had happened. They stood with me, bought me drinks, and talked to me so that I didn't feel alone.

After they left I finished my fourth large glass of red wine and I was totally pissed I hadn't eaten for nearly two weeks so the wine had just gone straight to my head. I staggered back home crying all the way. I didn't care what the people who passed me thought, I just looked like a sad drunk woman to them. I felt so lost that I just didn't give a shit. Everyone was laughing at me anyway: the sad bitch whose husband went off with the woman who tried it on with so many other husbands; but mine was the one who left. What did that say about me?

When I walked into the home that I had cherished the door slammed shut and the sound echoed up the hall. I realised that now it was just an empty house, constantly taunting me with the memories of the past; of the happiness that was a sham, and all it contained now was the sound of crying.

Snowy our Westie was pleased to see 'mummy', as always. I put on my new CD's and danced around the kitchen; I played Justin Timberlake, "What goes around" over and over again. Then Nelly Furtado's album, 'Loose', but I didn't know all of the tracks on the CD and suddenly the track 'In God's hands' started to play and it hit me like a hammer. As I listened to the words of that song I just sat on the kitchen floor sobbing, playing it again and again for over two hours; whilst the beautiful Snowy tried to kiss my tears away; but he couldn't keep up with the volume and they plopped onto the floor forming a puddle.

We forgot about love
We forgot about faith
We forgot about trust
We forgot about us

Our love floated out the window
By Nelly Furtado and Rick Nowles

CHAPTER 20

'The War' – Day 12 - Wide Searching Eyes

A Saturday in April 2007

On the Saturday morning Della came over to tell me that Danny had called to arrange the collection of his stuff; he had asked if it was still in Della's garage because 'she' had told him that I had given it all away to charity.

It appeared that Danny's sister in law was going to collect his stuff on the Monday. I felt so sad: I had always held onto the belief that all the time Danny didn't collect his stuff we had a chance, and now that chance was gone, and it was all becoming a reality: Danny was going to live with 'her'.

After Della left 'her' partner came over and I asked him why 'she' thought I had given Danny's things away to charity. He said that it was because he had told 'her' that I had. 'When I asked him why he said that he had given 'her' stuff away, and he wanted Danny to think that I had done the same. He then told me that he had also told 'her' that I had started divorce proceedings against Danny because he wanted Danny 'to pay'.

I was getting angry with him, in fact I was fucking angry with all of them. None of them had given one thought to me; I had just been their fucking pawn to push around, and I had let them. Well they had seriously underestimated me; I realised that my friend Toni was right when she had told me to stay away from 'her' partner at the very beginning of this 'War'.

Ethan came home and his friend Adam was with him. It was the night of the 'Soul' music disco that Jess had invited me to and I was dreading going to it. But the boys told me that I had to get out of the house and start to make a life.

As I was getting ready I just cried: I didn't want to go. I asked the boys if I looked okay and they said I looked great (bless them) I had made my eyes up heavily with blue make up in a seventies style, and as I was about to leave my eyes filled up with tears again; but both the boys stopped me. Ethan looked at me and said 'don't cry mum, be strong.' They were seventeen years old and were supporting me, just another skewed thing in this fucked up world that I found myself.

Even the journey down to the venue was a nightmare. I was sitting in a car with three other happy couples who were all trying to make me feel better. I felt as if I was floating in space; how was I ever going to deal with Saturday nights without Danny?

After we got to the venue we went up to the bar; I looked around me and all I could see were middle aged women, looking their best, none dressed up in seventies clothes; they all appeared to have wide searching eyes, it seemed as if they were searching for 'Mr Right'; they seemed terrified of remaining single forever. I realised that I was back in the realm of those women and I didn't want to be there. I just wanted to go home.

Poor Jess did all that she could for me and tried to involve me; but it was all I could do to stop the tears. The music was my saviour: old school seventies soul; so I lost myself on the dancefloor, nobody could see me crying there. I just danced like a woman possessed until I eventually fell asleep on one of the sofas around the side of the room. The lack of food, copious amounts of alcohol and dancing had finally allowed me some sleep.

All the way home Jess just kept saying sorry; she hadn't realised how devastated I was and she thought it would help me. I felt so ungrateful and so sorry for her, she was just trying to be kind but I didn't think anyone understood how I felt. I was lost.

But the good thing that came from it was that when I got home I did actually sleep for some of the night, and didn't wake up until 4am, which was a good nights sleep for me in this new life.

CHAPTER 21

'The War' – Day 13 - Gaining Ground

A Sunday in April 2007

It was fantastic weather, the type of weather you could rejoice in – if you were happy. I decided that I needed to face going down to the beach and lying amongst all the tourists that would have flocked there. It was something that Danny and I had always done. The beach was at the end of our road and we would lie in the same spot for hours just 'being'. I knew that I had to face that hurdle; I had to be able to go the beach again in the future on my own.

When I got to the beach it was busy and I found myself surrounded by people who were happy, laughing and spending time with each other; I felt so alone. I lay in the same spot that Danny and I would always lay in and thought of all the times I had been there with Danny. Next to me were a couple and he had a patch of hair in the small of his back, the same as Danny; it made me think of all the times I had laid there and stroked Danny's back and I realised that was lost to me, that I would never stroke Danny's back again.

As I lay there surrounded by people I felt so alone. The tears rolled down the side of my face and onto the stones; I was grateful that I had sunglasses on so that nobody could see I was crying.

Jess and Matt were at their beach hut and Jess came over and gently suggested that I go and sit with them; I knew that she felt sorry for me and just didn't know what to do to help me. I was hesitant about going because I was conscious that I was the party pooper for everyone, but Jess insisted.

Bless Jess, she poured me a large glass of red wine and started to talk about what had happened. Matt was a laid back and intuitive man and he said that things 'just didn't add up.' He said that he thought that there was more to it than we knew and that he believed that Danny had got caught up in something that he couldn't get out of. Both of them told me to stop talking to 'her' partner, or letting him into the house because they thought that both him and 'her' were playing games with each other and just using me to make sure that Danny and I didn't get back together. Jess said that she thought they were the type of people who if they were unhappy they wanted everyone else to be unhappy.

I thought about the conversation I had with 'her' partner the day before, of how he had put words into my mouth, and I realised that I was being played. It was true; I had not played games since the shit had hit the fan; I had simply focused on trying to stay afloat and make sure I was going to be able to put a roof over Ethan's head. I realised they had all played games, including Danny; and I was sick of it. In fact I was above it; so I sent a text to Danny that said: 'Despite what you have been told I have not played games, and neither am I going to. I am better than that.' Danny didn't reply.

When I got back from the beach I thought about how things were going to change the next day because Danny's belongings were being collected to be taken to his new life with 'her'.

As always, the stepper was my saving grace and I got on that stepper for the third time that day. I was looking good, and I had lost twenty four pounds now.

CHAPTER 22

'The War' – Day 14 - The Debris of War

A Monday in April 2007

Driving into work on my first day back since Danny had left I found myself sitting in the inevitable traffic jam, and I thought about the fact that Danny's clothes were being collected. I had the obligatory music blaring out of the stereo because it filled my mind and helped to stop some of the madness that was going on in there. Nelly Furtado was playing and 'Te Busque' (I looked for you) came on and I remember just sitting in that traffic jam with tears running down my face. I didn't care what anyone in the surrounding cars thought: my heart was broken.

When I arrived at work everyone rallied around me and was so kind. My two closest colleagues and friends, Sherri and Hannah, acted the part of bouncers; not letting anyone near me who might make me cry; but nobody wanted to make me cry, they didn't need to, because my eyes were doing that all by themselves.

So many people came to see me and hug me; some told me how the same had happened to them, reassured me that I could get through it; even today I cannot begin to describe the kindness I felt from those people.

I needed to work, I needed money; my contract at the time was only for twenty hours a week and it was not going to enable Ethan and I to survive, let alone pay the huge mortgage I was going to take on. Even on the first day my colleagues rallied round and immediately offered me an increase to my working hours: all on a flexible basis because they knew that there was a high possibility that I would not be able to do every day, and some days I would just have to go home.

I was walking around in a daze, the last time I had been at work I had been happily married to a man I loved more than anything in the world; and I believed that he loved me. It seemed as if someone had picked me up and planted me in a parallel universe, one without Danny.

It was one of the people who I worked closely with that suggested that I ask for an urgent referral to a counsellor; but I was so upset I couldn't even call the counselling services, so she did it for me. I don't know what she had said to them but they called me back that afternoon and explained that they had an appointment with a counsellor in two days' time. But when I got home I got another call from the counsellor to ask me to go to see her the next day. To this day I believe that my wonderful boss had called them and asked them to see me as soon as possible. I know that she was worried about me because the weight was literally falling off me, and it terrified her.

I went to Della's and she confirmed that that my sister in law had collected Danny's stuff. I asked her if my sister in law had made any comment and Della said she didn't seem bothered that we had split up that she just didn't seem to care.

I felt as if the last nine years of my life had just been a complete lie where Danny and his family were concerned. From their behaviour it seemed clear that they never really liked me or Ethan. I hadn't heard a thing from them, they hadn't even sent a text to Ethan; and that actually upset me more than anything because Ethan had seen them as his family.

When I got back home I got on my stepper, I needed to burn off the anger that was inside me.

CHAPTER 23

'The War' – Day 13 – The Counsellor

A Tuesday in April 2007

There had been a hole in our kitchen ceiling for nearly a year prior to 'The War'. Our shower and bath had leaked and had rotted the ceiling. Ethan had been going on and on about it, and how it seemed to represent a 'wound' in our house, and I realised that it had happened just as we had become closer "*friends*" with 'her'. So I made a resolve to get it fixed and called a plasterer and arranged for him to come to repair it the following week. It was my house and it was time that I took control of it. Ethan was right: it was like a festering sore, and it needed to go.

I was still not sleeping so I got up at two in the morning and decided to be constructive: I did some more ironing. I smiled to myself that there I was again, like a mad woman, doing her ironing at two o clock in the morning. It was the day I was going to my first session with the counsellor and I hoped that she would be able to at least allow me some sleep without the images that kept invading my dreams.

My boss May kept bringing different types of food into work and trying to persuade me to eat them; at times she was almost pleading with me to at least take a bite, but I couldn't, the food just turned to cardboard in my mouth. My eyes were still permanently brimming with tears. That afternoon I left work to see the counsellor. I had the same dress on that I had worn to the solicitor's office because the dress had started to represent my new self, or even the old me: someone I had left behind, had let go. It gave me comfort because every time I put it on I knew that I looked better and better in it.

At the Counselling session I just cried throughout it. The counsellor explained to me that she thought that Danny had thought that I was too good for him; that this was often the case in situation such as ours. She thought that Danny had left me for someone who was not as pretty or intelligent as me; because he would then be able to feel superior to them; which he couldn't do with me. He had left me for someone who he had confidence he could keep because he was not confident that he would keep me. I can remember how she indicated with her hands, that I was 'up here' and Danny was 'down here'; and how with 'her' the situation was reversed.

Where 'her' and I were concerned that made sense. I understood: Danny needed to feel like the 'Top Dog' and he was never going to feel like that with me. I thought back to how 'she' was never the fucking brightest button in the box, and I smiled to myself when I remembered that one of 'her' favourite sayings was "I don't get it!"

When I got home I called my sister to tell her this revelation and she told me that she had known that all along!

I realised that what the counsellor had said was probably on the ball: of how Danny had said how much he had hated it when I got an admiring glance; I thought back to a conversation before 'The War' broke out, when Danny said that ever since we had been married he wondered if I would be there when he came home, expected me to have packed my bags and left. He always felt that I was too good for him; the counsellor had got it spot on.

I remembered when Danny left he had said as he was leaving because he was terrified that I would do to him what he had done to me; and he that he just couldn't bear the thought of it. It was starting to make sense now: Danny had run away because he was afraid, so he thought that he would take the easy option. What a stupid fucking mistake to make!

I felt that I was getting stronger all the time and I wondered if wearing the dress was an omen. I felt good in that dress because it made me think of all the times 'she' had brought up my weight and how 'she' was thinner than me. Well there I was: thinner than 'her' now, and to match me she would need a head transplant!

I was determined to get stronger, get my career back, and become my own person and to look good as I was doing it. Then Danny would realise exactly how much he had lost!!

So I got on the stepper and made sure that I worked off over two hundred calories by stepping to 'I don't need a man' by the Pussy Cat Dolls. How apt!

CHAPTER 24

'The War' – Day 16 - Echoes of War

A Wednesday in April 2007

It was my last day at work for the week, and although I needed to do more hours, I couldn't cope with it, just my actual twenty hours were enough.

When I got home I was on my own because Ethan had gone to his girlfriend's house. I still found it hard being in the house on my own; despite it being full of furniture and all of the beautiful things that we had accumulated over the years it still felt so empty.

When I was in the house alone I would start to picture all the times 'she' was here: of the time 'she' sat in my snug, crying and telling me of the awful life 'she'd had, whilst Danny entertained 'her' small child in the kitchen and brought 'her' in drinks. I remembered how 'she' had said to me then that one day I would hate 'her'; now I knew why: because they had been seeing each other then and probably finding it so funny that I was offering her sympathy whilst 'she' was meeting my husband and kissing him.

I thought of the time that Danny had sat at the breakfast bar and held my hand and told me that I had nothing to worry about; of how he had promised me that he was not having an affair with 'her'; it made me furious when I thought of how he had laughed and said 'Do you really think that I would leave you for 'her'?' So when I was in the house alone I felt as if I was going to drown in that sea of lies and I just couldn't stay in my own house.

I went to see a friend that I used to work with; I seemed to have forgotten to call people I would just turn up. I had called my friend the day after Danny left to tell her what had happened and she couldn't believe it. She had been in a similar situation and understood why I couldn't be on my own; she invited me in and listened. She understood the need to do anything to stop you from being on your own and able to think.

I was so conscious that Sunday would be the anniversary of my mum's death; it would have been ten years since I spoke to her and I had wished that she was there to talk to. I needed her to wrap her arms around me and tell me it would be alright.

When I got home I tried to watch some television and as I sat on the sofa Snowy sat one side of me, and my beautiful cat Molly sat the other; effectively sandwiching me between them. I knew that they were trying to tell me I would be okay, that they loved me and that everything would be alright.

But when I went to bed I couldn't sleep because I was afraid to shut my eyes and see the pictures that were waiting for me.

CHAPTER 25

'The War'- Day 17 - Ghosts

A Thursday in April 2007

I had begun to feel as if there was a presence in the house. Strange things had started to happen since 'The War' had begun and things kept going wrong: pictures would just fall off the wall, the blind fell down, the bathroom door lock had begun to stick. It was as if the house was out of kilter.

I was starting to get annoyed with myself when I cried, I wanted to stop crying; so I thought back to a time when my heart had been broken; when I was younger and engaged to someone else, and I tried to channel all of my inner strength and focus on what I did then and how I had survived.

When 'her' partner knocked on the door to tell me that 'she' and Danny were moving into their house at the weekend; that 'she' had told him how in love 'she' and Danny were, that Danny was going to support 'her' children. I just said 'good for him!' I told him that I didn't need to know because I needed to move on now; that I knew that he was trying to drag me backwards all the time, and I asked him to leave.

Two friends that Danny and I used to know came to see me, and so did Della; we played music and I opened a bottle of wine. I put on music that I had listened to before: 'The Greatest Love of all' by George Benson. I had listened to that song so often in the past;

especially the line 'no matter what they take from me, they can't take away my dignity'. As it played I started to cry because I knew that I would have to find the greatest love of all - me.

As I got more and more pissed I started to contemplate things; I started to run scenarios through my head: Was Danny really gay? A young bloke he worked with had kept bringing him back watches from his holiday, was Danny really in love with him? The things that I considered got more and more ludicrous because I just couldn't believe that Danny would leave me for someone like 'her'.

CHAPTER 26

'The War' – Day 18 - Gaining strength and Ground

A Friday in April 2007

It was Friday night and I had been invited to go out with my friend Debbie and her sister. They were going on a pub crawl of the pubs in town and I knew that I had to face that I was now a single woman and that I needed to find a life of my own. So I decided that if I was going out I was going to enjoy it and I went to the hairdressers to get my hair cut.

I didn't care who knew about Danny and I, in fact I was more afraid of hiding it because I knew that it would then control my life as I would be terrified that people would find out from someone else. So I continued to tell everyone what had happened. It was almost cathartic and when I told the hairdresser; he was lovely and offered to run a colour rinse through my hair free of charge. It never ceased to amaze me how kind people were, or how many people had been in a similar position – including my hairdresser.

I had boots in the shoe repair shop that I needed to collect; it made me smile when the man who owned the shop gave me my boots free of charge and then came around the counter and put his arms around me; he said "I am so sorry, he will regret that as you were always too good for him anyway." Danny had always been jealous of this man and the attention that he always gave me when I went into his shop; so to hear him say that made me feel good.

It did make me wonder why so many people kept saying to me that I was too good for Danny because I never felt that I was.

As I started to get ready for my night out I was already drinking vodka when my friend's sister called to collect me; and I was on my way to being pissed. I had on a pair of jeans that I had not been able to fit into for years, and a white low cut top: I felt good in the way that I looked, but shit in the way that I felt.

As we went into the first pub I realised that I was still at odds in the world of singletons. What was really noticeable was how men who had known me for so long suddenly thought that I was easy pickings because someone had left me. It was as if they thought I would take anything; they were wrong I wasn't going to. There was one man who Danny and I knew; he approached me and told me how he had always been attracted to me and that I knew where he was if I needed him. He had no teeth for fucks sake! Why would I want him?

But as the alcohol kicked in I just started to feel sadder and sadder. All the pubs seemed to be full of arseholes and whilst I knew that blokes were looking at me I just didn't want to be there. This was not my life; this was not what I wanted.

We went to the disco (see, who calls it a disco?!) and it was packed with people my son's age. As always music was my saviour and I just danced and danced. A young man came up to us and told my friends that he really fancied me; it was a compliment, but the cougar scene wasn't my thing, and never would be; he looked younger than my son and it just made the whole ludicrous situation worse.

Eventually we meandered back to my friend's for drinks; I just felt lost: three weeks ago Danny and I had started to play music together in our snug, we had been getting ready to celebrate the Easter weekend and now he was moving into a house with another woman. How the hell did it happen? It hit me like a wave and I started sobbing. My poor friend and her sister were mortified because they couldn't console me. When I got home and I just walked around my beautiful house and it meant nothing; everything that I had worked for in the last nine years meant nothing.

I felt as if I had lost my soul.

CHAPTER 27

'The War' – Day 19 - Sunshine on the battlefields of War

A Saturday in April 2007

When I woke up the sun was streaming through the bank of windows across our beautiful bedroom. It would have been my dad's birthday (God rest his soul) and I knew that if he were with me then he would have told me that I was worth more; that I was strong, that I would get through it.

I went downstairs and made myself a cup of tea and decided to take it back to bed. It was a simple thing that I loved to do but when I had done it in the past nine years Danny had been there with me; so sitting in my bed alone just made me start to cry.

I had made arrangements to go to London to spend the weekend with my sister and family. I didn't want to be alone on the tenth anniversary of my mum's death. When she died I had felt so lost and I never thought that I would feel pain like that again; but that was exactly the pain that I was feeling; in fact it was worse because my mum never meant to break my heart, she had never stopped loving me. Danny had.

I still felt so lost, but I put on a brave front as I drove to my sisters. When I arrived Ethan was there and he persuaded me to go to local garden centre and encouraged me to buy a lantern with crystals on it – something new, something that only I had owned. Everything was symbolic I knew that.

Various friends and relatives arrived but I just sat there with my eyes brimming with tears that occasionally escaped and ran down my face no matter how hard I tried. But I still had that strong feeling that Danny was also crying somewhere; despite what I was being told Danny was not happy: I could feel it.

I could see that my sister Louise was really worried about me; she had seen me with break ups before and normally I would have got back up at this point; but this one had broken me: I just didn't see it coming. I had put all my trust in Danny, we had seemed so much in love and none of it made any sense; the only option I had was to just get really pissed and blot it out.

CHAPTER 28

The War – Day 20 - A day of remembrance

A sad Sunday in April 2007

It was the tenth anniversary of my mum's death. I had been dreading this day because it marked a depth of time since I had seen and spoken to my mum. But because of the pain I was in the pain I anticipated just blended in with the rest. I had stayed at my sister's house and when we got up she just didn't know what to do with me; and I really felt for her.

Nel had invited me to dinner and as I left Louise she reminded me that our mum had always loved my strength; told me that she believed that this was a test from my mum: something to jolt me back to the person I had once been: A strong independent woman. Because somewhere I had lost myself in Danny and I had been lost for too long; so on the tenth anniversary of her death my mum had intervened and given me the 'kick up the arse' that I needed. I knew that she was right.

Poor Nel, all I did was cry and I couldn't eat the dinner she had cooked me; I was getting thinner by the moment and had lost thirty pounds.

After leaving Nel's I picked Ethan up from his girlfriend's house and went to see my Aunt. She and my late Uncle had always been a great support to me, always there when I needed them, and I trusted what she had to say. I got upset when I was there as Auntie Joyce told me that I was too good for Danny because it was a constant that people were saying to me; even the counsellor had said that Danny had thought that himself. I was starting to realise just how insecure Danny must have felt with me, through no fault of my own.

I looked at my aunt and told her that I wanted to stop crying, that I was sick of crying and she just looked back at me and said 'Then why are you then? Just stop.' It was if she had pressed a button: I looked at this lady who had always been there for me, always believed in me, but who always told me it like it was, and it all made sense: if I wanted to stop crying then I could. I stopped crying.

When I got home I put on Simon and Garfunkel's 'Bridge Over Troubled Water' in memory of my mum. It was the last song she sang with me, and I knew that my mum and dad were there with me; I could feel them.

CHAPTER 29

'The War' – Day 21 - Repairing the Ramparts

A Monday in April 2007

It was the beginning of another week without Danny, and the day that the plasterer was coming to repair the ceiling in the kitchen; in my haste to get everything out of his way I forgot my phone. I didn't even know I had forgotten it until I was at work for over half an hour, and as soon as I realised I knew that it was a sign that I was moving on, and in a way I was glad. My phone had been attached, almost surgically, to my hand since 'The War' began; and yet there I was without it, and it meant that there had been a turning point in my situation. I was getting stronger.

I went to the counsellor on the way home and she confirmed that forgetting my phone was a step forward; in addition I didn't cry all the way through the session and when I left I felt better than I had in a long time.

When I got home it was gone seven in the evening and Ethan came down the stairs moaning that the alert on my phone had been going off since ten that morning. At that moment I knew that it was going to be a message from Danny.

When I checked the phone it was showing me that 'The Arsehole', as Danny was now saved as in my phone, had sent me a text to say 'I thought that I would text you as I need to collect some of my stuff. Hope that you're okay, I am worried about you.'

My initial response to this was: 'Yes! Fucking Yes! You fucking bastard! I knew that you would come crawling back, I fucking knew it!'

My next response was 'What Fucking stuff?!'

But I didn't text him back instead I called Louise; when I told her about the text she said that she knew he would come crawling back as well. She asked what time he had sent the text and when I told her it had been late morning she advised not to reply because it was clear he had sent the text when he was alone. Louise also told me not to tell 'her' partner if he came over, because they were playing a game and I should look after myself now. She was right; I needed to remember that nobody had given a shit about me.

I put some music on and danced for an hour around the kitchen; and then I drank a bottle of wine. It was only then that I realised that the hole in the ceiling had been fixed and I realised that Ethan was right: it had been a festering sore in the house; a sign of how bad things had been, and now the bad things were finally going to get better.

And now you want somebody
To cure the lonely nights
You wish you had somebody
That could come and make it right

**What goes around comes around part 2.
Performed by Justin Timberlake
Written by Nathaniel Hills, Justin Timberlake, Timothy Mosley**

MAY 2007

CHAPTER 30

'The War' – Day 22 - The Surrender Part I

When I got up I had changed my mind: I didn't know if I wanted to respond to the text Danny had sent the night before. I was tired of it all, I needed to move forward and extract myself from the 'daytime soap opera' that Danny had dragged me into. I was worth more than that.

I had booked a day's leave from work to clean up the house after the repairs that had been made by the plasterer. It was starting to feel like just my house now, and I felt that things were changing and I was starting to feel that I was now able to make it on my own. I noticed that I didn't tend to hear the echo of my own footsteps following me anymore; it was as if the house had soundproofed the floorboards to allow me to come to terms with being there on my own; the house had become my ally.

But as I started to make my first cup of tea of the morning the tears started to form, and my eyes started to well up. This time they were because I knew that it wouldn't be long before it was too late for Danny to come back. I have always been the type of person who seems to have an internal switch, it is not something that I can control, it just 'flips' where my feelings are concerned; and once it has 'flipped' I cannot get those feelings back; even if I wanted to. I knew that this was starting to happen where Danny was concerned.

Jess knocked at the door and when I opened it I was crying. I explained that I was afraid that if I responded to Danny then he would ignore my text and it would bring back all those memories from three weeks ago, when he had just ignored me. I couldn't bear the thought that he would drag me back and make me feel like shit again. I wondered if I was just better off leaving it now, because clearly I was starting to take small steps to move forward without him. But at the same time I was angry that he seemed to feel that he was entitled to anything else from the house; and I was angry that I was back to checking my phone again.

Jess suggested that I text Danny to ask him what stuff he thought he was entitled to, and then totally delete his number from my phone book so that I couldn't look for his name, or his alias of 'The Arsehole', on my screen. So I sent the text and then deleted his number. But Danny replied immediately with a text saying that he wanted a television, a stereo, some furniture and his bike; it made me laugh, as there was no fucking bike!

I was incensed that he thought that he was entitled to anything and I called him, and he answered after the first ring! I knew, I had always known, that he was not happy, no matter what I was being told. I had always known that somewhere Danny had been crying for what he had lost in the same way that I had.

When he answered the phone I could hear that he had been crying and I was so fucking glad. I asked him whether he was still in love and he started to cry. I was on a roll:

'Are you still happy Danny?'

He answered clearly 'No'

'Have you realized what a terrible fucking mistake you have made now Danny? How you have lost everything: me, Ethan, the animals, the house? And now you are living in a tiny little terrace house I hear; with a door that leads straight out onto the street; I understand how you must be so fucking happy!'

Danny said that he wasn't; he knew that he had made a terrible mistake and he didn't really want anything from the house, he was just using it as a way of getting in touch with me because he thought if he just approached me in any other way that I would just tell him to 'fuck off'. I was still tempted! Instead I told him that all of the TV's and stereos belonged to Ethan now and he cannot touch any of them; and that his bike had been stolen.

I asked Danny what he actually wanted and he said that he just wanted to talk to me face to face; that he knew that he had treated me so badly and that he felt really ashamed of the way that he had behaved. He asked if we could meet up that evening to talk about what had happened and how we had come to be where we were. He explained that he was afraid to come back and knock on the door, afraid that I would get my revenge and he had thought that 'she' was the easier option. That 'she' was in fact driving him mad, because 'she' was so thick and had nothing to say. Through it all Danny just kept saying how sorry he was for all he had done.

I asked him if he was still in love with 'her' and he said 'no'. He said that he was never in love with her, that he had always been in love with me. So I asked him why he had told me he was in love with 'her', and I couldn't believe it when he said that he was trying to make it easier for me to move on! I didn't believe that for one minute; didn't believe that he could have possibly been thinking of my welfare as he acted like a cunt, and broke my heart into smithereens. Although I had always known in my heart of hearts that he still loved me I was not prepared to accept this bullshit of an excuse.

I suggested to Danny that he should come home if he was so unhappy and perhaps we could work it out. But Danny said that he didn't know if he could!

I was so confused: he had approached me, said that he loved me, but was then saying that he didn't know if he could come back. One minute he was saying he was unhappy with 'her', and not in love with 'her', that he had always been in love with me; and then he was saying that he didn't know if he wanted to come home. Surely it was simple: If you're unhappy you would come home. All Danny kept saying was how he was afraid that if he came back to me I would just throw him out once I knew that he had nowhere to go.

Despite feeling really angry I knew that I had to meet him; I had to try and have some sort of understanding about what the fuck had happened to us, what the fuck had happened to me to enable me to move forward with or without Danny. We needed to talk face to face. But Danny wouldn't come to the house because he thought it was being watched and he didn't want anyone to find out or be able to interfere in something that should be between him and me.

I agreed to meet that evening in a car park by the beach away from anyone who may know us. 'she' had arranged for Danny to collect a chair that they had bought and 'she' didn't know that Danny had contacted me; Danny sounded afraid of 'her' when he explained that if 'she' had found out he had spoken to me that 'she' wouldn't let him out of 'her' sight. I was dumbfounded when Danny then said that he was afraid of 'her' I didn't realise how afraid of 'her' he actually was. I also knew that it worked in my favour because it meant that Danny had started to realise how much trouble 'she' had caused and how much he should not have listened to 'her' and all the things that 'she' had told him about me. But it pissed me off that he still he seemed to be worried about 'her'.

As it turned out my Sister had been right when she had said that she thought that Danny's phone was being checked by 'her' and Danny said that even when he had gone to work (which had not been often because he had been such a mess) 'she' would then ring his work to make sure he was there. I was starting to think I was dealing with a 'bunny boiler'!

All the time I was talking to Danny I was pacing back and forth across my living room. I felt a mixture of anger, relief, elation, satisfaction and fear: Anger because I could have still just punched Danny for what he had put me through; relief because I had been right all along when I had said that Danny was not happy; that I believed that he had been crying somewhere. I felt elation because we had the chance to get back together; and also because Danny was now hiding things from 'her.' I felt satisfaction because the happy little home that 'she' clearly thought 'she' was building with Danny (really buying a fucking chair!) was actually starting to crash down around 'her' fucking ears and 'she' didn't even know. I felt fear because I didn't know if Danny would let me down again.

After I hung up 'her' partner came over; he picked up from my behaviour that something was different and asked me if I blamed him for any of what had happened. I lost it! I told him that I did blame him as well as 'her': for the games they played; for the fact that he had known for some time before he told me; for the lies that they both told, for the fact that none of them had thought of me. The more I said the angrier I became until in the end I was screaming at him. I pointed out that the mistake that they had all made was to underestimate me and how I would now make them all pay. Then I told him to 'get the fuck out of my house.'

I thought I told ya, hey
(What goes around comes back around)

What Goes Around – Justin Timberlake
Written by Nathaniel Hills, Justin Timberlake, Timothy Mosley

CHAPTER 31

'The War' - The Surrender Part II

After throwing 'her' partner out I called Susan; she had been with me through all of this: listening to my never ending tears and madness whilst I had tried to make sense of what had happened to me. At the time Susan was over an hour's drive away but she made the journey back home and arrived at my house a couple of hours before I was due to meet Danny, simply because she just wanted to give me moral support.

I knew that I had to look good for me. I had now lost over two stone and was more toned than I had been in years thanks to the hours on the stepper. When Susan arrived she sat in my bedroom and we chatted; she said that she had always known that Danny would come back; because there were so many things that didn't add up. She had seen his face at the dreaded BBQ, seen how he had looked at me, and seen that he was devastated.

After Susan left I wandered around the house trying to occupy my racing mind. I couldn't have a drink to steady my nerves because I had to drive. My heart was back to beating its way out of my chest, feeling as if it was going to burst. I had nearly an hour to fill before I had to leave to meet Danny and I couldn't stand it because I knew that if this meeting didn't work then Danny and I were going to be lost forever.

When I got to the car park where we had arranged to meet, Danny was already there. I was surprised to see that he had lost as much weight as I had. Danny asked me to get into his car but I refused; it was contaminated by 'her' now; so I insisted that Danny got into my car. After a long silence I asked him what he wanted to tell me and he said he wanted to explain what had happened over the past few months: wanted me to know the truth about everything.

Danny explained it had started in the July of the previous year: they had kissed at 'her' party; the very party where I had pulled Danny away from 'her' when 'she' had been pulling him towards the dance floor. I had left the party before Danny that night and after everyone had left and 'her' partner had gone to bed 'she' and Danny had kissed in the kitchen. Danny said that after that night he had looked for 'her' phone number in my phone; supposedly so that he could text her to say that the kiss shouldn't have happened, and that he wanted to forget it all. I didn't think for one minute that was the reason Danny had contacted 'her', because by doing that 'she' had his number and Danny knew that 'she' would pursue him; and that is exactly what 'she' did: bombarding him with texts, calling him as he drove to work, and when he was driving home; even today I believe that is why Danny had sent her a text: because he wanted someone to idolise him; he wanted the ego boost.

But the next thing that Danny told me was the bombshell: he had met 'her' in London at 'her' sister's house, the previous October whilst he was meant to have been working overtime on a night shift at work. Danny had clearly agreed to the overtime so that he could meet 'her', and I wouldn't have suspected. I felt sick as he told me that it was with the intention of having sex, but that he couldn't perform and they only had a fumble.

My brain started to put it all together now: It was in the month leading up to the Halloween party; the party where I had found 'her' sitting on Danny's lap. No wonder, Danny had already fucked her! The fact that he couldn't get it up was neither here nor there!

Danny told me that after that meeting he had stopped at a service station on the way home and thrown up because he knew that if I ever found out he would lose me, forever. And that was it: 'she' had him trapped now because 'she' had something that could be used to blackmail him; and that is exactly what 'she' did. If 'she' sent him a text and he didn't reply 'she' would make up an excuse to come over to our house; and then when they were alone 'she' would threaten that 'she' was going to tell me. Now this was unlikely because I would have fucking punched 'her' in 'her' goofy face, but Danny believed 'her'.

The whole time Danny was telling me his story I was just sitting there looking out to sea, my eyes brimming with tears. I was struggling to understand how my life had changed. There we were sitting in a car park by the beach, with people walking past with their dogs, something that we used to do; and now we were two strangers. It was a hot sunny evening, people were on the beach, sitting outside the pub just behind us, all of them happy and laughing, all of them doing the things we used to do; and there we were sitting in a car surrounded by the debris of our lives and I was wondering what the fuck had happened to me.

Danny said that he had tried to stop things; that he had stopped sending 'her' texts stopped responding to 'her' texts for months; but that it had started up again in the March of this year. I thought back to that month: it was the month I had been really ill and Danny had come to the Doctors with me. As I sat there, listening to Danny, I realised why I had become so ill: because I had been ignoring the very things that were under my nose. I couldn't understand why Danny had gone back to responding to 'her' texts in March if he had broken contact with her before. Why? For fuck's sake why?

Danny said that in March it had escalated and they had started to meet up in the next town along the coast; a pretty small seaside town called Lowly; they would both drive there separately and then sit in Danny's car kissing.

I just sat there numb. Here was my husband telling me how he would meet someone else to kiss and caress 'her'. I couldn't understand how Danny could meet her; I didn't want to believe him. But when I asked him when because he seemed to spend all of his time at work or with me; he said that he would leave for work earlier than he had to, and tell me he was leaving work later than he actually was. I looked back and could remember noticing how 'her' car would always be gone from its parking place not long after Danny had left for work. I had been such a fucking idiot. It all seemed to make sense: the text that had been sent to our house in March had been for Danny; and Danny had just barefaced lied to me when we had sat at our breakfast bar. In fact Danny had gaslighted me when he had said 'Do you really think that I would leave you for her?'

I thought back to all the times that 'she' would 'just come over to see us' because 'she' needed someone to speak to; I thought of the day that 'she' told me that one day I would hate 'her'.

I asked Danny what he wanted to do; did he want to come home? When Danny then said the he wasn't sure he could to that to 'her', that he couldn't leave 'her' in such a mess, I freaked. I started to scream at him about how he had no worries about leaving Ethan and I in a fucking mess. Danny jumped out of the car, and I followed him. All the people enjoying the sunny evening were looking at us now and I didn't care. I was so fucking angry with Danny: he left Ethan and I without a second thought and now, after the conversation we had that morning on the phone: when he had said that he had never loved 'her', had always loved me, now he was telling me that he was concerned for 'her'. I lost it! I punched him so hard around the head, forgetting that I had the car keys in my hand. I punched him four or five times, with everyone watching; and I didn't fucking care. Danny just stood there and let me.

I'd had enough; really, really, had enough! Enough of being in a soap opera with a bunch of skanks, Danny included! I walked back to my car and got in and just before I drove away I opened the window and said "if you're not home before midnight tonight, don't ever fucking contact me again." And with that I drove away.

I drove straight back to Susan's house. She opened the wine and as I talked to her I realised that I was worth more than Danny. I thought of all of the people who had told me that in the past three weeks: of how they had been right. I was worth more than the treatment I had received; worth more than what Danny had put me through. I was no longer afraid to go home; it was my house: and I was no longer seeing it as a home that had belonged to Danny and I.

When I got home I opened some wine and rang my sister. I told her what had happened and that I felt as if had never really known Danny at all; that I could see he was beneath me and that the counsellor and everyone else who had said it were right: I was too good for him. I decided at that moment that I didn't actually want Danny back; I thought I did but after our meeting he had shown himself to be so weak and I didn't need that.

When I told my sister Louise she calmly asked me "So what will you do if he walks down the path later then? You have asked him to come back and to give up the house with 'her' and I think you need to consider that; because although he didn't consider you that doesn't mean that you have to stoop to his level."

My sister was a clever cow, because she knew that I had prided myself on the fact that I had not engaged in any of the games that they had all played: in fact, I saw them all as beneath me: like characters from a daytime show where they all lie and attack each other. Louise knew by pointing that out to me that I would let Danny in if he came back. I decided that I would have to let him sleep in the spare room until he found somewhere else to live.

For the first time in a long time I just felt tired, physically tired; and I went to bed by ten. I wasn't prepared to wait for Danny anymore, or worry about if he would come back or not. My life was moving on and for the first time in three weeks I fell asleep quickly and I didn't wake up until my phone rang at ten past eleven, it was Danny.

When I answered he explained that he had left 'her' and was in the next road to our house and wanted to come home. I asked him why he was parked in the next road and he said that it was because he didn't want to be seen; the games were continuing then! I got up and waited for him to walk to our house. He had no key because of the locks being changed; and it seemed quite satisfying that when he arrived he had to ring the doorbell.

It seemed really weird when I opened the door, because although Danny was standing there on the doorstep, wanting to come back to me, I still felt that I was on my own. When he walked into the house it all seemed really strange because Danny looked so uncomfortable in what had been his home. As we both sat on different sofas looking at each other it was as if we were strangers. I was in my pyjamas; I didn't care how I looked, because I was getting to a place that I didn't care about what Danny thought about me anymore; and I was fucking sure I wasn't going to compete with 'her'.

Suddenly Danny asked me if I had an affair with my old boss James. I was incredulous! Where the hell did that come from? I answered with an immediate 'No' and asked him why the hell he had asked me. Danny started to cry and explained that 'she' had told him that I had told 'her' that I had an affair with James. Danny had started to realise that he had been lied to: that he may well have lost everything because he had listened to the lies 'she' had told him. Everything that he had done over the past three weeks had been because of his insecurities and 'she' had played him like a fiddle.

I asked Danny to be honest with me and tell me if it was him who had called my phone on the night he had left and he confirmed that it was. I asked him why he had called and he said that they had been in a crummy bed and breakfast place, with a payphone on the wall in the hall, and he had called me from there. I asked why he hadn't called from his mobile and he said that he couldn't because 'she' had taken it. He had called because he was worried about me: had found himself sitting in this awful place and just wanted to come home. But when I didn't answer he thought that he had lost me; thought that I didn't care and that 'she' had told him the truth when 'she' had said that I only wanted the house and hadn't wanted him.

I just didn't know whether to believe him. If Danny had wanted to come home and was worried about me, then why did he not just get in his car and come home? Why did he put me through three weeks of hell? Why did he let us get to this place we were in now? Why did he say he loved her? Why did he say he didn't love me? None of it made any sense, none of it added up. I didn't bother to ask him if he had sex with her, he had already told me he had in one of our conversations when he was being a cunt.

I asked Danny where he wanted to be and he said with me. So I told him that there were two conditions: he had to step up to the plate and face his fears about whether he was good enough for me; and he had to change his phone, the number, everything. Danny handed me his mobile immediately and said that I could have it. He knew that 'she' would just keep sending him texts until he answered because that is what 'she' always did. He wanted me to take control of the situation so I took the phone off him and turned it off.

I then told him that he had to sleep in the spare room; but in all honesty I was just getting to the point that I just wanted to get back to normal and I wanted him to sleep with me; I felt so exhausted, as if all the fight had gone out of me and I decided to just let him sleep in our bed.

I didn't want his phone anywhere near us; so I put it in the spare room as far away from us as I could get it.

As we lay in bed we just talked and talked; suddenly Danny kissed me, not a full on kiss but a tentative kiss, as if he was waiting to see if I would smash him in the face. But it told me so much: that Danny had wanted to be where he was now for so long, wanted to be with me, and kiss me. It fold me how much he had missed me; and it told me that he was afraid of me and what I could do. I kissed him back, because I was too exhausted to feel angry. We then started to kiss passionately and it was clear that Danny had an erection; but I just couldn't do it, I couldn't have sex with him. I had worked too hard to get myself respect back and I was not prepared to just throw it away again. I pushed Danny away and started to cry, and he lay there mortified that he had even tried; he understood.

For the first time in a long time we both slept!

CHAPTER 32

Fighting for Survival

When I woke the next morning the first thing I did was go into our spare bedroom, where I had left Danny's phone (I couldn't bear to have it near me, even though I had turned it off!) As I turned it back on it just started to ping constantly, as if it was broken and the notifications button was stuck.

I smiled to myself when I saw how many missed calls and texts there were - over three hundred - all from 'her'. I smiled because it was 'her' turn now to be on the receiving end of Danny not answering his phone or responding to texts. In fact I had the phone so the only person she could contact was me!

As I looked at all the messages I realised that the woman really was delusional. The texts were all asking Danny where he was, who was he with, when was he 'coming home.'

I knew from our conversations that Danny had told 'her' that he was coming back to me, and it was clear that 'she' was in total denial. I started to think that 'she' was a fucking lunatic, but little did I know at the time how much!

As I sat looking at the phone 'she' called, I could feel my heart beating and the anger build up inside me so I composed myself before I answered, although I could not keep the smugness out of my voice. 'She' sounded shocked that I had answered, shocked that I had Danny's phone; but it did not stop her having the audacity to ask to speak to Danny; as if I was going to say 'Oh okay, of course' and pass the phone over.

Instead I told 'her' that Danny did not want to speak to 'her'; he was sitting on the side of the bed shaking his head, he did not want to deal with 'her' in any way.

I took great delight in saying that Danny didn't want to have anything do with 'her' and had asked me to speak to 'her' and deal with 'her'. 'Her' response was "You know he has had sex with me don't you?"

"Yes" I said "I know."

"Then how can you have him back knowing he has had sex with someone else?" 'She' said.

It was clear that this was 'her' trump card; 'she' thought that if 'she' rammed home to me that Danny had fucked 'her', then I could never stay. - Little did 'she' know that her doing that just made me all the more determined to stay, just to fuck up 'her' biggest weapon.

I took a deep breath and said "Because sex is not love and you don't seem to realise that. You can have sex with anyone it does not necessarily mean anything. But you would never understand that, because you think that when you have sex with people it means that they love you that is why you sleep around so much. Look at you, nothing but a fucking slag, who still has nobody, because Danny is not with you now is he?" I hung up and turned the phone off.

Danny looked at me and said he was worried about going back to the house he had rented with 'her' to collect his belongings; that he needed me to go with him because he was afraid of what 'she' would do. He said that 'she' would not leave him alone and would follow him about and go on and on at him, as she had over the past six months; and I could see at that moment just how weak Danny was.

I started to realise that this woman was a fucking maniac, and that a lot of what had happened was because 'she' hated me and all that I had; things that 'she' had never had and would never have. So 'she' had set out to destroy me. 'She' had played the game well, but clearly not well enough; 'she' had underestimated love; but perhaps more importantly 'she' had underestimated me!

I was in disbelief that despite all the shit Danny had put me through I was going to have to go with him to collect his stuff; and help him extricate himself from the quagmire he had got himself into. So I found myself taking control of a situation that I had not created and taking Danny to collect his things.

I took my car; I could never get in Danny's car again. It was the place that he had met 'her', had made a fool of me, and had kissed 'her'. Whilst they had been together 'She' had driven it and it was contaminated with everything about Danny's time with 'her'.

I can't explain how I felt on that drive. I wondered how my life changed so much in less than a month? And it was all Danny's fault. There I was, two stone slimmer from the last time 'she' had seen me (all hail the divorce diet), driving down the motorway to the house that Danny had rented with 'her'. Adrenalin was seriously getting me through at that moment in time and I could hear the blood pounding in my ears.

When we arrived at the house, a tiny little two up two down terrace, with a front door opening directly onto the street, it just compounded my feelings of confusion; how could Danny have left our beautiful home to come and live here? How could he have thought this was a better option, that he would be happy?

Rubbing salt into the wound Danny used his key to open the door, and as we walked into the house I could hear 'her' calling the police and asking them to come and remove me from the house.

'She' had the audacity to shout down the stairs to me and ask me to leave, and I immediately thought of all the times 'she' had been in my house, and invaded my personal space. I cannot tell you how much I hated that woman at that moment in time, I wanted to fucking kill 'her.' I told 'her' to "fuck off and make me!"

Danny began collecting his things and I went to the CD player; I could see all of the CD's that had been in Danny's car, CD's I had bought. I looked through the window and saw Danny's shirts blowing on the washing line and knew that 'she' did not believe that he would leave 'her'. It reinforced my gut feeling that 'She' was seriously deluded, and that it was not going to be easy to get 'her' out of our lives. I felt completely out of place in that house, I did not belong there, I was quite simply too good for it.

Moving between rooms collecting clothes was surreal: Danny's dressing gown where it was hung in a 'his and her' fashion on the back of a door, aftershaves from the dressing table, I was scooping up clothes out of drawers, shoes from under the bed; all the fucking things I had packed up three weeks earlier!

I remember feeling as if it was happening to someone else. I looked at the bed that they had been in together, had sex in, and it made me feel sick, it really was like being in a bad dream.

All the time the sun was shining outside, and a light breeze was blowing, and the summer was on its way; everyone seemed happy and here I was in a house that my husband had rented with someone else. I was so fucking angry I was shaking and I just wanted to get out of there before I killed 'her'.

All the while 'she' followed me saying how Danny loved 'her' and not me, how I was not enough for him, goading me. I knew that I could really hurt 'her' so I tried to ignore 'her', but in the end it got the better of me and I pointed out to 'her' that he would never have loved 'her' in the way he loved me, because she was too fucking ugly!

'Look at my face' I said, 'and then look at your face, there really is no comparison.'

Clearly I had touched a nerve and 'she' flew at me scratching the front of my chest and face, which was not a good idea, given how I felt!

I cannot remember what I did, but suddenly I had 'her' by 'her' hair, it was wound tightly around my hand and 'she' could not move 'her' head, which I had by now shoved into the carpet on the floor; and she' was screaming that I was hurting 'her'. I remember thinking 'hurting you! I haven't even started!'.

As I lifted 'her' head I had every intention of elbowing 'her' in the face until 'she' had no face left. At that point Danny pulled me off 'her' and pleaded with me to let go because I would be the one who was arrested. As I let go 'she' ran to the bathroom and locked herself in.

However 'she' had not finished and whilst I contemplated the steep stairs, with my arms full of clothes, 'she' came up behind me and punched me hard in the back and pushed me down the stairs. (I had the bruise between my shoulder blades for over six weeks after the incident.) It was only Danny's quick thinking that saved me from breaking my neck; because he caught me, stopping me hitting my head on the wall at the bottom of the stairs, his hand taking the full force.

As I got up I made for the stairs again planning to go back after 'her', but Danny grabbed me, he knew that I would have kicked the bathroom door in this time, and he was right.

I couldn't believe my life had come to this: fighting with someone for the person I thought really loved me, who would never let me down. I really was in an episode of Jerry Springer.

The police arrived and 'she' accused me of assault, until I showed them the large red and black weal on my back where 'she' had punched me. Ironically the policeman then asked me if I wanted to press charges! But I said no. I could not bear the whole situation; I could see the policeman looking at me with pity in his eyes and I could see that he was looking at Danny with contempt. I needed to take myself out of the situation; I needed to hold on to the dignity that I maintained throughout the three weeks that Danny had been gone.

I asked the policemen if we could just get the rest of Danny's stuff and I took great joy in the fact that they escorted 'her' out into the garden and would not let 'her' in the house again.

After another two trips to the car I couldn't bear it any longer and I said to Danny that I wanted to go and "fuck what is left behind."

Our world was burning around us and the things in that house just did not matter. So we left behind the shirts that we had chosen when we were on honeymoon in Turkey, the CD's that we had danced to over the years; but most importantly we had left behind Danny's Filofax that had all his future shifts for work written in it, his email address and his work phone numbers. Leaving that behind would be something that we would come to regret.

As we made our way back home in the car 'she' was constantly sending texts to Danny, asking him to come back, telling him that I would not stay with him; that I would make him pay, would leave him for someone else. 'She' really knew how to tap into all of the things that he was afraid of, as 'she' had done so many times before; manipulating the situation so that he would consider leaving me for 'her'.

I could see from the look on Danny's face that he was starting to wonder if 'she' was right so I pulled over and got out of the car. I looked at Danny, this man in turmoil, and asked him to send 'her' a text and tell 'her' to 'fuck off.' But Danny just looked at me and said "I can't, I don't want to hurt her."

I started to cry and said that he had best walk back to 'her' then, but Danny just stood there looking at me; he clearly did not know what to do and said "I don't want 'her', I want you!'

I just couldn't understand why he would not tell 'her' to 'fuck off', or why could he not treat 'her' like he had treated me? If he loved me why did he not want to hurt 'her'? He had hurt me enough! I thought of all the times that Danny had laughed at me, told me he didn't love me. told me that he loved 'her'; I thought about the fact that my husband had fucked someone else; of all the things he had done to me, the worst things in the world, and here he was telling me that he could not do the same to the person who had been the main instigator of all this trouble.

But I was not prepared to give 'her' what 'she' wanted this time. I didn't know if I wanted Danny but I was pretty fucking sure that 'she' wasn't having him either. This time I would play 'The Game'. So I told Danny to get back in the car and I carried on driving away.

All the way home 'she' continued to send texts every ten seconds and I wondered what the hell had Danny got me into.

As I had told Danny when he came back giving up his phone was one of the main things that he had to do if he wanted to stay with me; it was a done deal: he changed his phone or he fucked off! I drove straight from that house to a phone shop and bought a new phone.

There we sat in the phone shop, with the young salesman giving Danny the 'spin' about the latest phones available when in fact we didn't give a shit what phone it was, as long as it was not the phone Danny had been using to cheat on me.

When we got back to our house Danny passed his old phone chip to me and I took great pleasure in snapping it in half.

After we arrived back from the shopping outlet it was late afternoon, and within an hour of our return there was a knock at the door. As I opened it 'her' partner barged past me and ran through to the back garden where Danny was standing on the decking smoking, and punched Danny in the face. As Danny fell down 'her' partner then proceeded to kick hell out of Danny; and Danny just lay there letting him.

I understood that Danny thought that he deserved it, I understood 'her' partner's anger, but I was not going to let him beat hell out of Danny. I had put up with enough, it was up to Danny and I to resolve what we were going to do and 'her' partner was not going to just do what he wanted, not anymore.

I lost it as I had walked through my kitchen after him; I found a strength in me that enabled me to pull him off Danny and I looked in his eyes and said "If you take one more kick at him I will hit you so hard you won't get up. Then I will call the police and I will press charges, and then you will never get custody of the child you have with 'her'." I knew that this was paramount to him. He looked at me and said "you wouldn't do that." To which I replied "Try me. I will do what I have to do to keep my family together and the rest of you can go fuck yourselves. Now get out of my house." He left.

I had stomached enough of all the games and the bad behaviour of all of the people involved in that crappy soap opera that was their lives; and I didn't care who I hurt anymore. When I threatened him with jeopardising the custody case he looked at me and could finally see that I was not the 'stupid little woman' that they all thought that I was.

Half an hour later he came back again; he stood at the doorstep and told me that 'she' had gone to Danny's sister's house and that Danny's family were supporting 'her'. I just told him to "fuck off"

And then the phone calls began.....

CHAPTER 33

May 2007 - Realisation: It's not what you thought

The evening after the eventful day full of fights our phone started to ring:

The first call was from Danny's stepdad and I answered the phone; he was quite off with me; said that he didn't want to speak to me and just asked for Danny. I could hear Danny on the phone to him, arguing with him, and then Danny hung up on him. When I asked Danny what he had said Danny said that he and Danny's mum thought that it was awful what Danny had done to 'her' and how he had left 'her' in the lurch; and they believed the least Danny could do was pay half 'her' rent and buy 'her' a car!

I just couldn't believe what I was hearing; they didn't give a shit about me or Ethan when Danny left us. They didn't call, wouldn't speak to me or tell me where Danny was when I called them; yet here they were saying that Danny owed 'her' something. I knew exactly where I stood now.

What I wasn't prepared for was the next phone call: it was from the police. Danny's family had called the police and asked them to call our house to make sure that Danny was okay. It was as if they thought that I was holding him against his will or something.

I couldn't believe the nightmare that I was in. I was crying when Danny finished talking to the police and he immediately called his mum to ask her what the hell she was doing. I don't know even today what was said but Danny ended up shouting at his mum and putting the phone down on her. All the while he just looked terrified because he knew that every little thing that happened like these phone calls, were making me reconsider taking him back. He started to cry and said he couldn't understand why his family were doing it.

Then the phone just started to ring and ring, with calls from 'her'. Intermittently there were calls from Danny's stepdad, who shouted at him for making his mum cry. Then there was the call from his brother, which I answered. I thought that he would be okay with me, but he wasn't, he was cold and said that he wanted to speak to Danny and not me. When Danny spoke to him I could tell that he was asking Danny if he had done the right thing coming back to me; and I could hear the disbelief in Danny's voice when he asked his brother why he was asking him when his brother knew that he had not been happy.

To get away from the constant phone calls from both 'her' and Danny's family, we went next door to Jess and Matt's house. They had been supportive throughout what we had been through and we just needed some people who were happy that we were trying to make it work. But an hour after we went there Ethan came around to say that the police were at our house and were insisting that they speak to Danny to ensure that he was safe. Danny's family had called them and said that he was in danger. Danny looked mortified as he went to see them; I just sat there numb. I didn't cry, I think at that point I felt that I had cried enough that day because of all the arseholes that I had dealt with, and I wasn't going to cry for them anymore.

I can remember Jess looking at me and saying "Methinks that you have too much of a strong personality for them and they didn't want him to come back to you." All of their actions suggested she was right.

As time wore on we had to change our home number to an unlisted number to stop the constant bombardment of phone calls from both 'her'; 'her' teenage child; and Danny's family. Sadly Danny didn't speak to his mum for over a year. Just another shitty thing about infidelity!

I went to visit the girls in the office. They were all so pleased for me, so pleased that Danny was home. They laughed about how much I had been underestimated by all of the characters in the charade that I had found myself, May, my boss came to see me and hugged me;

she could see that I was so happy that Danny had come back, and she knew that I thought that we were just going to go back to 'normal'. I remember clearly her looking at me and saying "I am so glad that Danny is back; but remember when I say that you are at the bottom of a huge mountain and you will have to climb to the top and go back down the other side before you are safe. This is just the beginning." I couldn't see how anything could be worse than I had just been through. I was wrong.

CHAPTER 34

May 2007 - I don't think I can do this
- The beginning of finding myself

Because of the constant intrusion from the phone calls Jess and Matt suggested we get out of the house and away from all the turmoil and drama. So we found ourselves in a small village just off the coast, a village we had never visited before 'The War'. It was something new, something that had not been contaminated by the past. The village had a windmill and we found ourselves in the coffee shop sitting opposite each other in silence. I thought to myself that we must have looked like a couple who had just met and were not comfortable with each other, or a couple on the verge of splitting up; you could tell from the glances we were getting from the staff that they knew that there was something very wrong with us. They were right: we didn't know each other at all, there was that distance between us; and I felt as if we were strangers.

We ended up a pub called The George Inn. It was a beautiful thirteenth century pub with wood panelling and oak beams; it was so pretty and it should have been somewhere where we could enjoy the ambience and relax. But Danny was different: more confident in how attractive he was; after all why wouldn't he be? He had two people who wanted him, and one was making it much clearer than the other that 'she' would do anything for him; whilst the other didn't know what she wanted with regard to Danny.

I wasn't sure that I even liked this Danny that was with me; I wanted the gentle and loving man who I had married, not the arrogant fucking twat that was standing with me now!

We sat at the bar and I watched Danny holding court with the barmaids, appearing to be full of himself. I didn't recognise this man anymore and I toyed with going out to my car and driving off without him; instead I went to the toilet to get away from the swaggering arsehole that I was with. I had no idea where my husband had gone, but I was pretty sure that this man with me now was not a man I liked.

I can vividly remember that the toilets had a bank of mirrors across one wall opposite the cubicles. As I came out of the cubicle I caught site of a woman in the mirrors: She looked like me, but was a much thinner version, and she had clearly been crying a lot recently. My eyes brimmed with tears as I looked at her; and I was full of sadness for her: that she had come to this.

She however seemed to be looking at me as if to say "Are you going to stay with that idiot outside? "I looked back at her, my eyes brimming with tears and said "I don't think I can do this." The woman in the mirror looked back at me, as the tears rolled down her cheeks and said "But you have to try to know if you will be doing the right thing if you leave. You have to give it time."

I still don't know to this day how I found the strength to overcome my pride and go back into that bar. It's as if people can pick up when someone is wounded emotionally, in the same way that animals can pick up when an animal is wounded physically: they smell that the person is easy prey. The barmaids knew that I was desperately holding onto something; and by Danny's behaviour it looked as if he didn't give a shit about me either way; so the barmaids played up to it. But I knew one day the tables would turn, because Danny didn't seem to realise that they were turning every second, and they were turning in my favour.

When we got home Danny took a selfie of us both together because he wanted a photo of us both for his phone. When I looked at it I noticed that Danny looked ill: he had lost so much weight and his skin was grey. I looked sad, thinner, and younger than him. I can remember looking at it and thinking 'this is killing him.'

As usual we turned to music and alcohol that night: anything to drown out our thoughts. But it was music that would become one of our saviours and that is why I am sharing some of it with you in this book; I cannot urge you enough to immerse yourself in music: sometimes to make you dance, sometimes to make you think and sometimes to make you cry. It really was a contributing factor to our survival.

CHAPTER 35

Joint Counselling – I Struggled

The day after Danny got back I called the counsellor to tell her and to ask if I could change my next appointment so that we could attend the counselling sessions together.

I was shocked when the counsellor informed me that before we could attend a session together Danny had to attend a session on his own. My immediate reaction was why? What right did Danny have to anything? Surely this was about me and about what Danny had done to me: how he could make it right. What a fucking cheek that Danny was being given any help when he deserved everything that he got! But the counsellor was insistent so I reluctantly booked Danny in to see her the following week.

Whilst Danny was at the session I was on high alert: what would he say to the counsellor about me? Would he slag me off and laugh about me as he had done in the past few weeks? Was he going to talk about 'her' and how much he still loved 'her'? After all he wouldn't say a bad word about 'her', despite the fact that 'she' had started to call his place of work to try and make contact with him.

When Danny returned I immediately asked him what he had told the counsellor; I couldn't bear the thought that he might be lying to me again, or that I wouldn't know all I needed to know to enable me to make a decision. So I was absolutely gob smacked when Danny told me that the counsellor had told him that he was not allowed to tell me what had been discussed; he told me that there were things that he had told her that he didn't want to tell me, or didn't feel comfortable telling me.

What the fuck! There I was: I had been lied to for at least six months, maybe more; I had been made a fool of, and laughed at; and yet Danny was telling me that there were things that he still didn't want to tell me. So why had he come back? What was the point of all this? How could there still be things that Danny could tell the counsellor but not tell me?

At that moment in time I needed to seriously consider my position and whether I really wanted to be there. I started to realise that what we had was gone, it was all gone and it wasn't coming back. I had been deluding myself to think that it was. I didn't know if Danny was really worth swallowing my pride for any more. It pissed me off that instead of being really honest, Danny had gone to MY counsellor and talked about me behind my back again! I had started to really dislike this man that had come back and questioned whether I was making a massive fucking mistake and whether it was going to just be easier to walk away.

Danny was watching me and it was as if he could see the thoughts going through my mind: as if he knew that I was on the verge of getting out of the hellhole he had dragged me into. So Danny told me that one of the things that they had discussed was that he didn't want a joint bank account anymore; and that he thought that I only wanted him for the money that he brought into the house.

I was shocked, because I thought that we would just be what we were before, and more and more it was becoming clear that we would never be that again; in fact it was another thing that made me question if we were ever what I thought we were in the first place.

There was nothing I could say, Danny had already opened a new bank account in just his name when he was with 'her'; I suppose that was one thing: he didn't open a bank account with 'her', especially given how important it seemed to be to him. But he didn't want one with me either, and it was because he thought that I only wanted him for his money; that hurt.

I had loved Danny so much, he seemed to have forgotten all the times that I had worked hard and worked overtime; seemed to forget that it was he who wanted me to work part-time; in fact it was he who had protested when I had taken the full time job for nearly a year. I wondered if he really understood me at all.

When we visited the counsellor the week after Danny's solo visit it was different: I felt alienated and no longer safe in that environment; as if Danny and the counsellor now shared a secret that I was not allowed to know; it was all too reminiscent of the year I had just experienced: with secrets and being made to feel uncomfortable.

I was so pissed off because now I didn't know if I could trust the counsellor because it felt as if she was on Danny's side; so from the minute I sat down I started to cry.

The counsellor asked Danny to tell me what he had told her, all of the things that he was actually frightened to say to me. When she said this I just looked at Danny; why was he afraid to say things to me?

Danny just sat there mute; so the counsellor suggested that he tell me about the things that were upsetting him. I just looked at them both because I couldn't believe what I was hearing: why did Danny get to tell me about what was upsetting him? What about all the pain he had put me through? When did I get to tell Danny about my pain?

Danny proceeded to tell me how he thought that I was only with him for the money that he brought into the house every month; that I was only interested in the house and only wanted him so that I could pay the mortgage and pay for the renovations. He brought up the fact that I only worked twenty hours a week and that he thought that I didn't want to work more hours than that. He said that it was putting more and more pressure on him and that I didn't listen when it came to anything to do with the house.

I sat there numb; it felt like the Danny who had come back had never really liked me in the first place. He was saying all the things that had made him want to leave and I just felt so 'ganged up on' and alone. I thought back to when Danny had told me that he had been falling out of love with me since the year before; and as he sat there saying all of these things I realised that had probably been true. He said that I had wanted him to do more and more overtime and then moaned when he was at work all the time. I thought back to conversations we had about me working more hours and it had always been Danny who didn't want me to increase my hours.

But it was when Danny then told me that he felt guilt towards 'her' for leaving 'her', abandoning 'her', that my world started to reel. Danny said that he was upset that he had broken 'her' heart and upset for messing up 'her' life; and as I sat there listening to that all I could think was 'what about my life? What about how much you hurt and upset me? What about the fact that you had not given a fucking shit about me or Ethan? When do you start to care about us?'

Danny explained that he felt as if, because of his actions, he had destroyed two people's lives now; and that it was his entire fault. I just sat there numb, thinking: finally something that was his fucking fault, I was waiting for him to try and blame that one on me as well, because he had decided to come back to me.

I questioned in my mind how he could have feelings for 'her' equal to the ones that he supposedly had for me. How could he not see just what a manipulative cow 'she' had been? That 'she' had been lying to him and telling him that I had told 'her' I had an affair hoping to turn him against me. But no! Danny just sat there telling me all of the things that he didn't like about me: the things that had made him leave; and clearly not seeing anything wrong in 'her'.

I had thought that when he came back Danny would just be so sorry, just want to make things up to me, as he always had done in the past; but it seemed as if this was not the case; that he thought that it had all been my fault.

I sat there and sobbed. There was nothing I could say. The man who I thought had loved me unconditionally had actually not really liked me at all. The man who had said he wanted to come back to me was now telling me all the things that were wrong with me; so why the fuck did he want to come back? And, more importantly, why the fuck was I having him back? I was worth more.

By the time I left the counsellors office I was crying so much I couldn't drive; so we just sat in the car, Danny in a terrified silence, whilst I sat and sobbed because I couldn't do it; I couldn't have him back.

I had to hold onto the ounce of self-respect that I had left; I WAS worth more. So I turned to Danny and told him I couldn't do it, and gave him back my wedding and engagement ring. I meant it.

For the first time since Danny had come back he started to sob: big, heart wrenching, struggling for breath sobs. He was holding onto my rings so tightly they cut into his hand. As I sat and watched him I knew he was in pain, and yes, I felt glad that he was finally showing the pain that I had been feeling for the past seven weeks. Cry me a fucking river!

But as I looked at him, a crying a wreck in front of me; I knew that I couldn't break up with him; although I still felt such anger, I still loved him, and I knew I had to try. I realised that if we were going to survive it would be me who made the ultimate choice.

Instead of going straight home I drove us up to the downs, a place where the sea just stretched out into infinity in front of you. There is something about looking out to sea, with its vast skies, that enables you to understand that you are just a tiny piece of the world; and that all of the things that you think are important don't really mean anything at all in comparison. It made me realise that we should try an overcome our problems; because you only get one life and I had to give it my best, so that if I walked away in the future I would know that I had done all that I could.

It was late evening and quiet and we just sat in the car in a stunned silence. Eventually I asked Danny to just talk to me and I promised that I would listen and not interrupt.

Danny asked me not to leave him, asked me to wear my rings and he cried and just kept saying how sorry he was. I explained that I felt as if I didn't know him, and that I was not even sure if I liked him anymore; but for what we had in the past I knew that I had to try, to ensure that eventually the decision that I made would be the right one.

Danny had returned to work the night that we saw the counsellor and the next day as he lay in bed my head went into overdrive. The voice in my head had begun its very long conversation with me, a conversation that would go on for years to come. I wondered if I really could stay with Danny, or if I would be happier by leaving and starting anew.

I was in turmoil, going over and over what Danny had said in the counsellor's office. It was clear that he still had feelings for 'her' and I was struggling; I have to admit that at that moment in time the main thing that kept me there was that I was not going to let 'her' win.

I called the counsellor because I felt that I needed to attend an appointment on my own. I needed to feel safe in that environment and I felt that the evening before had been so disastrous that I may not be able to attend again if I couldn't feel safe. When she answered the phone she said that in actual fact she was going to call me because she felt that she needed to see me on my own because of how badly the previous session had gone. The counsellor explained that she didn't think that the previous session had been good for me and that she had not fully understood the strength of my personality.

I arranged to see her early that afternoon; Danny was still in bed when I left but I didn't leave a note to tell him where I was. It was the start of a cruel game that I would play, when I would disappear for hours, and turn my phone off just to teach him a lesson for the three weeks he had left me alone and not answering his phone.

It was as if I was using the knowledge that Danny always thought I was going to leave him as payback for all the things that he had done to me: If he thought that I was always going to leave him before 'The War', then that would be nothing to what he would feel now. It was the start of the turmoil I would find myself in for nearly a year to come: where one minute I was so angry with Danny I would want to punch him in the face, and the next I could be so calm and rational; over time I came to learn that despite this I was the key that was going to keep us together.

At the session with the counsellor I was surprised when she advised me to consider whether staying with Danny was going to be the right decision for me. She explained that she had not fully understood just how strong a personality I had and that she was unsure if I would be able to stay, because it was highly likely that I would move on without Danny and leave him behind.

But instead of making me want to leave Danny, this triggered something in me and I came away realising that pride was my deadly sin, and I was not going to let it beat me.

CHAPTER 36

'Triggers'

For the first two weeks after Danny came back we both struggled to do anything normal, including going to work. It was as if nothing mattered, neither of us cared if we lost our jobs, our house, anything; because everything was already lost.

One morning Danny suggested that we go out, get out of the house, and away from all the memories. So we decided to walk to the seaside town of Bexhill, about three miles from where we lived. To get there we had to go through Lowly, the place where Danny had met 'her' in his car when he was supposedly driving down the motorway for work.

As we approached the slipway from the beach that would lead us up to the promenade I could feel my heart in my chest beating harder and harder and working its way up into my mouth. I found myself thinking 'did they park there and snog, or was it there? Did they go in that café? Do those people who run the café know that they were making a fool of me?' As we made our way into Bexhill I wondered if they had visited any of the pubs we were going to. Did everyone know Danny? Know that he had been there with 'her'?

Over the afternoon we visited lots of pubs and as I got more and more pissed the more that voice in my head played games with me. As normal we had not eaten; and Danny suggested that we go to an Indian restaurant. Once seated we ordered more alcohol and a ton of food. But the longer I sat there the more I started to wonder if Danny had brought 'her' to this Indian restaurant and whether the waiters all knew about them and were laughing at me with the chefs in the kitchen.

By the time the food was brought to the table my eyes were brimming with tears; I could that see Danny was terrified: he sat there with his head down because he just didn't know what I was going to do at any given time.

I just knew that I couldn't stay in the restaurant or eat any of the food; I couldn't bear the thought of any more people laughing at me; so I just got up and left. Danny quickly threw money on the table and ran after me; but I was nowhere to be seen. I had run down a small alley between the old houses, an alley that had been used by smugglers years ago; I just needed to get away from Danny.

But when he eventually caught me up, I had this rage in me. I couldn't believe that we were here in this place, desperately trying to get something back that had gone. In fact that had perhaps never existed in the first place. So I turned on Danny with the age old questions: Why he had done it? Why had he made me look such a fool? Why had he gone off with 'her' the person who tried it on with everyone's husband? Why did it have to be mine that went with 'her'?

As I asked him I just got more and more angry. Danny kept saying that he didn't know why he had done it; he didn't know why he had made a fool of me.

How could you not fucking know? How could you do something that was so bad, so cruel and then say that you didn't know why you had done it? I was screaming at him by then and when he said he was sorry I just punched him, and then I punched him again, a right hook; and then I just punched and punched and punched him; and he let me.

Eventually Danny got hold of my hands because I think he was close to losing consciousness. We made our way out of the alley and hailed a taxi, and by the time we got home Danny had two black eyes.

CHAPTER 37

France – The start of something new

After the disastrous night in Bexhill we knew that we couldn't make things better in our surroundings because 'she' was everywhere. If I had told 'her' about a pub I wanted to visit 'she' would visit it and then tell us 'she' had been there so I had memories of 'her' in places that I hadn't visited. If we visited somewhere new I would wonder if Danny had been there with 'her'; 'she' had, quite simply, ruined every place for me.

Danny suggested that we get away, I immediately thought that he meant somewhere like Greece, given that I had to cancel the holiday that we had booked because we had split up. But Danny suggested somewhere simpler, like France. I can remember how that caused an argument because I had got some brochures for other countries and Danny said that he thought that I was taking over again: wanted him to spend a fortune on a holiday. Eventually we agreed on France because it was a simple choice.

So we set off on what was to be a life changing holiday in France. We didn't book anywhere to stay, didn't have a sat nav, and simply followed the coast road. It was so peaceful, no-one knew us; I didn't feel as if anyone was looking at me and thinking 'look at her, the silly bitch, she had her husband back.'

Our first night we spent in Wimereaux, and stayed in a small boutique hotel. It was a beautiful, tiny hotel in the heart of the town. We then drove down the coast road and found the beautiful town of

Le Touquet and our love affair with France and its people truly started. There was a tiny champagne bar, where all the French people visited, and I loved it, loved the atmosphere. We would spend hours in there, welcomed by all, nobody knowing what had happened.

It was what we needed, to just get away from what was an oppressive environment at home; and it started to help us because we knew that this was somewhere we could escape to easily on a joint adventure that had not been tainted by the past, something new that we could build together.

Over the month of May we would go on to visit Le Touquet three times, nearly every weekend in fact. Although it brought us away from the memories at home, what happened continued to haunt us: From the young guy who tried to chat me up when Danny was in the toilet (I let him); to the middle aged Frenchman who told Danny that I was magnifique and did he know how lucky he was. Oh he knew!

It was as if karma was really teaching Danny a lesson all on its own, it tapped into his prime insecurity: that he couldn't keep me and kept reminding him of the high possibility that this was now true.

CHAPTER 38

Coping Mechanisms – The Demon

I went back to work towards the end of the month of May. I wanted to take on the extra hours and I needed to be independent financially from Danny. I had come to realise that I was never going to allow myself to be that vulnerable again. When Danny had left me I had to consider full time work and a change of job, and as far as I was concerned Danny coming back and saying the things he had said about me wanting him for his money, had just compounded that.

But every day I struggled. I was still not eating and permanently had tears in my eyes and I kept finding myself in the toilet crying.

I felt such a fool and so humiliated. I had a voice in my head that kept telling me that I shouldn't be sitting at my desk with tears in my eyes; and telling me it was all Danny's fault.

It told me that if I left him now I could have my sense of pride back and people would not pity me anymore, that I wouldn't cry any more. I started to believe it; I just wanted to stop crying, to not feel a fool; I wanted my self-respect back, and I believed that all of that was impossible to achieve if I stayed with Danny.

Once a week a man from another department, we'll call him Josh, would come to our offices for his weekly meeting with his boss. He was a lovely gentle man, who had a strong sense of faith in God. He came to see me to give me a hug and some moral support for what had happened.

Josh said that I had done the right thing: in having Danny back. That trials are sent to test us, to help us become stronger and different people. I told him I was struggling, and I explained that it was as if there was a voice in my head, I called it a demon, that was constantly whispering to me to leave Danny, telling me what a bastard he was and how he didn't deserve me; more than anything reminding me of the fool that they had made of me: of how they had laughed at me.

Josh looked at me and said 'I am glad that you have called it a demon, because that is exactly what it is: it is evil. Evil doesn't want you to be happy, doesn't want Danny to be happy, it doesn't want anyone to be happy. It will tell you that if you leave Danny you will feel better because your sense of pride will come back, because you will have distanced yourself from what Danny has done. It will tell you that you will feel better because you are not with Danny anymore and that you will be able to leave the situation behind. But will you? Will you feel happier? Will you stop crying? Will you get your pride back? Just remember, evil wants to destroy any possibility that you have for happiness, destroy the possibility of anyone else's happiness, and the only true possibility for happiness is to stay with Danny and try.'

Now this is where my strong personality came into its own: I thought about it, about what Josh had said and I knew that it was true. If I left I would not feel any happier than I did now; I would still be broken hearted and so would Danny. Ethan's life would be affected, as would everyone who was supporting us. What was I going to achieve by leaving? Just more devastation!

I could move away from Danny, sell our house and walk away but I also knew that I would be consumed with bitterness for what Danny had done to us, and that over time that bitterness would destroy me; whether Danny was with me or not.

I was not prepared to let that happen to me; I didn't want to become a vindictive vicious person who trusted nobody. I was not going to let that bitch do that to me.

After my conversation with Josh, when the voice started to whisper in my brain, I would imagine it as a green evil imp-like demon. Something that just wanted to cause mischief, hurt and pain; I knew we had all been through enough of that already and I could see what it was trying to do, it was clear it was lying to me.

Now getting this demon under control was hard, trust me it was so hard; but visualising the demon to which the voice belonged helped me tell it to 'FUCK OFF'. I would literally shout it out loud when I was in the car.

Getting a coping mechanism for that voice in my head was one of the things that saved me and us. I realised that it was my own voice, my own brain and that I couldn't let it beat me, and visualisation enabled me to fight it at every turn.

What happened to us all those years ago led me to read many psychiatry books, 'Counselling for Toads' being the first (for those Wind in the Willows fans - careful you will never look at the in the same way again) I know now that the demon was in fact what psychiatrists now refer to as the left hand side of your brain. Byron Katie gives an explanation in her book 'Loving What Is':

'...perhaps the most important revelation is precisely this: That the left cerebral hemisphere of humans is prone to fabricating verbal narratives that do not necessarily accord with the truth.'

In the same book there is a quote from Michael Gassaniga:

'It is like 'having what amounts to a spin doctor in the left brain...'

For me over the years I have learnt that it is in fact my ego, and that can be your worst enemy when it comes to overcoming infidelity!.

It was the first coping mechanism that I put into place and it was because of Josh's advice. I know if I had not listened to him Danny and I would not be here today. We have a lot to thank that man for.

JUNE 2007

CHAPTER 39

I don't know you

This is the event that started my journal. When I look at my husband now I cannot relate him to the person I am about to describe. In fact when we discuss it now Danny just shakes his head in disbelief at what an arsehole he had become.

It was the first Friday of June and although Danny had been trying hard I was still in a state of shock at where I was. I didn't really know the man that was with me; what he had done to me had proved that, and I was unsure of a lot of things about Danny and whether we really should stay together:

Danny picked chavvy clothes: trainers, Fred Perry shirts. He smoked, he would be defensive and sometimes arrogant; and let us not forget he went off with a woman with half of my intelligence and goofy teeth, whose favourite saying was 'I don't get it.'

Where before I could overlook the clothes and the smoking and the defensiveness after 'The War' I couldn't; I didn't want to. I had also realised just how much Danny had changed in the years we had been together with regard to his arrogance; he had never been arrogant when I met him but leading up to 'The War' and just after it he was an arrogant twat.

In this particular part of our story Danny was due to start a night shift and we were talking about 'The War' and what had happened when we had gone to the house we had rented with 'her' to pick up his clothes. I said that I had wanted to kill 'her', and it was a good job he had stopped me. Danny then looked at me and smiled, smirked even, and said "I have to be honest; I thought it was a real ego boost that two women were fighting over me."

I looked at him in disbelief and my mouth fell open. I can remember just thinking 'I don't fucking like you.' I stayed calm and just said "I cannot believe that you have just said that! I can assure you that I was not fighting 'her' over you, I was fighting 'her' because of what 'she' had done to me; 'she' could fucking have you!"

I couldn't kiss Danny goodbye when he left for work, I didn't want to. In fact as soon as he left I called my sister Louise and I cried. I said that I didn't think that I could stay and that I just couldn't see how things were getting any better; that I couldn't live like this. I didn't see why I should put myself through all of this pain when I didn't actually like Danny anymore. Perhaps I had changed too much in the time he was gone.

Louise told me that she could see that things were getting better but I just couldn't see it because my brain was in such turmoil. She told me to buy a book and write in it how I felt that day, and then write in it whenever I felt the need; and to then go back and re-read what I had written a month later. She assured me that I would be able to see that some things (however small) had changed.

I bought that book, and it saved us.

MY JOURNAL

A test of time

Pride – A measure one has of their appearance
both to themselves and others

Self—respect – A belief in oneself without
letting what others think influence it

CHAPTER 40

Journal Entries - June 2007

A Saturday in June 2007

Last night Danny and I had been talking and he had told me that he had found it an ego boost that two women had been fighting over him. When he said it I looked at him in shock because I couldn't believe what a fucking wanker he is.

I rang my sister and told her that I couldn't do this; I didn't think I could stay, I couldn't see how things were getting any better. She suggested that I keep a weekly journal of my thoughts and feelings; mainly as a comparison, to enable me to establish whether I was moving on or not; whether I could stay with Danny, and whether things were getting better or easier; or whether I couldn't forgive. I thought it was a good idea; I needed anything that would help me.

When Danny had said about his 'ego boost' I pointed out to him that I was fighting with FGB (Fucking goofy bitch) because of what 'she' had done to me. I wasn't fighting for him! FGB could fucking have him!

However it really got to me – as I should never have been in that position, and I was; and I am worth more than that!

Yes, Ethan is right that some of that is my pride. However it is also my self-respect.

I cried over it, coming back from Tesco; I cried over my situation. I sat on The Downs for forty five minutes, but once I had cried I felt better. It made me realise that 'she' was prepared to fight for Danny, but he still came back to me; knowing I could reject him at any time. That told me something.

But it also makes me wonder if I really knew Danny at all; if that is the way that he thinks do I really like him? Or want to be with him? Perhaps I had just never noticed the arsehole in him before; and now I am starting to! I have to step back and become my own person. I cannot be totally absorbed in Danny like before. That is how things have changed. I must stop craving affection from him.

I could still have a good life financially, with security and companionship; it just won't be that 'all-consuming love' anymore. I am sad about that.

That is what I feel

Rosie

Reflections Here & Now

The picture of me writing this entry is clearly etched in my mind: I had gone down to the beach on my own and I was laying in the sunshine, with all the happy holiday makers around me, writing a book that may put pay to my marriage. The sky was blue, the breeze was blowing, people were laughing and I had tears in my eyes.

Before I started to write my book I had not read this journal in nearly ten years. The first thing that struck me was how controlled I was in this entry; because I know that I was totally mad. Perhaps that was part of the madness: it was making me afraid to write my true emotions down.

I didn't know if I actually liked Danny or not, or if he was someone who could say something like that then he was not a person that I wanted to be with. Add to that all the other pain and I was on the verge of walking away. It made me want to run and, yes, I thought Danny really was 'beneath' me.

I can remember the conversation that I had with my sister; I told her that I couldn't see that things were getting any better; in fact every day they seemed to be getting worse because my dislike for the person that Danny was just grew and grew.

I still felt like shit, because I felt that I was selling myself short in staying with him; and I thought that the only way to get over those feelings was to split up with Danny and move on to a new life. The advice from my sister was good advice. She knew me well: I was a person who needed time to think and reflect; and I hadn't had time, in the nightmare of the previous two months to process anything. I felt as if I was drowning in waves of emotion. My mind whizzed from one thing to another and I was literally going insane.

This journal enabled me to see how I had felt at the time in comparison to how I felt when I re-read an entry days or weeks later; more importantly the voice in my head couldn't put as much of a spin on the things that I had written down, because they were there on the paper in front of me. Over time it enabled me see a clearer picture of myself as well as the person that Danny became.

At this point in time I was doing what most people do when their lives are blown apart by infidelity: I just thought that things would go back to normal. What was normal? The love we had for each other, or the lies that had been told? How could I go back to normal when I didn't actually know what 'normal' was?

I believe that we hold on to what we can: material things, the kids, at that moment in time they are the only solid things that exists. Even at this early stage I was considering the fact that I could 'still have a good life, with security and companionship'.

The important thing that I had realised was that I needed to 'step back and be my own person' and never be 'totally absorbed in Danny' in the same way I had been before. I was still craving affection from him; and it was making me feel worse; because I still felt like someone waiting for someone else's approval. I had actually lost respect for myself: I had chosen not to see the things that were under my nose and then I had allowed Danny to come back.

I had to get my self-respect back; it was different to ego, it was about liking me without caring what Danny thought. Realising this enabled me to become my own person and stop expecting Danny to make me what I was. To a degree I lost myself in the years leading up to 'The War': I had given up my career, put everything into Danny and his career; leaving myself financially insecure and vulnerable. So I had to find myself and look after myself first; whilst knowing that this may mean that I would leave Danny behind as I became a different person that I may walk away.

It was a chance I had to take, because right at that moment I felt as if I had nothing anyway.

Rosie

A Tuesday in June 2007

Felt very positive today, after feeling very sad yesterday.

Danny and I had a big chat yesterday and I decided that Danny was as sad as I was for what we have lost. That he wants back what we have lost. That made me feel better, because I realised that Danny still treasures what we had.

He doesn't' believe that I will be able to do this (have him back). But I will try because I do believe that we have too much to throw away.

I told Danny that he had to have the courage of his convictions and fight for me if that is what he really wants. I have to say that saying all of it has helped, and Danny has made every effort.

When you know that someone loves you that much, is that sad for what they have done, what do you do? Throw it away? Look back in a years' time and regret it?

But every now and again Danny having sex with 'her' creeps into my head, and it is like a wave coming over me.

Things are better, but I wonder if that will ever stop; and will I ever be able to say I am one hundred per cent happy which I was before?

I am sure that is a question that has been asked over and over again "Why"

Rosie

Reflections Here & Now

The night before I wrote this entry Danny and I had been in the garden drinking (which was de-rigour to ensure that we didn't think too much!). I was watering the few flower pots that I had bothered to pot up and Danny was watching me with tears in his eyes. I looked good, and I knew it.

I asked Danny what he was thinking, because I remember looking at him and he was trying not to cry. I found myself wondering what the hell was going on in his head. His behaviour at that moment was at complete odds with the person who had treated me so badly just weeks, even days before.

Danny just looked at me and said that he was upset because he was so very sorry; and that he couldn't understand why he had done it to me. He asked if we could get back what we had before, and if I would ever be happy with him. I told him that I only felt eighty per cent happy in comparison to how I had felt before 'The War'. But I was lying to him because at that moment I didn't feel happy at all.

Ironically I couldn't hurt Danny, despite how much he had hurt me. I remember looking at him and he just seemed so lost; I couldn't break him any more than he had broken himself. I could see that to hurt him wouldn't achieve anything; it would not change where I was, it wouldn't make me feel any better, and I starting to become worried about Danny's sanity.

I remember that he started to cry; despite what he had done whenever he cried I found myself looking at him and feeling so sorry for him; whilst at the same time wondering why the hell he done it to us.

Given Danny's reaction to me being eighty per cent happy then I was right to embellish the truth. It was like a see-saw: I couldn't hurt him when he looked so hurt but at other times the urge to hurt him was so strong it felt as if it was burning in my soul.

I could see that Danny did love me and that was something; one of the foundation bricks on which to try and build a new relationship. I knew that what we had was lost and that we would have to build something new; but I didn't tell Danny it was lost at that time because I knew that he couldn't have handled the truth.

It seems to be one of the ironies in these types of situations: that often the person who has had their heart broken ends up being the person who pulls it all back together. I know that when I stood in the garden with Danny that night I could not hurt him any more than he was already.

Rosie

A Thursday in June 2007

I cried at work again yesterday because of the thoughts in my head about things I cannot change.

When I came home Danny and I were fine, but eventually I decided that he should know I had cried at work, and that I cry at work every day. The counsellor had told him that there would be things I would say that he would not want to hear.

I explained about the things in my head. Danny said that he didn't cry anymore, but had waves of depression come over him – because he eventually feels he will lose me.

I had realised that Danny is my defence against my demons; that only he can drive them away by putting his arms around me and just saying sorry. If he wants to keep me he must have the courage of his convictions and fight his fear to keep me.

I reminded him again of the wedding speech and that I don't feel he is a 'loser'.

I feel we have moved onto the next phase. I am happy for the first time.

Rosie

Reflections Here & Now

My first reaction to this entry was 'Oh My God!' we had so much further to go, we had not moved on to the next phase, we had not even begun this phase!

I know that I had said that we had moved on to the next phase because I just wanted it all to be over. I wanted it to 'move on', to not be in my head anymore and to just be 'normal' again. I was struggling with my inability to 'move on'. Over time, as you will see, I realised that by trying to make it move forward faster, I was just adding to my madness; I had to learn to accept where I was.

Although I was wrong and we were nowhere near the next phase what I did have at that time was hope, and if I hadn't had that hope then I couldn't have stayed. I had to believe that things would get better; and you will see that I hope often during this journey. Don't ever let hope go.

For me it was important that Danny understood how much pain I was in. I still believe that the person who has caused the heartache needs to accept the responsibility and all that entails: that they have caused pain that they have put someone in a position where they cry every day, often throughout the day, that the person they are trying to reconcile with has been driven insane by what they have done.

I had told Danny that I cried because I knew that it would upset him and make him afraid that I would leave. More and more I was realising that we were never going to be what we were before; that what we had was dead; and I blamed Danny for destroying it. Yet, Danny just seemed to want to bury his head in the sand and pretend that everything was 'normal'; which just made me really angry: he had betrayed me, made a complete fool of me; allowed someone else to make fool of me, slept with someone else, set up home with them, even rented a fucking washing machine! Nothing was 'normal, there was no normal anymore.

I can remember being furious with Danny when he told me that he didn't cry anymore, how dare he, when I was crying all the time: in the car (the worst place), in the shower, at work, on the toilet!

As the words go I expected him to "cry me a river". I can honestly say now that the reason I say I was happy was because I had told Danny that I cried at work and that I had upset him. I had made him feel as insecure as I felt and that was exactly what I wanted to achieve.

One of the boundaries that I put into place at the very beginning was that Danny needed to have the 'courage of his convictions' or that he needed to 'step up to the plate' and all are true. He had allowed his insecurities to destroy us and I expected him to overcome them, a hard task given that I played on them virtually every day.

Danny had done the damage and only he could make it better. I have been asked by people who have committed adultery what they can do to make it better and the only advice I can give them is to accept and own what you have done. If you are not prepared to do that then how can you make it better?

At the time I wrote this journal entry 'Just Say, Just Say by Diana Ross and Marvin Gaye (Written by Ashford and Simpson) was our go to song; it still is and it still brings tears to my eyes.

When Danny first came back we sat opposite each other one night at the breakfast bar as this song came on. It said it all.

'Just say Just say that you'll forgive me and make it better
Just say Just say that you you'll stay near me
and make it alright, make it alright
Just say just say that life without me would be impossible
Just say just say you'll never doubt me and make it alright. make it alright

Diana & Marvin
Written by Ashford and Simpson

A Wednesday in June 2007

I now feel the need to write in my journal, as it helps me sort the thoughts out that run through my head (like lunatics sometimes!)

We had a lovely time in France, apart from me having an outburst on the Saturday night: hormonal and drunk, not a good combination! I said some horrible things to Danny, (like he was just a shag and nothing more!), too much- just to hurt him. But we got through it, although he has told me that he feels he has lost me.

Danny wants back the love affair that we had. So do I; and, at times, I do feel that we have that. But of course that total trust and belief that I felt before 'The War' has gone. I want it back, and yes I do believe that I can get it back.

I explained to Danny that he will have to woo me again to get me back. I hope he can.

I find driving in the car the hardest thing. That is the time when the thoughts just run around and around in my head. It appears that it is the same for Danny.

We put some music on last night and he told me that he still cries to it when he drives to and from work. I know that Danny finds it all as hard as me. That he cannot understand why he did it. But that does not help me; and although I know he wants to be able to tell me why, he cannot. That is something I have got to deal with.

I asked Danny if he hated 'her' for what 'she' has done to us, and it hurt when he said "No." I was so mad. How could he not hate 'her'? Especially for all the awful things 'she' did to me? It really made me take a step back. Danny got angry because he said I wanted him to say what I wanted to hear, that he was "just being honest."

I got angry and said that if he didn't hate 'her' then it didn't match up to the things he said: crying in the car, always loving me, losing the best thing he ever had. That he was contradicting himself. He thought about it, and said that what he felt towards 'her' was anger, for what 'she' had done to us.

That is a start.

At times I have a physical pain in my heart; as if someone is squeezing it tight. I do realise that six weeks ago I had it all the time. Now I only have it every now and again. I see that as a way forward. I know that Danny has that pain too.

Last night I asked Danny if he won the lottery would he stay; he said he would, but he doesn't think I would. At times I don't think I would either, but at other times I do. The lottery couldn't buy me the love that Danny has for me. That is the one thing I am sure of, and at times that breaks my heart because I feel that I am responsible for that love.

I am hopefully going to be okay at work today, and not cry.

Rosie

Reflections Here & Now

My journal had now turned into my saviour; something to keep me sane; and it would become something that I wrote almost on a daily basis for some time, whenever the madness took me.

When I read other people's blogs now, I understand why they post sometimes two or three times a day: it is quite simply like a Fury running around your head, and writing it down gives you some sort of release. I too found that once I had written it on the page it would no longer torment me. I would urge anyone who finds themselves in this situation to get a book and write down how you feel. It helped me to see that I was moving forward when my mind was playing tricks on me and whispering to me that I wasn't.

Danny and I were now visiting France as often as we could; it was somewhere to escape to, where there were no memories of what had happened. Everything we did there was new, everything created a new memory, and this helped. But as this entry shows what has happened will always be with you and I can remember clearly the time I have mentioned in this entry when I lost my temper with Danny and walked away because I had been triggered: A James Morrison song had played in the bar we had been sitting in and the aperitif in my mouth had turned to cardboard. ('She' had bought tickets for his concert and planned on taking Danny, so as soon as the tune played it was all back in my head.). I had walked out of the bar, leaving Danny there. Stumbling down to the beach I heard Danny behind me and I screamed at him to leave me alone; that I didn't love him, that he was 'just a shag.' Danny had just sat on a bench opposite me until I had calmed down; he would not leave me, and eventually I had agreed to go back to the hotel room with him.

Oh I remember that physical pain so well; literally as if someone was squeezing my heart.

Someone once asked if, although I could see all the things that Danny was doing to get me back, were there still times that I just didn't care? It made me smile because in the first year of getting back with Danny I can honestly say 'yes every day!'. That is what Danny picked up on when he said to me that he didn't think that I would stay if I had won the lottery; and what I have written in this journal entry is true: neither did I.

But the important thing was that I could see that we had something; that I had something: I had a man who loved me in the here and now; and that was something to hold on to, and I was right, I did have a responsibility not to just throw it all away.

Rosie

A Thursday in June 2007

Yesterday was a good day. For the first time I was able to drive home in the car without it permanently being in my mind. I cannot begin to express the relief that I felt.

I also missed Danny too. Not because I was wondering what he was doing; but just because I missed him. When I text him and told him I knew it made him really happy from the text he sent me.

When I came home Danny had written me a love note on the blackboard in French and when Danny came home we actually acted normally and didn't talk about it all.

It felt good.

Today was also a good day. I actually felt like the 'real Rosie ', joking about, laughing and making other people laugh.

I have given Danny the confidence to sit in the car and ring me, even if he felt that people in the road would be looking at him. I gave him the confidence to make a point, and not care about what other people thought; and he rang me and he said "his beautiful wife."

But then the demon came: I got the thought in my head that Danny had been seeing 'her' for two years. I needed to ask him immediately because my concern is that Danny says things that he thinks I want to hear. As I explained to him that is not the right thing to do where I am concerned, because I will remember what he has said before and then pick him up on small things that do not add up to his original explanation; or if they don't get their story exactly right. Danny swears he wasn't. (Seeing 'her' for two years) I believe him. But now I have upset him at work.

To my surprise though I didn't think about it all the time in the car as I drove home; I'm not crying for what I have lost, I have only realised today that it is because I don't want that back. Although I love Danny I really don't want to be that person again. I like the person I have become when I am on my own; but perhaps not always the person I am when I am with Danny, but I think that will change.

I am going to ring Danny now to make him feel better. I have got a handle on it.

Rosie

Reflections Here & Now

Driving in my car was one of the hardest things for me. I can remember dreading going to my car at night after work because the demon was waiting for me every time. It was as if it sat in the passenger seat just waiting to say 'hello', and then it would ask me what music I was going to play tonight to try and drown him out.

I would drive home in what seemed like a little world all of my own; a world that only the demon and I lived in; and the demon would do the talking: asking questions about things that didn't add up in Danny's story.

It would remind me of times that 'she' and Danny were together; of how they would stand outside smoking together, laughing; and it would tell me that they were laughing about me.

It would berate me for lying to myself, and tell me how it was here now to make sure that I never did that again. It would enter my thoughts and run a film of what had happened through my head over and over again. Then it would tell me how other people were laughing at me, or pitied me. That they thought that I was stupid for having Danny back and for believing him; that I was so stupid for feeling sorry for him now.

I often felt as if it was poking my head and asking me if I was listening. It knew to tap into my deadly sin: pride. Every song I played from any CD (and I was buying them as if they were going out of fashion now) would relate to what I was going through at that time. I would cry at so many but the Sugar Babes 'Stronger' was a song that resonated with me, because I knew one thing for certain: I was strong; and all of the other players in this comedy of errors had made one big mistake: they had underestimated me.

That song was the angel in my head; reminding me of what I had gained because of what had happened.

Due to where we lived I often felt as if I was being watched when I was in the car and for obvious reasons Danny felt the same; in fact he was intimidated by it. This entry shows the fighter in me: I was not prepared to be intimidated; and over time this gave Danny the confidence to not be intimidated either.

Hope is ever present in my journal entries as always. This entry is only two weeks after I started to keep my journal but as I have said hope was the only thing I had. So I held onto everything: every good day, every day that felt as if we were getting back to normal. Although, as I have said in my entry, this was so early in our recovery there was no 'normal' it had not been created yet.

I know, now, that we were never going to go back, we couldn't go back because what we had was gone; and what we were going to have was going to be new, but based on what we had learnt from this life changing, mind blowing, excruciatingly heart breaking and painful experience. I also know that 'Rosie' who wrote this journal didn't know any of what I know now, but she still hung on to hope.

Danny was so afraid to approach me in many ways, in fact he was just afraid all the time. Before 'The War' he had always called me his 'beautiful wife', even had me saved in his phone under 'beautiful wifey.' But when they had been together 'she' had found out and insisted that he save 'her' in his phone as 'gorgeous girlfriend' That meant that what Danny had called me, named me in his phone, was meaningless: At the beginning Danny calling me beautiful wifey meant nothing to me anymore. I told him to just save me in his phone under Rose (he was still not allowed to call me Rosie) because I felt that any term of endearment was just a load of crap! So for Danny to have the courage to call me his 'beautiful wife' was immense, and I knew it.

My biggest fear though, was if I caught Danny out on a lie I would leave. That is why when I thought of a discrepancy in his story I had to know the truth immediately. But now I know that I was never really going to know the truth. I often refer to the truth as 'The Unicorn of Truth': it only exists if you believe it. I do believe that Danny was lying to me because he was afraid to tell me all of the truth and hurt me all over again. As the years have gone by I know that I don't need to know because I should base my life on the here and now and not what happened in the past. Even then this applied but I was far too insane to see that.

Over the years I learnt that if I left Danny when I caught him out on a lie I would be leaving the man who was working hard to keep me; that he was lying because of the fear of losing me. The man working hard to keep me was not the man who had left me; that man was gone.

Danny had faced all of his demons in his fight to get me to stay and was a different man; I couldn't break that new man's heart.

I was changing and was starting to realise it. I could see that I was a different and stronger person when I was not with Danny; I was 'my own person'. I had at this point gone back to work full-time, becoming more independent financially, and was starting to realise that I didn't want back what we had before. This was fundamental to our survival, although neither of us realised that at the time. Why was it fundamental? Because we had to create something new based on our love for each other in the here and now. I had never doubted Danny's love for me, even when he was setting up home with 'her' I always knew he was crying somewhere.

Only the other day I was talking to someone about this book, recounting a story of something that happens later and she said "did you do that because you hated him at that time?" My immediate response was "No, I never stopped loving him." And do you know what? That was true, and that was the foundation on which we have built our new relationship, which is all the stronger for the mistakes we made.

Rosie

A Monday in June 2007

I told Danny on Saturday that I wanted to get 'that' love affair' back – and I do. We had a good evening this evening and Danny took my car to work because he hates driving his so much.

But yesterday I had a bad day, and that is what gets to me so much, the highs and then the terrible lows.

Danny told me on Saturday that he had cried at work with the boys in his gang. He had told them about our argument on Friday, but we did laugh that I had lobbed his phone at his head!

But yesterday I just had a really bad day. I was decorating (not good because the thoughts keep whizzing round your head). Why did he do it? Why did he start to see 'her' again in March?

I checked his phone bill right back to last June, as Danny had told me to do, to prove he had not been texting 'her'. But of course 'she' had a different phone then – how could I check? And that made me angry, because Danny knew that. So does that mean that he is still lying to me about what happened?

I could also see that it all started again on the 28th of February. All the texts, and it really upset me, my heart was pounding in my chest again.

I had a big chat with Ethan (always so astute)! He told me I must let it go and see what I have now. But the hurt is so bad. Ethan said I that he could see that Danny loved me so much; and I just looked at him as if to say 'you're joking right?' But I had to laugh when he said to me "Mum! You're not an easy person to come back to!"

Anyway I got the decorating done and never rang Danny all day. He didn't ring me, apart from to say he was on his way home. I swore to myself that I wouldn't bring it up; that I could act. But I couldn't.

I did bring up not being able to find the number and that I thought that Danny had deliberately set me up to look; thinking I was still a silly bitch and wouldn't remember that 'she' had changed 'her' phone.

I told Danny that for us to survive I have to know he is not still lying to me about anything. But he swears he is not. I explained and showed him how I remember things – like he now says that he didn't meet up with 'her' at Lowly until the March. That they had only communicated by phone in the September and October. But then I remembered that he said she had asked him to meet 'her' when he first text 'her' in the July, to say the kiss was a mistake. So is he now lying again? Why did he ever text her? Why did he contact 'her' at all? None of it added up.

See!! What do I do? I know in my heart of hearts that I need to let it go and concentrate on now.

I explained to Danny how it has affected me: my wedding photos mean nothing; you might as well throw my dress away because when I look at them they mean nothing. That I look back on the last nine years and feel that what I had never actually existed, it was just crap. (But as I am writing this I realise that there must be something, or I would not be here.)I want to stay but that is how I feel.

I know that Danny went up to the toilet and cried. I cried.

When Danny came back down we talked – something that Danny must continue to do. Even though he told me he does not cry anymore he told me he had lied. That he needs to go to the Doctor for anti-depressants because he feels so down; that he cried yesterday when he had sent his gang home from work. That he cried every day because his gut feeling is that he has lost me, that he is picking up that vibe, and that he cannot live without me; that he has suicidal thoughts – that he was thinking that if he got run over by a train whilst at work I would be able to get over him because it is a different bereavement, and financially I would be ok. That he sat on track yesterday without his high-visibility gear on, crying.

So now I have written all this down and now I realise that I must help us. That only I can. Do I let that fucking cunt destroy us any more than 'she' has already?

I know that Danny cannot live without me – something that Ethan predicted at the very beginning when he first left. I know that Danny is so sorry, that he was so manipulated; got caught up in something.

I must move on, I must leave it in the past and concentrate on now. I need to prove that to myself.

God/Mum please help me.

Rosie

Reflections Here & Now

Reading my journal now is like reading another person's story: I know that person, I know how much she was suffering, I know that she made me the person that I am today; and her strength, courage and determination brings tears to my eyes. Especially when she asks her mum for help; because I know that to do that she was in a really bad place. When I read this entry I cried for the person who was writing this journal; I cried because I remember her pain.

I was right when I wrote that our son Ethan was astute when he told me to focus on the here and now. He knew me so well when he said that I was not an easy person to come back to, and he was right; because it took a lot of courage for Danny to come back and fight for me. What Ethan had said made me take a step back and think; and his words echoed in my ears, often at times, when Danny would sometimes look so lost; or when I could see how hard he was trying:

even when I was mainly being a bitch. In fact I still quote them back to myself today because I have learnt that you have to see yourself and your actions, after all none of us are perfect.

In this entry I notice that my language is changing, and my madness and anger is starting to emerge. It was just over a month in, and I think that the initial shock and disbelief were starting to fade; making room for the reality, and the anger and rage that comes with it. I was starting on the journey of trying to find out the truth.

With infidelity comes lies, lies, and more lies; or as Danny would have had me believe at the time of this entry: the truth, truth and more truth!

I think that an easy way for me to explain what I went through is this:

What I said to Danny about the importance of not lying to me, and always telling me the truth, was true at that time. He had lied to me so much over the year before (or however long it was) that I couldn't bear the fact that he may still be lying, keeping secrets that he could only share with 'her'. The thought that I may be lying to myself by accepting what he told me terrified me; and made me angry at times. So at that time Danny telling me the truth was so important. But here is the crux: How do you even know if someone is telling you the truth?

At the moment that I am writing this journal entry I wanted to believe that I could get the truth out of Danny. I needed to know; but over time I came to realise that no matter what Danny said I didn't believe him. I would try and catch him out in a lie at every turn, I would ruminate over things he had said and how they didn't add up and I would drive myself insane doing it.

Danny was in a no-win situation. You will see as our story unfolds that this continued for years; and it was only when I realized that the truth was in fact like a unicorn (it only existed if you believed it) that I was able to move forward: I had to decide what I believed to be the truth, based not only on what Danny told me but on things I knew and had chosen to ignore, and my gut instinct. Basically I had to stop lying to myself. Then once I had decided what I believed to be true I then had to decide if I could live with it. When I finally realised this only then I was able to fully move forward.

Over the years I came to the decision that that Danny had been sending 'her' texts ever since they had kissed in the July the previous year. In fact looking back now, I think that he had been seeing 'her' long before we went on our holiday to Skiathos: I think that it had started in about the June before we went. The only difference now is that I know that the when and where, and what happened doesn't matter in the here and now.

I can honestly say that if I were to be able to conclusively establish what happened back then: to have it proved to me; would not make any difference to how I feel in the here and now. But…

The important thing is I do not lie to myself, no matter how painful. I face what may be the truth and I deal with the worst case scenario. That way nothing can bite me on the arse. However at the time I wrote this entry in my journal I could never have made these decisions about the truth; because at that moment in time if I had believed that Danny had been cheating on me that long I would not have stayed. I was in a 'catch 22' situation: I wanted the truth because I didn't want to be made a fool of anymore; but I didn't want the truth because I would not have stayed, and ultimately I wanted to.

I believe that is one of the hardest things to understand when you have been betrayed, you pursue the truth, whilst terrified you will find it.

I can only hope that reading my book about our experiences and how we got to where we are today will give you hope that one day, as time progresses, you can face up to this reality: and then you can make the decision on whether you want to pursue the 'truth' forever, or make your own decisions based on what you know in the here and now, and move on from there. Only you can make that decision.

Because this is a journey that both Danny and I went on it is important that I explain to you the impact all of this was having on Danny: This entry starts to touch on the turmoil that Danny was actually experiencing every day. He found it so hard because one day I was telling him I could do it and we could survive, and the next I was telling him that I couldn't do it, and I didn't know if I could stay. It had started to drive him mad. At that point in time I know that it was part of my revenge: I punished Danny every day. But over time I stopped wanting to take revenge because I could see the damage that was being done.

Danny was in turmoil because he couldn't understand his own actions: why he had jeopardised our relationship, or why he had left me, and for so long. He had disappointed himself, he had lied to himself, he had lost his self-respect and I know that he hated himself for what he had done.

Often we are so hurt that we cannot see the pain that the other person is in; after all at the outset of the journey you undertake why the fuck should you? They did the damage they should get all they deserve right? .....

Rosie

A Tuesday in June 2007

Dear Danny

I thought that rather than write in my journal today I would write to you. (I hope that the writing is big enough!)

Yesterday I wrote in my journal that I realised that you cannot live without me, that you are so sorry, that you were so manipulated and caught up in something. That I must move on and leave it in the past and concentrate on now; I realised that only I could really help you and us.

And yesterday I really was ok. If you think about it, although some things came up we talked about them and they were done, we didn't go on. It was good.

But when we went to bed and you were kissing me, you closed your eyes in a way that said you couldn't look at me. You said it was because of the guilt, and I know, and understand that. But it makes me feel as if you don't want to be with me. Or that you are thinking of what you have done with 'her'. I know in a way you regret it, wish it wasn't in your head; and whilst I know that you cannot help it, a chain reaction is set off in my head and I think of something that I really don't want to, and it made me cry.

I know that you want to make love (we can just have sex anytime) to me. I want you to. I can help with your guilt: if you make me happy you will feel less guilty.

I do have a handle on most of it now: meaning I can keep it under control. I am happy that you are back with me, happy that you love me so much, happy that you want to make it up to me in any

way you can. But you must overcome and get control of your guilt –
or that can actually destroy us because it stops you from doing the
things that will make me happy.

You want that great 'love affair' back – then we need to make
love, you need to be able to look at me and not shut your eyes. We
need to stop letting it interfere and affect our lives anymore.

We need to work together – I am, by getting control of it in my
head. Now you have to. I will help you but you must talk to me about
what goes on in your head; like I am now: I am writing you a letter
in my journal. Please darling, if you want us to work, talk to me.

In the words of Diana and Marvin

"All I want to do is make it up to you, because I need you more
than life itself."

"All I want to know, is you still care that nothing's changed, and
it's the same as it used to be."

**Just say Just say Diana Ross and Marvin Gaye
Written by Ashford and Simpson**

I love you.
Rosie

Reflections Here & Now

I wrote this open letter to Danny in my journal, and left my
journal open on the side for him to read when I wasn't there.

I wrote it because whenever we were in bed together I could see the
pain on Danny's face; even only recently he told me that if I shut my
eyes he thinks that I am thinking of someone else because he does not
deserve me; even now, even all these years later.

Although I had written this in my journal I hadn't put it behind
me when I wrote this; it was way too soon, and I was just hanging on
to hope.

Leaving my journal open for Danny to read was an immense thing
for both of us: me because my journal was my safe place; a place that
only I visited, and a place where I could be really honest with myself. It
was uncontaminated and the first thing that I had in a long time that
didn't include Danny. For Danny because he knew that my journal

was my sanctuary, he understood the importance of the symbolic gesture I had offered in allowing him to read it; including him in the power that it had to heal us.

I knew when I left it open that Danny wouldn't read any of the other entries because he was afraid of them, afraid of what I had written. Danny knew that my journal was a way for me to try and stop myself from running away from our relationship; and he knew that what I had written on any particular day determined if I would be there with him that evening.

In addition he didn't want to read it because he was afraid of what it showed: which was the damage that he had inflicted on us as a couple. That is how Danny saw it, and still sees it now. I don't. I know now that it took two of us to cause what had happened: We had stopped communicating, and I had become so caught up in my 'happy life' that I couldn't see the fear that Danny felt every day, fear that he would lose me some day.

I was so caught up at the time in believing that Danny loved me so much, was confident in our relationship; so happy that I didn't consider for one moment if Danny felt the same; and because of that it allowed another manipulative and evil person to come into our lives and use what I couldn't see against us.

I know that some people reading this will say that it was all Danny's fault because he was the one who had the affair, had sex with someone else, even moved into a house with her. But here is my take on it:

If during the first seven years that we were together (yes how cliché it was the seven year itch!) I had understood that Danny never thought that he was good enough for me; noticed that he had asked me if I would turn up to our wedding; noticed that he had felt that one day he would come home and I would not be there; that he had in fact felt that way the whole time we were together. If I had picked up on that insecurity then we would not have had that crack that 'she' had been able to crawl between to get to us. If I had listened to my friend Lucy all those years ago when she told me to stop talking about my boss James because it was worrying Danny, would 'she' have found it so easy to tell Danny that I had an affair with James when I didn't?

If I had not sent Danny to Coventry so many times when I was upset about something (often something that had nothing to do with

Danny) sometimes not speaking to him for days on end: feeding into his insecurity that he was not good enough, would 'she' have been able to get between us?

No, the answer is no!

Yes Danny broke my heart; he made a fool of me; he left me for someone else and acted as if he didn't care; he told me that he didn't love me and that he loved somebody else; he held court with the barmaids in the pub when we first got back together and, yes, for all that he was an arsehole. But I would be a fool if I couldn't see the arrogance of my actions when we were together before 'The War'. 'She' did get into Danny's brain and tell him that I would leave him one day, and my actions had unlocked the door to let 'her' in.

Danny's biggest problem had always been his fear, fed by his own insecurity; or as I have come to learn his vulnerability. So when he came back that is what he had to face every day, on an even bigger scale because of what he had done. That was Danny's Karma: it was not me doing back to him exactly what he had done to me, it was having his fear and insecurity increased by a hundred because now I was independent of him; and more importantly I no longer trusted Danny to provide my happiness. I had realised that I had to provide my own. I am still like that today, what happened to me made me find myself and never lose her again and even today that frightens Danny. But he still stays because he knows that despite it all I am what he wants.

Only recently in the years that I have been writing this book has Danny picked up my journal and read some of it. He has read some of my blog, although hardly any, and he does engage and listen to other's stories. I think that has helped him realise that he is not alone. When someone asked Danny why he had done what he did he simply said that it was because he never thought that he would keep me, that he still felt that I was too good for him and that sometimes he still wondered why I love him. Now I am conscious of that, and I do remind Danny of how much I love him and to not listen to that 'demon' in his head.

I have said in this journal entry how when Danny closed his eyes it set of a chain reaction in me which made me cry. Now I know that he closed his eyes through guilt.

Rosie

A Saturday in June 2007 (very late and technically Sunday)

So here I am, in Louise's spare bedroom, and I am happy. We have discovered that I am the type of person who needs to know the truth, no matter how hard it is; and that Danny is the type of person who doesn't want to know the truth because he cannot deal with it. We have to respect that in the future.

Last week I told Danny that I have a problem with what he says he felt like during 'The War', and want to understand (wanted) to piece the jigsaw together. So Danny talked to me, and I could piece the jigsaw together. I don't even need to go into the ins and outs.

On Thursday Danny talked about it without being prompted. He started to cry and said that he was "so sorry." I know that. Now I have been able to piece the jigsaw together I can see how manipulated we both were. I know my husband loves me so much and just wants to keep me.

We have had three good days since Wednesday. I can now easily keep my demon under control. It hasn't permanently been on my mind (hardly at all), and it's chased away when it does come into my mind.

I feel like we are getting back to normal now. I hope so. I am hopeful. I am looking forward to the future. I am eighty per cent happy, perhaps ninety per cent.

Let's be positive.

Rosie

Reflections Here & Now

When I wrote this entry I was in my Sister Louise's spare bedroom I had taken on board my sister's observation that I had been 'Princess Fucking Tippy Toes'. That Danny had been working too much overtime whilst I worked part time and that I needed to take some of the burden away from him. Louise's observations had been fair, so when Danny and I got back together one of the things we agreed was that when Danny worked his first night shift I would stay at Louise's house near to where Danny worked; it meant that I could drive him home the next morning and relieve some of the pressure. I didn't do this forever as my career started to take off, but I did it for at least five months.

It was hard for me to do because I was back at work full time, but it was essential so that I could show Danny that I supported him; because he had felt unsupported in the past. I know that some people would question why I owed Danny anything after what he had done to me; but as someone else who has been in a similar position said to me recently: 'if you want it to work you both have to do the work.'

I was aware that one of the lies and stories that 'she' had spun to Danny was that I only wanted him for the money that he earnt, so that I could renovate our beautiful house; and that I only wanted the house and not Danny.

Before 'The War' when we visited each other's houses 'she' would ask Danny how he felt about us, and Danny told 'her' his insecurities: that I would leave him one day, and that he thought that I only wanted him for what he earnt so that I could spend it on the house, that really I was only with him to keep the house. 'She' then manipulated this information, feeding on Danny's insecurities, by telling him that I had told her that I was only with him for the money he earnt, that I didn't love him, that I only wanted the house. Telling him things that I hadn't said; and Danny's insecurities allowed him to believe 'her'. So after Danny came back I knew that I had to show Danny that I did want him and that I understood the pressures on him and would help him wherever I could.

When I wrote this entry I took the fact that there is a gap between entries as a good thing; but I know that it was just me holding on to any small thing to give me hope. I went on to write in my journal like a maniac again at times. All the time when this happens to you the thing that drives you insane are the ups and downs. One minute everything is okay the next everything is in despair – just another part of the grieving process that I truly believe only time can really help. It is an ocean of despair (not a sea, because it goes on for so long) and I found that I just had to ride the waves and use hope as my buoyancy aid.

Was I eighty per cent happy when I wrote that entry? I felt that I was, but I would then feel twenty per cent happy the next day, or the day after that. I only started to feel close to one hundred per cent happy when I had gained myself back fully; because then I would no longer feel vulnerable. Over the years I have come to understand that no one person can make you happy; you have to look to yourself for that.

As part of my blogging journey and interaction with some really wonderful and brave people I always say that to move forward in this you have to hold on to every tiny thing, small steps. Imagine it as a jigsaw of tiny, tiny pieces and when you find a piece, something small that can give you hope, place it in the jigsaw until in the end it makes a bigger picture. That's what I did.

Rosie

A Sunday in June 2007

I had a nightmare last night: I dreamt that Danny left me again and went off with 'her'. It was one of those awful dreams that just kept coming back every time you go to sleep. I don't know if that was why I felt sad today. Not the wave of despair that I used to feel (I pulled the plug on that bath a long time ago) but still sad.

As I am writing this I realise that one of the reasons for it is that Danny seems so happy because I am happy (happier); and that just emphasises how much he loves me. So it brought it home to me tonight what he was so frightened of when he first came back: – which is why all he kept saying at the time was "I am so frightened." He was frightened that he would never get me back, that he had lost me forever.

But that makes me sad. Because although I understand the manipulation, the mistakes that he and I made, the circumstances that led us to it all, I still cannot understand why he let me down. I loved him so much, implicitly, without doubt or question. Now that has gone; and I am sad because I want to get that back – but I can't; and yes to a degree Danny has lost me. I can never one hundred per cent rely on him again. That man has gone for me; and I know that he desperately wants to come back, and I want him back, but I can't let him back. It is something that neither of us have any control over; and for what? Something so stupid, so trivial; is that how much we meant to him?

Why wasn't it enough? Why did he have to nearly lose me to realise what he had? And now he doesn't have that anymore.

I don't know. Will it get better with time? Will the sadness go away?

Rosie

Reflections Here & Now

When I started this journal I had written in it often because it helped to take the thoughts out of my head and stop them from tormenting me. Just before this entry there had been periods of up to three days where I hadn't written in it because things had actually started to calm down (or so I thought!). But here I was back to writing in my journal again – every day.

The dream happened because I was clearly struggling with feeling as if I would be back in that vulnerable place again. The torment of feeling that one minute you are back to being 'a little bit normal' and then WHAM! It is all back stronger than before, for me it was one of the main things that nearly made me walk away – many, many times. But the ups and downs are the norm, and that is why people so often use references of the sea when referring to how they feel: with waves of emotion, feeling as if you are drowning, going up and down, fighting for breath. I always refer to this time of my life as my journey on the ocean of despair.

I have come to often ask the question: 'what is normal?' And I have realised that what you have in the here and now IS the 'normal', that's it! It is no good looking back and believing that what you used to have was normal, or looking forward in the hope that normal will be in the future, none of those things exist, neither the past nor the future. The only moment is here and now and the only 'normal' is what you are experiencing here and now. If you can get your head around that then it will help you immensely as you move forward.

Clearly from my introduction you know that for me it did get better but I did put into place lots of coping mechanisms to help me deal with it. In the very early days I used visualisation (the demon – although I still use him today), and the bath of despair was one of these: When I found myself spiralling downward I would stop and visualize myself sitting in a bath full of blackness. I imagined that blackness holding me there trying to pull me under and then I pictured myself pulling myself upwards and stepping out of that bath. In the early days it stopped me spiralling when I felt overwhelmed.

I was right when I have said that when something is lost you will never get it back. I can remember that immense sadness and pain so implicitly and the fear that they would never would never go away and I would feel like that forever. This is one of the reasons I wrote this book, to help the person reading this understand that it does go, it does get better. To give them hope.

When I read this entry my eyes filled with tears when I read that I had written 'I loved him so much, implicitly, without doubt or question' and how that had gone. I have stopped to consider whether I love him without question now, all these years later, and the answer is yes I do. He did the work, he made it better.

I asked myself if what I had said in this entry was true: would I ever one hundred per cent rely on Danny again? The answer is clear because I live in rural France with him, on a very small monthly budget and we have to trust each other to make it work. So yes I do one hundred per cent rely on Danny, in the same way that he relies on me. Do I trust him? Yes I do, but I believe it is a different trust, because now I will never ignore my gut instinct, and that applies to all aspects of my life.

I have often been asked "Aren't you frightened that he will do it again?" I have always said no because I watched Danny pull himself through hell to keep me, and I know that there is no way that he is ever going to risk losing me again.

I asked recently on social media this question of the people who have had their hearts broken:

'If you were in their shoes could you keep going? Be honest: if you felt like a cheat, was with someone who cried every day, sometimes all day, because of what you had done; someone who screamed at you, hated you, loved you, blamed you for everything including rainy days would you stay?'

I asked myself that question, and the answers from other people were interesting because most said 'no'.

When Danny came back he did say nearly every day, from the first day he returned, that he was 'so frightened'. I had forgotten that until now, he would whisper it often

"I am so frightened".

Over the years I have watched Danny face every fear he had, never give up, cry rivers- even now – but he has carried on, and for that I have respect.

Rosie

A Friday in June 2007

Ethan is being really difficult; perhaps because he and Annie aren't getting on. But yesterday we had a row and he threw up in my face what Danny had done, for the third time. That really hurt me.

It frightened the life out of Danny as well, because he thought that it would drag it all up, and we haven't spoken about it for a week now. We had finally got back to some normality: had our tea at a normal time, snuggled on the sofa. I think it also made Danny feel guilty because he realised that he has given people ammunition to fire at me now – even Ethan.

I went to Susan's and spoke to Louise on the phone because I was so upset. When she realised what Ethan had said she rang him and had a go at him. When I came home I pointed out to him that if Danny and I don't make it I will sell up and go anyway. I can't keep living my life for other people, and that includes both Danny and Ethan. I need to worry about me now, or I won't survive.

I really cried when I went to bed. But surprisingly I feel okay; felt okay last night after I cried.

Danny was on a night shift and had rang me at Susan's because he was so worried and I rang him back at about 1am to tell him I was okay, but he was still really worried, but I do feel okay.

Over the week I have come to realise that, where before, I totally relied on Danny for my emotional support it was unhealthy; and to be honest I don't think that Danny can supply that, definitely not now.

But where before I would feel totally alone and withdraw now I don't'; I realise all the people, not Danny, who care about me are there for me. I used to think that Danny was my greatest ally, and now I realise that he never was. I am.

Instead of feeling totally alone, I now feel stronger and able to cope on my own - know I can. I am still sad that I cannot have that person I can totally rely on – thought I could rely on. But the person I have to totally rely on is me. I have to spread any other reliance around others because it can never be totally on Danny. Ironically now Danny does totally rely on me! I know that if we do not make it, that it will be the end of Danny and he will just throw his life away.

I still feel sad, but not as bad as I did at the beginning of the week. That is what this journal shows – how much easier it is getting, even in a week; I know that the sadness will get easier, as Danny makes it up to me and we make new memories. Like any bereavement it will fade. In fact I have just realised that we should be on the plane to Skiathos now. At the beginning of the month that would have really upset me, but I didn't even think of it today.

Rosie

Reflections Here & Now

And there it is! I had started to find me. I had realised that I couldn't rely on one person for my emotional support, and more importantly I had started to realise that the only person I could ever fully rely on was me. That sums it all up. As the years have gone by I do rely on Danny more than at the time of this entry but I can assure you that I have never ever forgotten that I am my greatest ally.

I have come to realise that we often put so much pressure on people to always be there for us: always be our emotional crutch, to sort things out for us. Is that fair? I don't think it is. Other people are not responsible for us they cannot make everything right; only we can do that for ourselves.

I have said something in this entry which is poignant, given that I am now sitting in France writing this; I said I couldn't continue to live my life for other people, and I know that this was the small spark that took me on a personal journey and led me to be the person that I am today.

I don't think that anyone realises that when someone has an affair it impacts on everyone they know. In this entry the impact on Ethan, who was only seventeen when this happened, is clear. How could I have expected him to be able to deal with it? I was hardly dealing with it myself; I was only getting through it day by day, as were both of us, all of us.

Yes, Ethan hurt me when he threw up in my face that I could forgive Danny but not forgive him for something so small that I cannot even remember what it was. But he was a teenager and I was still trying to be the mum who taught him what was right from wrong. Looking back now I can understand how he thought that, I had a bloody cheek.

Ethan was angry with Danny, angry with me: not for having Danny back, but for becoming this person who didn't have it all together. For Ethan his mum always had it all together, and now she was this manic person who seemed to always have tears in her eyes. I can remember how Ethan would seek reassurance that we would be alright; that we would have somewhere to live and be able to still live in our home. It was me he sought reassurance from because all his life it was me that had always made everything alright. It was only as I went further up the career ladder and got stronger that Ethan became reassured that all would be okay.

Danny was afraid because he still thought that if we didn't talk about it, then it was all over, and we could go back to living normally (that bloody word again!)

It was only my poor sister Louise who really understood all of the implications if Danny and I split up; and at times it was Louise who was the only voice of reason in this whole sorry scenario. So try and have someone who you can talk to who will not emote with you; but will listen and consider and then give you a measured response and leave their own emotions out of it.

God knows in this situation you don't need anyone else's emotions in the mix!

Rosie

CHAPTER 41

Stories to Tell – June 2007

In my journal entry of 18th June 2007 I have said about an argument that Danny and I had when I had threw his new phone at his head. The argument just highlighted how mad we were: as all of the players tend to be in the infidelity saga: We act like children, do things that we would have done when we were teenagers. I can remember thinking at the time that it was as if I had gone back in time, to when I was selfish and only thought of myself; a time when I didn't consider others feelings before I said harsh words.

We had been to Susan and Malcolm's house for the evening. They only lived ten minutes from us and so we always walked so that we could have a drink. I have only realised as I write this book that it was as if their house was a 'safe house'. It was a place where the people understood but would also call us out if one of us was behaving irrationally.

We had a good evening but walking home we argued, over what I do not know, but I know that as we approached a road leading off the road we were on I walked off and told Danny to 'fuck off.' But he came after me and when he caught up he gave me his new phone and told me to give it to Ethan because he was leaving.

I can remember looking at him incredulously as he walked away, he was leaving AGAIN!! I was so angry that I just took the phone and threw it at his head; and it hit his head, hard, and then bounced off and landed on the floor breaking into pieces. That phone had just cost us the best part of one hundred and fifty pounds, but I didn't care. It was just a fucking phone.

Danny just stood there looking at me as I said "Don't think that I will ask you to stay this time, because trust me I fucking won't! If you walk away now you will never come back." He knew that I meant it, I did. So he bent down and started to pick up all the pieces of the phone and as he was doing it he just kept saying 'I can't believe you did that!'

I just walked away from him and went home. But I poured myself a wine and waited on tenterhooks to see if Danny came home too.

This time he did.

Rosie

June 2007 A Story: Finally getting the message across

There is another important part of our story here that I have not written about in my journal, which really surprises me because it was a key incident in our story. I am sharing it because it's important to show how we worked together, and what Danny did to reassure me which enabled us to get to where we are today.

By June 'she' could no longer call our landline or contact Danny other than to call his place of work; and 'she' had been constantly leaving messages on the answer phone at Danny's depot. One particular day the office had phoned Danny, who was on a night shift, to say that 'she' had left another message saying that if he didn't call 'her' 'she' would turn up at the depot on that night.

Now the phone 'she' had been ringing was the incident line so the Depot Manager had told Danny that he had to resolve it, or the Depot Manager would call the police because 'she' was blocking up the incident answer machine.

Danny called me at work and asked me to come home; he didn't want to call 'her' without me being there: he was still afraid of 'her' and the damage 'she' could do. So I went home and Danny asked me to call 'her' using my phone because I had not changed my number and 'she' would know it was my phone but think that it was Danny calling. (I have come to realise over time that Danny must have used my phone sometimes to call her, I wouldn't have checked before 'The

War', I thought that I was safe) I knew that once 'she' heard my voice 'she' would put the phone down; and that is exactly what 'she' did.

I turned to Danny and told him that he had to call 'her', using my phone, because she wouldn't listen to anyone else other than him. So Danny called 'her' and 'her' phone went to answer machine, because 'she' clearly thought it was me. Danny left a message saying that if 'she' kept trying to contact him he would report 'her' to the police as a stalker; reminding 'her' how this may impact on the custody battle that was going to take place with 'her' ex. He also said something that was so important to me at that time: he told 'her' that he loved me, had always loved me, had never loved 'her', and that he just wanted 'her' to "fuck off" and leave him alone.

Now I look back I know that it was one of the things that made me stay at such a difficult time. I needed to know that Danny was on my side, and to hear him say that in front of me gave me assurance that he was: Danny had reversed what he had said to me and said it to 'her.'

'She' never rang Danny's Depot again and never left any more messages on the answer machine. In fact I heard about a month later that another man had moved in with 'her'; ironic really: 'she' didn't waste any time for someone who had been so 'in love' with Danny!

CHAPTER 42

Journal Entries - July 2007

A Monday in July 2007

After writing my journal and getting into the car the awful thoughts that I have tried hard to get rid of were back in my head again. That really got to me, and when I got to work (later than I said I would be) I rang Louise from the car before I went into work. I was upset about what Ethan had done and what Danny had done to put me in this position. I said that I felt that I had spent the last nineteen years looking after other people, including Ethan and Danny, and now I need to look after me.

Hannah my friend from work then text me to make sure I was okay, as all the people that I worked for were worried about me. That said a lot.

I did manage to get it under control since my last entry, and Danny and I had a lovely weekend and a brilliant Friday night. But yesterday I just felt sad. I am sad that I am in this position, sad that Danny did what he did; still cannot understand that if he loved me that much how he could do it. Sad that we have lost what we had; and that no matter how much we want it to come back, it has gone and will never come back. But I know that it is bereavement and that with time that sadness will fade but never go away. Or will it? Can we achieve something new something better?

I was quiet yesterday evening when I sat in the garden and Danny asked me why. I told him I was eighty per cent happy but twenty per cent sad; that I knew that I could never totally rely on him; that sometimes when I felt like this I needed to go away from him for a short time to grieve on my own; how I had never felt like that before but I do now.

I am a different person – fully me for the first time since my mum died- when I had said that to Danny when we were apart it had been true. I do still love him and want us to work.

I do still love him and want us to work, but what Danny doesn't understand is that my love for him was so complete, so total – more than I have given to anyone else – and it is that which has been destroyed.

I know it really hurt Danny when I said that sometimes I needed to get away from him; he was upset that I was only eighty per cent happy. But as I said to him did he really expect one hundred per cent? He said that the reason that he thought he would lose me is because someone will sweep me off my feet; someone who has not hurt me like he has, someone who can give me that 'great love.' I said that I don't believe that 'great love' exists. What would stop them doing to me what Danny has done? Who is to say it would be any better?

Danny hit the vodka!

I told him that what I needed him to do was come to bed and cuddle. His state of mind worries me. It also shows me sometimes just how different Danny and I are. I used to think that I had changed Danny, that after meeting me and achieving all he has he thought differently to when I first met him. I now realise that he doesn't. It is me who keeps him there, and obviously from what has happened sometimes even I can't do that!

I didn't sleep well. I know that Danny didn't either. I do love him, I know he loves me, I hope that is enough, want it to be enough.

Time will tell.

Rosie

Reflections Here & Now

Here we are less than a month from my entry in June when I lied to Danny and told him I was eighty per cent happy when I was nowhere near that and yet in this entry (and previous entries) I have said that I am eighty per cent happy and meant it!

This is why I kept a journal: so that I could see that things were getting better. When this happened to me I frantically searched for other people's stories where affairs had taken place. I found some but none of them showed me the pain they had experienced: they had either not survived or had told the story of how they recovered, when I needed to understand their pain. But none shared their madness as I am now, and that is what I needed; because in this ocean full of storms I couldn't see how I was going to survive. So my only recourse was to write my own madness and then go back and read it and reflect and understand.

Since starting this book I have read many people's blogs about the way that infidelity has affected their lives: a common theme is how we all swing from one emotion to another and it re-enforced to me that I needed to write this book, because I am here, we are here many years later and I can show you all my pain, all our pain and then I can tell you how I feel now, honestly.

At the time that I wrote this entry a lot of my increased happiness was due to Danny's stubborn determination not to give up; that man was like a limpet! And I respect him immensely for that; as Ethan said 'I am not an easy person to come back to.'

But my increased happiness was not all due to Danny's actions. I was working more hours at work, earning more money and starting to feel as if I was becoming my own person again. A different person to the person who had been married to Danny before, I was no longer dependant on him financially or emotionally,

I will say this often: It was essential for my survival that I was my own person who was primarily dependent on herself, and I knew it, even then. If I was honest I was afraid of the implications of it because I was still struggling to stay, and the more independent I became the more the demon told me that I could leave if I wanted to, and I still struggled for a long time into the future as you will see.

It was bereavement: I had lost something that I had, and loved so much, something that was so precious to me; and what makes it worse is because of the nature of how I lost it I felt as if it was never really real in the first place.

I remember thinking that the last nine years of my life had been a lie, and even now I don't tend to look at my wedding pictures as much as the ones when we renewed our vows. But an important thing that I can see looking back on this entry is that I asked myself, even in the midst of all the madness, if there was a possibility that we could survive and find something new and better; despite the fact that at that time we were still teetering on the edge of the cliff into oblivion, hope was still there. For those people who are where I was when I wrote my journal if you have hope hold onto it in the dark days and nights it is your biggest ally.

It is interesting that I saw Danny as weak at that time, because I was the one that seemed to be able to pull us back together when Danny hit the vodka. It is true that I do have a stronger personality than Danny, put my back up against the wall and I will not be beaten, but now I see the strength it took from Danny to keep us together: He wouldn't give up even though for most of the darkest parts of 'The War' he was terrified.

Rosie

A Tuesday in July 2007

For the first time I feel the need to write in my journal, but don't actually know what I am going to write!

I had the day off with Danny yesterday, as I was worried about him. We had a long chat about what we had discussed yesterday and mainly Danny still feels that I don't need him. I do so need him. Danny is the rock on which the rest of my life is based.

Today I have that feeling: as if there is a hand on my heart and it is squeezing it with all its might. For the first time in a long time I feel afraid and I cannot put my finger on what it is.

We went for a long walk to Lowly (another hurdle). We were going to have a couple of drinks and come home. But we met a man, Peter, and we ended up drinking with him and going back to a pub in Smugglers Cove with him. We were having a good time, but Danny told Peter about what had happened, and obviously, when people have a drink they offer their opinion – perhaps one that you should not always listen to.

Peter liked me and told me how sorry Danny is, but he was talking to Danny and Danny looked really sad. I asked Danny what was the matter but he wouldn't say. The drink kicked in and we ended up arguing over everything.

As I am writing this what does it tell me? Drink was part of the thing that caused our problems before, and I have come to the conclusion that we have to be careful with it. Danny kept talking about committing suicide again, and that makes me afraid.

I don't want to be in the place that I am, but I am. I do believe that we can move forward, regain our life together and I know that is what Danny wants; but he must overcome his fear, must help me as I help him. I need him too.

I fear my rock is crumbling and I don't want that. But am I the cement that can hold him together? I believe I am, I hope I am.

It is a small thing that has come between us; surely our love for each other can overcome it. I am crying now as I write this. Although I didn't know what to say a lot has come out.

Addendum

Danny has just rung me.
Please God help us make it: Overcome the demons and move on.

Footnote 4.20pm

I realised why I felt like someone was squeezing my heart this morning. Because I thought there was a possibility that I would lose Danny, and that frightened me. I now understand that Danny lives with, and has lived with that fear every day for years; and I understand what he is so afraid of.

Rosie

Reflections Here & Now

I don't think that you ever forget that feeling of having your heart squeezed; it is something that stays with you forever. Or that feeling that you are drowning; I read people's posts and comments on help groups, and social media and my heart goes out to them when they say that they feel as if they are drowning. Because that is exactly what you are doing in the aftermath of an affair: drowning in a sea of emotions, feeling high one minute, low the next; gulping for air at times. It is so hard.

The place called Lowly that I refer to here is the small seaside town, a really pretty little place and it is the place where Danny would go to meet 'her' in his car. They would sit in his car by the seafront and talk and kiss and do God knows what else (I really don't and didn't need to know.) I couldn't bear to get in Danny's car ever again; in fact he sold it not long after we got back together. Because of all of this to walk to Lowly was a major hurdle, as I have said in my journal. But even then I knew that I had to face each hurdle full on because that was the only way that I was ever going to overcome them and overcome my fears. I often say 'take control of a situation don't let it take control of you' and I was applying that philosophy here without even realising it.

One of the things that I found after 'The War' was that people have a way of sniffing out when something is amiss between a couple; I have said it before: it is a bit like sniffing out a wounded animal; a weakness. On this occasion the man we were talking to sniffed out Danny's fear that he would lose me. By telling him what had happened Danny had enabled him to consider if I could be taken off Danny. I really think that they thought that because I had been brought to the brink of destruction and had my confidence destroyed that I would want payback: that I was 'easy pickings'. They were wrong.

Of course this also fed on Danny's fear of Karma, as they tried to take me away from him to score points on him (as 'she' had so often done to me). The age old adage is 'what goes around comes around' (still love that Justin Timberlake song) But I don't believe that Karma is about revenge. I believe that Karma teaches you about cause and effect: how your actions cause things to happen that will affect your life in the future.

I have found that Karma will pick up the thing that makes you the most insecure, your weakness if you like, your fear: the very thing that made you take the action in the first place (the cause) and remind you of it every day; and turn it around to bite you,(the effect).

I believe that Karma is a lesson that teaches you to not always listen to what your demon in your mind is telling you; but to listen to all of the little things that life shows you that we so often choose to ignore. I believe that Karma is not about revenge, Karma is about learning; but more often than not, the lessons are hard ones.

On this occasion the reason that Danny looked so sad was because the man 'Peter' had told Danny that he had no chance of keeping me; that 'women 'like me' wouldn't stay; and that someone else would steal me from him'; and of course Danny believed him.

Interestingly Peter then rang me himself days later. Seriously! He was about twenty years older than me and looked like someone who could be my dad; but he still thought that I would give him a chance! Obviously he didn't know me and he was firmly told no.

I did tell Danny he had called, mainly because I didn't want there to be any secrets between us; but I would be lying if I didn't say that at that time I didn't enjoy poking Danny with that stick a little bit myself.

I was never going to leave Danny for someone else, because I knew that wasn't the answer. But I was going to find myself and hold on tight.

Over the years I have realised how much Danny had to face his fear to stay and he never gave up. He learnt the lesson that Karma sent his way, and for that I have the utmost respect for him.

Rosie

A Friday in July 2007

I have just cried. I know I am hormonal, so that is a contributing factor, but sometimes I still feel like crying. The biggest thing for me, the thing that is constantly in my head, is the fact that Danny had sex with 'her'.

I think that at the beginning of this journal I said that it wasn't the main thing for me. That it was for Danny but not for me. I did mean it at the time; perhaps it was because I had so many other things in my head to deal with.

Now I don't have as many things in my head, which is a good thing, but it has also opened the way for me to deal with what was actually the worst thing of all. And perhaps at the beginning it was just too big for me to deal with, so I put it to the back of my mind. Now it is here and I know, as is my nature, I have to confront it to deal with it. But how do I do that? I am hoping that by writing this in my journal it will help me.

I know that Danny says that he thought he had lost me, and that he was only 'going through the motions'. That he had to shut his eyes and think of me. But although I really want to believe him I can't. I know Danny well enough, and if he had something on his mind he would not be able to get an erection. – It happened often enough with us. He had sex with 'her' on the night he text me (supposedly because he thought he had totally lost me, that I had changed my number, because I had not text back.) How did he do that?

Danny says that if I had not text back he would have come to work and waited for me by my car; when, in a day, a week, a month? I don't believe he ever would have.

I am crying now, but I know that I have to write these thoughts down to make some sense in my head. (That's the control freak in me!)

I know that Danny had a fumbling session with 'her' (crap) when they were together at 'her' sister's house. But if he loved me (loves me, sorry shouldn't use past tense.) how could he have sex with 'her' after he left when it was supposedly something he regretted from the minute he shut the front door? I want to believe so much, but can't. I am not that type of person (sometimes I wish I was) and that undermines us.

We went to the counsellor and she said that we had an 'inner couple' that not everybody has. I know that Danny loves me, I know that he is so happy we are back together, I know he got caught up in something; I know his weaknesses and guilt made him run away; but how come his grief at our break up, his guilt and his love for me didn't prevent him from being able to have sex with 'her? 'Something does not tie up.

I don't feel that I can talk to Danny about this; but I fear that if I don't it will destroy us. He thinks we are moving forward, and we are in a lot of things; but for me, right now, I feel this will always hold me back and eventually destroy us. I have found this really hard. I am hoping I can find some resolution. That I will look back in a couple of months and be able to see it has got better.

We have had lots of good points this week. But I can't write about them right now because this overshadows them.

5.15pm

I can't read what I have written because I have been upset all day. I spoke to Nel for an hour after writing it and we agreed that my hormones have a lot to do with how I feel, but I know, also, that this is the final and hardest hurdle.

I am going to provide a makeup party for Hannah's daughter's birthday, and I am looking forward to it. I promised Hannah I would be okay, and funny, like I used to be, how I normally am!

Danny has picked up that something is wrong; but I will stick to my plan that I drew up with Nel – wait until the hormones are gone and keep writing in here. Then see how I feel.

When I spoke to Hannah she said that Danny says those things to make things better, because he is so desperate not to lose me. But I think that it is more to make Danny feel better because he does not want to lose me, and hates what he has done. I suppose that in some way that should make me feel better: that is how little he thinks of 'her,' or what they did. In some ways it does.

I know that it may not be all that I am making it out to be in my head. But unless Danny talks to me about it I will never know. What if it was what I think in my head? How would I deal with that? And even if Danny told me it wasn't would I believe him?

Right now I don't want to kiss Danny let alone do anything else. I can use my tooth falling out as the perfect excuse.

This is going to be my hardest test. Because right now I feel that I need space from Danny; and for us to survive I have to overcome that. I have told him to have a sleep for half an hour.

How ironic that bloke from the pub called me today and left a message. I am not interested. But perhaps it now gives Danny a dose of the situation he has put himself in.

Rosie

Reflections Here & Now

This is the big one. I knew that I had to confront what I believed to be the most heart breaking thing of all; at least that was how I felt at the time.

When I think of it now it is still something that I have to dismiss in my head because the image would be too awful to contemplate; but despite that I know now that was not the most heart breaking thing; that was being lied to, and gas lighted and ghosted until I no-longer trusted myself and wondered about the person that I had spent so many years of my life with; because it was those things that caused the most destruction to our relationship; they caused most of the damage that took years to rebuild from.

But at the time I wrote this entry that was how I felt, and this entry shows how painful it was because I couldn't even read it at the time; couldn't write about the good things, because this one thing took over.

The thought of the person I loved being intimate with someone else is the thing that churned my stomach. Thinking of Danny and 'her' in 'the act' I imagined all sorts of things: mainly how wonderful and romantic it must have been. How they must have laughed about me and compared me.

Knowing and acknowledging that Danny had been intimate with someone else, done something with someone else that was only meant for us, meant that the intimacy in our relationship was lost. It was another thing that would have to be rebuilt because what we had before was just crap.

That is why I often told Danny that a 'shag was just a shag'. In fact that was how I was coping with it: I had sex with Danny, I didn't make love with him. I can remember on our holiday in the August of 2007 that he was so tender and loving; but it made no difference to me because I could not allow myself to give that intimacy to him. I could not allow myself to be that vulnerable again.

In fact if I were honest the intimacy is there but the vulnerability that I felt when I made love with Danny before 'The War' has never fully come back. I love Danny, I hug Danny, I caress and stroke him; but where the act itself is concerned it is sex.

I was right that I had to confront it, even though I was terrified that I wouldn't be able to move forward in my life with Danny when I had heard the details; I knew I would not be able to live my life with him at all without hearing them.

I learned that Danny was more afraid of this conversation than I was, although I didn't realise it at the time. He was afraid because I asked him why so many times and he himself did not know the answer; in fact as time wore on he found it harder and harder to answer. It was also because he didn't want to hurt me anymore than he had already, and he was terrified that if he answered honestly he would lose me; and he probably would have.

Coming from the point of view of the person who has been hurt, I needed to know, had to know. But looking back now how do I know if what Danny was telling me was the truth? How will I ever know? 'She' could crawl back out of the woodwork and say the 'truth' and how would I know if that were the truth either? That is one of the joys of infidelity: you have to be strong and make your own mind up about what you think happened – and having such a strong personality I went for the worse thing because if I could face that I could face anything.

Further entries will show that I asked about this over and over; I grilled Danny. He gave me answers, but I grilled him to such a degree that in the end he was giving me different answers: anything that he thought that I wanted to hear, and of course then I picked him up on the conflicting things he had said.

For years after we got back together I told Danny that if I ever found out that he was lying; found out that the foundation for whatever we rebuilt our relationship on, was based on more lies I would leave. I continued to say that even after we renewed our vows. I was, quite literally driving myself nuts.

It has taken me years to realise that it doesn't matter. Because what we have here and now is what's important and shouldn't be compromised because of something that happened in the past.

Over time I had to decide if I could live with this knowledge or not. I had to decide what was important to me: What I had in the here and now or what I had lost that had never been what I thought it was in the first place. I did consider whether I could live a life where I would never allow myself to be vulnerable in bed with Danny; or whether I should leave and find someone new. But I realised that what had happened meant that I was never going to allow myself that vulnerability with anyone again. When I realised that, then I decided to stay because I realised that sex was only one of the important aspects of our relationship.

Rosie

A Monday in July 2007

It's done!!

We went to Nel and Gus's on Saturday and as usual Nel and I chatted. In the evening when I had a drink I got upset because 'it' was on my mind. I said that I needed Danny (told Danny) to cuddle me and to be more affectionate to me. To not be afraid that I would pull away; and I swore on my mum's grave that I wouldn't pull away if he did this.

When I picked Danny up from work that day he told me about how he and another member of his gang had ended up crying in the works van together about the mistakes they had made. When Danny said that he was upset because he could lose me over a "fucking old shit" I liked it when he called 'her' that.

On the Sunday he was talking about FC (Fat Cunt, my new abbreviation for 'her') and again called 'her' a "fucking old shit." And that made me feel better.

My hormones had also calmed down, and I realised that what I had said to Danny about showing me more affection in some ways, was one of the keys to overcoming it. I knew that he was worrying about what was on my mind and that wasn't helping him; I knew that I had to speak to him that day.

I spoke to Auntie Joyce and Louise and they both agreed that this was something that had to be discussed, no matter how painful, to enable it to be boxed up and put away: because if I didn't discuss it I would never move on.

Louise suggested that I should show Danny what I had written in my journal. I don't think he could have coped with it all; but when we did talk I read him some bits: about closing his eyes and things like that, and the entry where I had said I didn't want him anywhere near me on Friday; to show him how it was affecting me.

On the Sunday when I picked Danny up from work we went down to East Hamden railway station which is a quiet place; Danny thought that I was going to tell him to go (Danny's biggest fear, as he always thinks that.) We talked about it. I know my husband well enough to be able to tell from his face if he is lying. I made it clear, that if there is one thing we have both learnt from this it's that I am the kind of person that needs to hear the truth, no matter how unpalatable; that is how I live my life – to deal with things head on.

Danny told me that throughout the whole time with 'her' he couldn't maintain a hard on. He swears that he did shut his eyes and think of me; but that sometimes that just made things worse; and that 'she' would get annoyed and say that he needed to learn to relax with 'her''. Silly bitch! 'She' just couldn't see what was under 'her' nose.!

I said about it making me feel better when he called 'her' a 'shit', and reminded him of when he said he didn't hate 'her'. But Danny interrupted me and said that was a long time ago (13th of June – it just seems so long ago because we have come so far forward.) That now he does hate 'her', that he "fucking hated 'her' for coming between us." For everything 'she' did to me. Because he has had to fight so long to keep me, in fact might still lose me because of 'her'. That he really hates 'her, 'her' partner because of the way he told me; hates that 'her' partner kept telling me things to try and make sure that Danny never got me back.

I said to Danny how both of them, and Danny to some degree, never took into account me: my life, or my feelings; but that with those two their biggest mistake was to underestimate me. They grossly underestimated me. Danny said "They sure did, so did!"

I promised Danny that was it now door closed. I thanked Nel and Louise. I know now it is time to move on. We toasted our future in the garden and Danny said "Thank you."

I did mean it. But then within an hour I found myself asking about why he started to see 'her' again in March, and it freaked Danny out.

But we have moved on, need to move on. It will still come up from time to time – sometimes Danny will need to talk about it (but he doesn't realise it now.)

I need to have the courage of my convictions. I want to close that door now, move forward now. To do that I must not only ensure all the lids are on the boxes but close the cupboard door. I must look at all the positives from now and use them as my tools. I will also continue to keep my journal until I no-longer feel the need. But hopefully most of what I write will be positive.

Positives for the future:

1. Danny said thank you.
2. Danny hates 'her,' regrets it so much.
3. Danny would do anything to keep me.
4. Danny is so sorry for what he has done.
5. Wants us to work so badly.
6. Is so happy when I am happy (what more could anyone want?!)
7. Danny maintains (big time) his erection with me
8. Loves me so much.
9. I love Danny so much.
10. Would give everything up for me.
11. I am the most important thing in Danny's life.
12. I have found myself. I understand my head for the first time ever.
13. I have lost weight and got fit.
14. I realise how many people I have who care about me/us.
15. We work well together as a team. Isn't that what life is really about? Isn't love just part of the equation?
16. Danny would never do it again.
17. Back, very closely now, with Louise. Better than we ever were.
18. Have a better relationship with Ethan.
19. Danny treasures everything about us, every good moment that we have.
20. Danny never wants to lose me.

I will use this list at times. But I am hoping that any future entries will mostly be positive (apart from the hormones!)

Rosie

Reflections Here & Now

It is noticeable that since the subject of Danny having sex with someone else started to play on my mind I went back to writing in my journal almost every day, sometimes twice a day. It was an indication of just how much that issue played on my mind; I was terrified of it.

My sister and aunt were right, of course: I did have to have the discussion with Danny, but it made me smile that we thought that it could be put in a box and locked in a cupboard.

What had happened to us was never going to be put in a box and put away. Oh how I know that now! In fact in my blog I have written a post entitled 'Little boxes made of ticky tacky' dealing with this very issue, and you can read it in some of the blog entries at the back of the book. (Thank you to the songwriter Malveena Reynolds for the words.)

I learned that everything needed to be confronted and dealt with to enable us to rebuild our lives and our relationship again. It was always going to be there, and part of 'dealing' with it was recognising that fact. I do believe that infidelity is not something that can be boxed up and never talked about again; as if doing this will make it like it didn't happen. It did happen. It changed everything and I truly believe that if you try to box it up and put it away you will be unhappy moving forward into the future. Acceptance is the key.

At the time I wrote this entry I wanted to believe that what Danny was telling me was true. I don't think it was now. Some of it perhaps: I can believe that he lost his erection with 'her' (I have no need to use the new name I had for her, not now). I believe that 'she' said he should learn to relax with 'her', because that was the Danny I knew: when he had something on his mind his penis couldn't perform. But the fact of the matter was that Danny had still 'tried' to have sex with her.

Now I know that Danny, as many people who leave their partners for another person do, wanted to keep 'her' happy because in his mind he had already ruined everything for us, and he needed to hold on to something. (The counsellor told me that when I visited her on my own, to help me to understand why Danny seemed to be defending 'her' at times.) But trust me, telling me he hated 'her', which as he said it I knew he meant, was a massive thing for me. I needed to hear that.

The conversation was also important to me because I had started to recognize my own strength: that even though they had all been players in the play, they had failed to recognise the strength of the leading lady, me!

The list of positives show how I clung to anything to keep me in the relationship; but it worked, I especially love number seven!

When I sit here now and I read what I hoped for:

Rosie

Journal entry

A Wednesday in July 2007

Why won't this sadness go away? Or am I asking too much?

It is still a bereavement, at times I feel I am still in shock at what has happened; because I was so sure of our love and commitment for each other, that nothing would ever tear something so good apart; that it was the most rock solid thing that I was ever going to have, and it wasn't!

All Danny says is that he does love me as much as I thought he did, because he came back. I suppose from that he means that he couldn't keep away. I understand that part; but why did he do it? I still at times (not all the time, not like before), feel an immense sadness about it all; and it does drive a wedge between us, but I am so hoping that will get less.

Danny did try so hard yesterday: Cleaned inside my car with lovely smelling cleaners, cuddled and kissed me; but as he said last night when we talked, it just never seems to be enough. I understand as I am writing this what he means, and I don't know if it will ever be enough.

I want it to be.

As I have said before, I cannot throw away the love that I know we do have. But perhaps I continually ask him to be over the top with his affection because I know that will make me stay; and I am afraid of myself, afraid that eventually I won't be able to.

Perhaps I do still want that 'special love'. Perhaps, if we can get through this, that is what Danny and I will achieve. But at the moment the wound is still so raw, I cannot see that happening. And perhaps it is 'the test of time' to see if we can / if I can stick it out.

I will try. Only time will tell. I will give it time.

Rosie

A Thursday in July 2007

I cried at work yesterday, but I do think some of it was my hormones. Danny cried at home. I think he was walking around the house, doing the housework, bawling his eyes out! What a pair! What does that say? I had rung him and told him I was upset.

When I got home he had done so much: mopped the floor, hoovered through, and cleaned our bedroom. He so wanted to show me what he had done. I know that this is a reflection of his love for me, I don't doubt Danny's love for me, especially now, and that it what I must focus on.

I gave him a big kiss, we kissed many times; I know we both feel the same. I played him an R Kelly song which has the lines

"...and you had enough love for both of us,
but I did you wrong, I admit I did,
and now I'm facing the rest of my life alone.
if I could turn back the hands of time........"

'If I could turn back the hands of time'
Written & performed by R Kelly

It made him cry, made me cry; and I kissed him and said "We will make it darling, it just takes time."

He grabbed me and said "We will won't we? Promise."

Rosie

Reflections Here & Now

I put these two entries together to show you how my days were full of huge ups, and even bigger downs. I know that one of the reasons that it was happening to me was because I wanted it to be over; wanted to 'move on', get back to 'normality.

Although we made it I feel so sad when I read some people's struggle, as I can still relate today to how hard it is; how you feel as if it will never go away; it will, but only if you let it.

By sharing my madness during the first five years after 'The War' I hope that people can relate to it, and have hope that they can survive too.

The thing was, I was not accepting the fact that I didn't actually know what normality was anymore. Everything that I thought was normal had in fact been blown apart by 'The 'War.' The 'Normal' as I had once known it had gone and it wasn't coming back. It was only when we both accepted that could we move forward.

Danny needed to accept the fact that what we had he had broken; and that no matter what he did he would never be able to fix what we had; he could only work hard and build something new. It was only once we had both understood and accepted that what we had was gone, and that we had to build something new, that things would get easier. But it took us a long time to get to that stage.

As well as realising that our 'normal' was gone we then had to allow ourselves time to grieve for it; whilst being careful not to fall into a trap of bitterness and self-pity. We were not alone at the infidelity circus; although it can be very easy to feel as if you are.

People have asked me how long it took to get over it; my answer is: I don't believe that you 'get over it'. I think you change and you get stronger from it, but this will depend on whether you can accept where you are. I have found that people often think it just takes a couple of months, or up to a year, but you will see from our story it took over two years before it no longer consumed our lives; and I would honestly say, for me, about five years before I no longer thought about it every day.

I can remember the counsellor saying to me that 'normally' at six months you should be able to go through a day without thinking about it; and there is that word again: Normally! I can remember panicking as October came our way because there was no way that I was going to stop thinking about it every day at that point; and in actual fact that was my 'normal'. I have a strong personality, and I had a lot of pride to deal with, so there was never any possibility that I was not going to be thinking about what had happened at the six month stage. I learnt not to compare myself to others. I used them as a benchmark to re-evaluate where I was, but I also learned that I was an individual with a different personality and how that would affect our recovery.

After the five years it just got easier and easier for me and now I can talk about it, laugh about it (yes I laugh about some of it!) and cry about it sometimes; mainly with Danny because he still cries, and I cry for him.

So these two entries are to show you all that I would have a day when I was convinced that the future would be bright, followed by two days of despair. That was my normal and I remembered May's advice:' You just have to keep walking forward, small steps'.

When I read this entry it did bring tears to my eyes for Danny. I found myself feeling so sorry for him. He went through as much hell as I did, if not more, but it took me years to realise that!

Rosie

A Sunday in July 2007

I couldn't find a card with the right words for Danny for the first birthday he had after his return; to me all the words seemed meaningless and trite. I couldn't say I would love him forever, I couldn't say he was the love of my life in fact none of them applied. So I bought him a card with a simple fine art picture on the front and wrote him my own poem, based on how I felt at that moment; and I also copied it into my journal so that I could read it to remind myself when I needed to.

As I try to write this poem
To think of what to say
The one thing that I know
Is that I love you all the way

Despite the things that happened
Despite the hurt and pain
I know we'll be together
That we have everything to gain
I know that you are frightened
I understand your fear
And I need to reassure you
Now that your birthdays Here
We'll see it as a beginning
A benchmark, if you like
The start of something new
A new phase in our lives
I know you can't believe it
Some things I say and do
So now I have decided
Here is my birthday gift to you
I promise to overcome
My heartache and my pain
I promise to work with you
To get us back on track again
I promise to use all the strength in me
To help support us both, emotionally
I promise that I love you
For us to work forever and always
To be with you my whole life through
To the end of my days
I promise that I never doubt
The love you have always had for me
How much you want me
Need me for eternity
I cannot replace the love that you feel
For what we have been through
We have something still
So happy birthday darling
I hope that you now know
Just how much I love you…..
So

Here is to the future
Let us always be together
let no-one come between us
To stay in love forever.

Rosie Joseph

Here & Now
I included this in my blog

I included this in my blog in 2019 when Danny found it in his bedside table. He had kept it all these years, even moving it to France with him!

Rosie

A Monday in July 2007

When I wrote that poem I truly meant it. Still want to be able to do it. But now I think the time has come for me to be brutally honest with myself, and perhaps that will sort my head out.

I still get images of the deceit; still have memories of the things that were said:

"You ring "her' as I don't have 'her' number."

"No. I don't love you anymore".

"I don't know when but I started to fall out of love with you a little while ago, because you always said that I didn't show you enough affection." (Danny said this to me over the phone when we were apart, when I asked him why he had left; funny that he shows me enough affection now!)

I remember the night, that night in March when I got drunk at 'her' house, of when Danny bought me home and then went back. I went back over to 'her' house in my drunken stupor because I knew, deep down, I knew something was going on.

I will always listen to myself in the future.

I don't feel the same about my house. I don't get that tingle that I used to have when I came through the door anymore. Next week when everyone comes down from London they can look around it, but I have no inclination to show them round.

I spoke to my sister Louise today and as always she made me laugh: she said that before 'The War' I had turned into that woman from the song 'Superwoman', a song that I always used to take the piss out of.

I said that despite everything I still have these thoughts come up in my head and I sometimes wonder if they will ever go away. Sometimes I wonder if I can live the rest of my life with them there. – As I am writing this I am thinking – if I didn't care for Danny anymore they wouldn't drive me nuts!!

But as Louise said I would still be distrustful of anyone because of what has happened, and I hate Danny for that. Louise made a valid point though: I am finding it so hard because I am fighting against all the morals and rules that I have lived my life by. My whole inclination is to maintain my self-respect, and no in some ways by doing this too I cannot maintain the morals and the rules that I have lived by. At the moment I will give it until January and then re-evaluate.

We had a good weekend and at Tom's party Danny got choked up just because he was there with me and said "Thank you."

I'll leave it there I think.

Rosie

Reflections Here & Now

There are a lot of things for me to say about this journal entry:

The thoughts that ran around my head were unbearable. There I was with someone so full of remorse and then the little voice in my head would say "How can he be like that now when he was such a fucking bastard before?" I didn't want to listen to it, I didn't want to remember what Danny had said, that he had told me that he didn't love me, told me he loved 'her'. But I did need to face it and the reality of what had been done, and only by facing it could I decide if I wanted to stay.

I have read blogs where people have struggled with whether their partner had told the other person that they loved them; and it made me realise how much I could help others because my husband had told me that, and yet here we are today.

In fact only recently I was discussing this issue with a friend: discussing other's struggles and how it had made me remember the cruel things that had been said to me, but that we still survived. So how did we? I cannot answer that in one response; because you will see as you read my story that there were many contributing factors but here are just some of the things that come to mind:

- In the beginning a big contributing factor was that I was not prepared to let 'her' dominate my thoughts for the rest of my life; or destroy our life together. That had all been part of 'her' plan: 'she' had wanted to ruin my life, and I realised that by letting my thoughts be dominated by what had happened then I was giving 'her' exactly what 'she' wanted. I still had a battle on my hands and I was not prepared to let' 'her' win.
- I took each day as it came and tried my best to deal with what was happening in the here and now.
- I became my own person – As you know I will always say 'if you don't have yourself you have nothing'. This was crucial to my survival because if I didn't like the person I was, If I didn't respect myself, how could anyone else?
  I held onto that always, and I realised that every time I started to panic at the thought of us not surviving; or considered leaving Danny I had lost myself and I made myself stop.
- With regard to 'making me look a fool' I realised that the only people who were looking like fools were the others in the whole sorry charade and not me; I had never lost my dignity.

What my sister Louise had said to me about fighting myself was true, I was. But I know now that the 'morals and rules' that I was referring to were not my self-respect, they were my ego; and as the years have gone by I have come to realise that ego is something so destructive that it should never be underestimated.

For me the definition of self-respect is that you have to like yourself: and this includes liking yourself and the actions you take.

I liked myself at this point in my journal: I had taken control of the situation, I had beaten them all in their little games; I was getting a career back on track, and I was thin again and I looked good. Shallow I know when I look back at it now; but at the time they were the things that were important to me because they were the things that had been taken away from me over time: by the lying and the gaslighting and the ghosting.

I suppose what I did was to behave with dignity (back to George Benson again) I was not prepared to be dragged into the behaviours of others, I knew that by behaving with decorum I would win; and let us not forget I was still in the middle of a major war here!

When I read this entry the part about our house made me sad. We had both loved that house, the beautiful Edwardian house by the sea. It had been our 'dream come true' when we had moved there; and I had always planned to approach an interiors magazine to show what we had done to it; I loved it so much. But the house was tainted because 'she' had been in it so many times; and whilst I came to love it again, and change the interior again, Danny never did fall back in love with it: there were too many memories and triggers for him that he didn't want in his mind.

For me this just highlights the irony that Danny had actually damaged himself as much as he had me, if not more.

With regard to the song my sister Louise laughed about: it is 'Superwoman' by Karen White. It had always annoyed me when I was younger because I would have just told the man (to who she is singing the song to) to fuck off! And yet that is the person that I had become leading up to 'The War': someone who was always trying to keep Danny happy; worked part-time so that I could support him, gave up my career, made the house a home. I still make the house a home, I still cook (especially now, in our life in France) but if Danny were to ever make me feel like he made me feel in those months leading up to 'The War' he would wear his dinner not eat it.

As you may have guessed, it was Danny's birthday; and he shares his birthday with my brother in law Tom, who was celebrating his fortieth birthday at the time. This was going to be the first time that Danny had to attend a big gathering with lots of people there that he had not seen for six years. With all of them knowing what he had done and what we were going through it was a very difficult situation for him.

When I look back I understand how much courage it took for Danny to go to my brother in laws party, when he himself believed that he was the biggest bastard in the world and believed that everyone else thought the same; he was right, some of the people at the party did think Danny was a bastard and wanted to kill him for what he had done. My sister and I were worried for him and we put our friend Joni on 'Danny Patrol' to make sure that nobody got to him or said anything to him. We all understood that Danny just couldn't have handled it and it may have been the last straw that broke the camel's back because were all aware that Danny had considered stepping in front of a train when he had been at work the week before; and actually needed help.

I know that it was understandable for people to feel that way at that time because they loved me and just wanted to protect me and stop me from hurting. But they couldn't, because only I could do that with the help of Danny; and they had to learn that they were not helping. The only way they could help was to give us support.

These last two journal entries highlight the highs and lows that can happen in the brain of the betrayed, literally within hours: I had written Danny a poem promising I would move on one day and then went back to thinking about what had happened the next. They show that you can really mean one thing one day and then feel something so completely different the next. Despite all of my promises to Danny in the poem I would still continue to put him through hell.

But I did keep one of my promises: I do still love him and it is more than I loved him before, a stronger 'real' love. I am still here with him and I don't plan on going anywhere.

Rosie

A Monday in July 2007

For the first time (apart from when I am in France) it has been a week since writing in my journal. In fact even today I don't feel a real 'need' like I normally do. I am writing this really to update it.

Over this week we have had some good talks; although they have been about 'The War' they have been constructive thoughts and talks.

After what my sister Louise said about me fighting against myself, I came to realise that it really did make sense. It also made me realise that it was all down to me now: if we are going to survive. I know that Danny desperately wants us to survive; and I decided that to enable me to deal with what was in my head, and the inner battle I am having, I needed to say what was bothering me when it was bothering me; so I told Danny what Louise had said.

I explained to Danny that he must not 'go insular' when I talk about certain things. That we now need to work together, talk it through together; Danny has things on his mind as well, mainly guilt; but as I explained some of the things on his mind that bother him probably don't even bother me anymore.

Danny volunteered to write a list, he can actually see that it would probably help him with all the things that make him feel guilty, and we could go through it together (as this would help me as well) and cross off all the things that no-longer bother me.

But we have talked so much now and gone through some of the painful things together and I now know that it was all such a mess. They never had full on sex, because Danny couldn't do it. For six days/nights of the twenty-one he was away Danny stayed away from 'her' at his mum's house or at his brothers. They only had sex five times in total.

I understand now that Danny was such a mess when he came back that sometimes he just gave me answers to shut me up. That he was so desperate to block out what he had done that even he couldn't remember. But now he understands how nit-picky my mind can be and how important it is for me to get the facts straight in my mind, no matter how painful; and he is working with me, we are working together.

On Thursday we got very drunk together. We cried and danced and laughed, and it was good. I did tell Danny about my January deadline; so he has now got it in his head that I am going to leave in January! On Saturday Susan reassured him that this was not the case.

Tom my brother in law had asked Louise why Danny shook so much and whether he had always done that and if it was because of what had happened. When Louise told me it made me realise just how upset and afraid Danny is of losing me. I don't want him to feel like that, I love him too much for that and I told him so.

On Friday we went shopping, we had a lovely day, and it hardly came into my mind at all, and when it did I could control it.

But on Saturday it was harder; I have come to expect that I will have 'downers' so they no longer take me by surprise. But I also found something that brought everything back: I needed to check Danny's old mobile bill and Danny was defensive, but I don't care. I know that I need to confront these things to enable me to control my head, and Danny now understands that. What I also realised was that when I last looked at his mobile bill I had sobbed, but this time I didn't cry at all. What a big improvement, what a giant step. When I came back downstairs Danny had made tea and I held his hand and reassured him, and then he was okay, we were okay.

Over the weekend we went out with Susan and Malcolm and had a lovely time. But this time it was Danny who got upset and Susan had a big chat with him. On the way home Danny and I talked; we sat on the seafront and talked about the deceit which I (did) still find so painful; so I was horrible to Danny and told him to leave me on my own.

When I got home Danny was playing love songs and kept singing to me. When I fell asleep on the sofa I kept waking up to find him staring at me, really close up to my face, with so much love on his face. He said he loved watching me sleep, loved me so much. It said everything. We danced and kissed.

I now realise that despite all the hurt and pain, which may occasionally come back to bite us on the arse sometimes (being realistic), nothing was destroyed: Danny has always loved me, but got caught up literally, in so much manipulation that it almost drove him mad. That during 'The War' I was right: all he had wanted was to be with me.

We had a beautiful day yesterday; walked down the seafront, pottered around the house together, Danny watched the golf, normal things. It was great.

I expected to get up today and have a 'downer', as this has normally been the case. But I didn't, I still feel the same. I said to Danny on Thursday that I am sick of it, sick of it affecting my life, bored with it almost. That I am not prepared for it to affect my life much longer; that is true: I am finally fucking it off.!

I told Danny yesterday that I am ninety five per cent happy; I am up fifteen per cent on the last time he asked, that's got to be a good thing.

I love you Danny.

Rosie

Reflections Here & Now

When I read my journal now I understand why I wanted to believe and had to believe in all the small things. As I have said before hope is essential if you want to survive.

One of the things in this entry that made me smile, all this time later, is my own self-denial. I have said that I understand Danny and believed that what he was telling me was the truth because I didn't want to face the reality and contemplate something that was too painful to contemplate at that time, but looking back now here is what I think:

I don't believe for one minute that they only had sex five times. Neither do I believe that Danny couldn't 'keep it up'. I can be this blunt about it all now because the 'sex issue' is way back in our filing cabinet labelled 'The War'. As I moved forward I realized that so many other things are important: our love for each other of course; our friendship, the fact that we make each other laugh, the understanding that we have of each other, the support we give each other.

I learnt that there are so many things you need to consider before you walk away. I have to say here that if we had not had all of these things then I would be writing a very different book today. But I had to be open to them, it could have been so easy for me to get caught up in the quagmire of despair that I felt; but as I have said in this entry (less than three months after Dday) I was sick of it. I wanted a life without it.

As part of this journey I learned that people can just have 'sex' it could be with anyone it doesn't mean anything. For me it wasn't the sex, it was the intimacy that I thought that they had. It was the feeling that someone I loved had been intimate with someone else. But as we moved forward I realised that Danny had sex with 'her' not intimacy.

I can honestly say now that they could have shagged twelve times a day, I don't give a shit. I will never know the truth and I know now that even if I am told it, in fact may well have been told it, I won't believe it. All I need to know is that they had sex. I am living in the here and now with a man who did everything he could to win me back, and keep me. What difference does it make to us in the overall picture how many times they had sex? None!

This was the first time that I didn't feel a 'need' to write in my journal. It was the first time that I had started to use it to update where my life was at that moment, not use it as a lifeline. To have not written in my journal for a week was a major milestone; but it wouldn't last. It was still early days in 'The War', and there would be many more battles to come. But we had made progress; we were starting to really talk to each other (at times).

Realising that if we were going to survive the onus was on me was also important: it is easy to get caught up in the belief that it is not up to the person who has been betrayed to make things 'right'. I realised that the onus was on me because it was my life and it was up to me where I wanted it to go. Despite all of his efforts Danny could not reassure me enough for me to stay. I knew that I had decide what I wanted and to face my fear where that was concerned. Nothing could hurt me more than I had been hurt already, in the worse way possible; and because of that knowledge it gave me total control over my fear. Things could only get better where I was concerned.

I smiled with sadness when I remember the conversation between my sister and brother in law. I had forgotten how terribly Danny shook after we got back together, because he was, as my dear old mum used to say: 'Living on his nerves.'

When Louise told me what Tom had said it was a wakeup call; it made me take a step back and stop just thinking about me. I really didn't want Danny to feel that afraid, no matter what he had done, because as I have said I loved him, and still do.

Looking back I can see how because I was the person who had been betrayed, I became self-absorbed. Some of this was a self-defence mechanism because I had to look after me first; but some of it was because I felt I had no responsibility in making things better. Writing this journal at the time, where I was honest with myself, I started to see the small things that were in front of me and it made me realise that it was not 'all about me.'

Over the years when we have talked about the 'The War' Danny has explained to me that when I interrogated him: asking him the same questions over and over again; he felt as if he was pinned against a wall terrified that he was going to give the wrong answer, even if that answer was the truth. He has explained that it was because all he wanted to do was keep me; and he was so afraid that the truth would drive me away; especially in those early days of recovery.

Rosie

A Tuesday in July 2007

And here it is: Not a downer as such – nothing like the downers I used to have.

I was fine yesterday but then Ethan and Danny had a row, a silly row like they have; only this time I didn't get involved like a would have before. (I didn't get involved at all in fact; they are both old enough they need to sort things out between themselves.) But it made me feel like, sometimes, I could just run away; and then it just made me think of the deceit and it made me feel sad; the bereavement, which is still what it is.

I asked Danny (as he was a bit arsy, because I had stayed downstairs and had five minutes to myself!) if he would ever do it again (the affair); because for a moment I thought he had been more distant; and thought that perhaps he was seeing 'her' again. He asked me how I could ask him that, even think that.

Why is he so surprised? I never thought he would do it to me before, but he did!

I suppose it's because I am afraid, was afraid, and because I had let my guard down in the past now my radar is up! That is the trust thing I suppose, and it has to come back slowly, and we both have to give it time.

We were talking yesterday, I said something and Danny said "I treasure every day I have with you" That was both lovely and really sad; as ultimately Danny believes his days with me are numbered. When we were talking later he even brought the bloody January deadline up again!

But he cuddled me and I fell asleep (I don't have enough sleep and I do need to catch up.)

I am okay today, not as happy as I have been the last two days, but not as sad as I have been before.

That's life isn't it?!

Rosie

Reflections Here & Now

Obviously reading my journal all these years later I know that the good days were still going to always be overshadowed by the bad; I know that no matter how much the 'Rosie ' writing this journal wants it all to be over at this stage she was such a long way off.

I had started to accept that I would have a good day, followed very quickly by a bad day, or even a good morning followed by a really bad afternoon, or a crap evening; and a night of no sleep. There was nothing I could do about it, and all the fighting that I did in my own mind with my thoughts was not going to change it: acceptance was the key to moving forward. but it took me years to realise that it would be a different acceptance for me in comparison to Danny.

Where the highs and lows were concerned I learnt to accept that they would be there, but that eventually they would no longer bite me as they had before; and believing that enabled the lows to get less and less as time went on. (But it was long time.)

But where Danny was concerned he had committed the betrayal and although he was truly sorry he couldn't accept that he hurt me in such an awful way; and he still cannot believe it today.

No matter how much Danny loves me now I am a different person to the person I was before 'The War'; I am no-longer a person who dotes on Danny I am my own person and that will never change.

Danny is often his own biggest critic. But he does not bury his head in the sand and try to pretend that the affair did not happen. Danny learnt over the years that talking about it, and processing it enabled us to move forward and be stronger. It had to be acknowledged because it was a major life event that made us the people that we are today. I asked him a long while ago to 'step up to the plate' and he did.

We both learnt that when infidelity comes into your life you have no choice but to keep moving forward and get through it, in whatever form that may take.

Even today years later, occasionally, some thoughts will creep into my head that would have made me angry, or made me cry years ago. But now I find myself saying "Oh yes, there is one of those thoughts that come up sometimes, bless it!' And then I shut my mind off to it and move on to something in the here and now.

Rosie

A Sunday in July 2007

It's over. I have to let it go.

I have to let go of what happened and look at what we can create: something new, better even. I do actually believe that.

I have come to a lot of conclusions this week and all in all, since about Wednesday, it has been a very difficult week.

I couldn't get out of my head what Danny had done; why Danny had done it, the deceit.

I know how much I have changed over the last three months...... so much.

When Danny first came back I had written in this journal that he wanted back what we had, and that I wanted the same. But now I know that we can never have that back; ever!

It has gone, died; Danny killed it by what he did.

I am different, stronger, me again. I know that I don't need Danny for materialistic things, because I could sell up and buy a really nice flat on my own. – But also that is why I stay: I love him, and ironically despite what happened I know that Danny loves me.

But I have also realised that I needed to talk to Danny about the 'Why?' Why did he do it, all of it? Tell him how it made/makes me feel. For the first time in my life take the monkey off my back and put it onto someone else's – Danny's, because he put it on my back in the first place.

So on Friday I did just that: I told him that we can never have back what we had (I don't actually want that back anymore. But Danny does because he is distraught at what he has lost.) I know that really hurt him, but tough!! I never asked to be where I am, and I do feel, at times, that I have been pussy footing around Danny and working so hard to make him feel alright that I have forgotten about me.

Now the time has come to sort me out, no matter how hard Danny finds it. It helped putting the monkey on his back, a lot! It upset him, but there you go, I am upset! And there was a time, not so long ago, when no-body worried about me.

I made Danny talk to me about London, and why he started seeing 'her' again in February. I told him when I thought he was lying, asked him when he thought of me! I know it really upset him, and perhaps part of me was happy he was so upset.

Toni came up from Cornwall this weekend and we went to see Susan. I took Susan to the front of her house to show her Danny's new car and we were talking. Danny's face when we came back into the garden was one of fear – he looked so worried and so alone. I don't want him to look like that, so I went over and kissed him.

But later, after Danny had gone to work, I started to think about the answers he gave about when he met 'her' in London at 'her' sister's house, and there have been three different versions so far! The one thing I need Danny to be now is honest, as he has lied to me too often and for too long; and then that fact in itself gets to me!

When Danny got home we ended up arguing over it. I ended up really upset about it all – it all came out, if you like. I told him how he wanted to run away from this part of our recovery, wanted to pretend and ignore it; but it is in my head all the time, and I can't ignore it; and he put it there!

Danny got defensive, the worst thing he can do. So I told him it was over, that I can't do it. Danny needs to make amends for what he has done and not keep being afraid. I gave him back my wedding ring.

One of the things that gets to me is when I am upset Danny just stands there. So I used what had happened in Susan's garden as a comparison: how I had gone up to him and reassured him when he was upset. I told him that it should not/cannot be me who does all the consoling and reassuring, because Danny fucked it up, so Danny has to fix it, not me!

So I told him that was his last chance and to have the courage of his convictions and face his fears. I walked away from him, and he came after me. He had my wedding ring on his little finger, and asked me to put it back on.

But I have said it all now; got all of my demons out. Danny has been honest, must still deal with his guilt, and I will help him, if he wants me to. But ultimately it's his problem.

This is a new beginning, a new relationship. I need to let go of what happened because it was in the past and I don't want it to affect my life anymore.

I always pride myself on being able to 'get a grip'; and I need to now. I need to step up to the line, have the courage of my convictions and look at what I have now.

I need to practice what I preach.

Rosie

Reflections Now

This was a major turning point of 'The War': I was right I had to think about me, and ensure that I was alright.

I have learnt that despite how much you love someone, the only one true person you have all your life is you; and if you're not okay then quite simply you are lost.

I realised that finding yourself is paramount to surviving infidelity whether your relationship survives or not. I found it could be anything: go to a yoga class, go for a walk every day on my own, anything to find myself, and not be dependent on Danny. In fact keeping the journal was the main thing that enabled me to find myself. It was mine, I wrote my innermost thoughts down and I did not share it with Danny.

Of course there was the fear that I would find myself to such a degree that I would leave Danny behind; and there were times that I was truly afraid that would happen to me; but I had to find myself I had no choice; I could not see how I could survive and move forward if I didn't.

I remember feeling so worthless: Initially I felt unattractive (hence the manic training), and stupid for letting Danny get away with it. I felt angry with myself for choosing to ignore things that were right 'under my nose'; and I had that awful feeling that people were pitying me for what Danny had done. Because of all of this I had to find myself again: a person in her own right and not part of a couple or dependent on another person. I was right that part of that was to stop feeling sorry for Danny, stop worrying that he would leave again, stop feeling as if I was being held to ransom; and more than anything to stop being a victim.

It was true that I was aware of how awful he felt, and the caring person in me (I was once told I was the rock that everyone else clung to) wanted to make things alright for him. When, in fact, I had to take care of me first, become really strong again before I could help Danny; and I can honestly say that if I had not done this then we would not have survived.

The monkey on the back scenario is a term used to describe situations where other people give you their problems which then, in their minds become your problem and not theirs. It is a good analogy. In fact I still use that analogy in my life now.

In psychology terms this is actually recognised as 'transference' when someone else's problem suddenly becomes your problem and not theirs. Danny did have to take responsibility for what he had done and face his fears, one of which was the fact that he didn't like himself and that is why he had let himself down.

Although it upset Danny to face up to what he had done, we all have to do that to move forward and the action that I took at this stage was the right one. Little did I know at the time just how hard it had hit Danny, and eventually I did ultimately become his rock that he clung to and when the time came I was there for him.

I cannot tell you the timeframe as to when I stopped asking Danny 'Why?' But I do know that I stopped asking him because I knew that he couldn't answer me, because he didn't know the answer and still doesn't to this day. This is one of the things that still affects him and causes so much guilt, because he cannot understand his own actions.

After three months I had changed so much. I could see that I had lost myself during our previous relationship and I had recognised that this was a new relationship with new people in it. But the key was: despite having come to terms with the fact that what we had was dead, I did (do) still love Danny; my love hadn't died; and I knew that we had too much to just walk away.

The time in London that I mentioned in this journal entry is referring to when Danny had said he had met 'her' in the October before 'The War' commenced: when they had met at 'her' sister's house. Ironically it had been our home town.

I had kept asking Danny about this episode because in my mind then it was when it had all started; when they had started to play me for the fool; and pride was my deadly sin. For me to think that it had been going on for over five months just poked that demon in my brain.

Rosie

"The future – a New Beginning!

A Sunday in July 2007

The Future
After what I have written on the previous page, I feel that I need to close that chapter. Start a new chapter, for a new beginning.

Reflections Here & Now

After my last journal entry I went back to my journal later in the day and decided to mark 'The End' of talking about what had happened. I had hoped that by doing that I would be able to concentrate on the future, and on a new page I wrote the above and marked a new section in my journal.

Three months is no time at all when you are dealing with grief and infidelity; I still struggled for a long time to come because I still had so much more that I had to accept and I was still struggling with that, despite what I had written in my journal. I had accepted that what we had was dead and gone and was not coming back. What I hadn't realised was that although I knew and understood that, I still needed to grieve for it.

But what I had realised was we were going to have to make something new; so I symbolically made a new section in my journal to show a commitment to it.

As William Blake said

"Hindsight is a wonderful thing but foresight is better, especially when it comes to saving life, or some pain!"

I lived in hope, and at this stage hope is the mainstay that will help you survive.

Rosie

A Tuesday in July 2007

It's not easy but I think I can do it – in getting the unwanted pictures out of my head.

I am now lying on the downs at Lowly. The sun is shining and the wind is blowing everything out of my mind.

I have had a difficult day today. Not in having those things on my mind, but with the sadness. There are two issues:

1. Getting the thoughts in my head under control.
2. The sadness for what I have lost. The grief for the bereavement, for the waste of that love that I had; that I had never had for anyone else.

Time will heal, I know it. How and what form that healing will take I don't know.

But as I am writing this, and although I have cried with sadness today, (a short cry, letting it all out like Sherri said. It's true it doesn't last long anymore; no more heaving sobs – not if I don't give way to it. There's just grief.) I also know that despite what I have lost I wouldn't want to go back to it:

- A big fat lump that had really let herself go.
- Someone who I am starting to see now was very frustrated, angry almost, inside. Because what did she have?

Everything centred on Danny; and although I was jolted out of that (kicking and screaming at the time) I never want to be that person again; I don't like her.

- A couple who had become so insular, so immersed in just themselves. I know that Danny would want to go back to that (because of his own securities, his own fear.) I don't!

Danny has changed since he has been with me; Louise was right when she said that I dragged him up with me. Although he is quite capable himself, he doesn't believe that unless he has me by his side.

In fact, perhaps sub-consciously he always knew I would come to my senses and that is why he thought he couldn't keep me.

So why am I with him now? I do find that thought popping into my head.

Because I know how much he loves me; and when someone loves you that much and you do love them, then why walk away? There is something to work on.

The life we have created together keeps me here as well. I enjoy his company, and he makes me laugh. Sometimes he also gets on my tits.

I had to get on my bike today and come here on my own. Regain my independence and do things on my own. I do notice that when I am with Danny we do both slot into that 'doing everything together' mode. I did, however, only realise today how many arrangements I make to do things with other people now. This has been a totally sub-conscious thing.

At the moment part of me still wants Danny to ring me, text me, reassure me. But the more I do things on my own the less that will get; and I need to do that. Danny will totally freak, just look hurt and say "Whatever you want." But not really mean it. That is no-longer my problem. I am enjoying myself, being myself, confident, self-sufficient, and not constantly thinking of someone else.

I am going to go to the pub on my own and have a glass of wine before I go home; and I haven't brought my mobile with me; this is me time.

This has really helped.

Rosie

Reflections Here & Now

I remember this day clearly: It was a beautiful sunny day, not hot because the wind had a slight chill in it; but there were bright blue skies with small puffs of cloud moving along quickly in the wind; and the sun was warm.

Lowly is a pretty place with rolling downs that lead down to the beach and sea, dotted with beach huts on stilts. There were lots of people there and as I watched them I was thinking how happy they all were; and here was I with my world in pieces, never knowing if I would really be happy again.

But I have learnt over the years that you see what you want to see, and I believed at that time that everyone was happier than me. Obviously that wasn't true, but when you are in a place where nothing seems to make sense, you believe that everyone else has their shit together when in fact it's just the good old demon in your head spinning you a line.

This was such an important entry for me because as part of the new beginning I also had to put things in place to find myself again. I had become 'lost' in Danny before 'The War' everything had revolved around him: I had renovated the house and managed the house and finances, so that Danny could focus on his career. I had lived my life for Danny and I knew that I could no longer do that; Danny could be part of my life but he could no longer be the centre of it – I had to be that.

So to start with I went somewhere on my own, and the choice was pertinent because I chose to go to the one place where Danny used to meet up with 'her' on his way to work: I had to face my fears to be able to move forward into my new life, and to not let my fears and memories beat me anymore.

There are four main things in this entry that resonate with me today:

- That I recognised that I didn't want to be the person that I was before; in fact I didn't even like the person that I was before. When I read this entry it did stop me in my tracks: the way I viewed myself from the past.

  Today we look back at the people that we were before 'The War' and we don't like them: we drank too much; mixed with people that we would never mix with now, put up with bad behaviours without question. We both agree that we really were a pair of arseholes.

- The fact that I have said that I was an angry and frustrated person; because I was: The Rosie who wrote this entry was absolutely right, I had been angry and frustrated; I hadn't been using my skills to their full potential and because of that I would get angry and lose my temper at things; or make small things more important than they really were.

- After 'The War', when I had begun to find myself again, someone had said to me that I had 'dumbed down' and they were right: I didn't want promotion at work, didn't want to work full time, didn't want to use my brain because that was the easy way out. 'The War' had made me see sense albeit 'kicking and screaming' at the time.

I believe today that everything does happen for a reason. That at times messages are sent to us and when we don't listen then a lesson is sent to us; and more often than not that lesson is a hard one. Even today I believe that my sister Louise was right; I was being sent a message, a kick up the arse if you like, to find myself again.

- The fourth and most important thing from this entry is that I can see that I wanted to stay with Danny because he made me laugh; because I enjoyed his company that we got on well together; and ultimately that I loved him. It wasn't the romantic things or the sex; it was the small everyday things that he did for me. I also love that fact that I could see that he got 'on my tits'. Isn't that life?

I did go to the pub and I sat in the garden on my own and showed myself that I didn't need to fear being on my own, in fact I needed to embrace it: to be an individual who didn't start and end with Danny, and this was the start of doing it. So I had two glasses of wine whilst I read my book.

Rosie had started to find herself again and it was crucial to our survival.

Rosie

CHAPTER 43 - JULY 2007

Stories to Tell

I am including this story to highlight the irrational way that I felt when this happened to me. I would literally act like a teenager at times. I know now that it is because I did not have control of my emotions, just like a teenager. I was experiencing the same levels of hormones, and the flight or fight response that they experience with regard to feedback and difficult situations. Here is my story:

Danny and I had spent an evening with Susan and Malcolm. They were safe people to be with because they knew what had happened, and had supported us in our recovery; we knew that we could spend time with them without fearing that what had happened would come out.

In fact when I look back we were still not eating properly and I can remember we had ordered a Chinese takeaway and Malcolm trying to persuade Danny to eat some of it; he literally fed him like a child.

But it seemed that whenever we came away from their house we argued. I think one of the reasons was because the road that led to our house was also the road those months before 'she' had walked up and Danny had followed her; so whenever we walked down that road the triggers would hit.

I cannot remember what was said in the argument but I do remember that I walked away. In fact I ran away from Danny, up one of the side streets, he called after me but as I turned a corner I ducked into someone's front garden and hid in a bush behind their caravan. I could hear Danny frantically calling for me but I just hid there, like a child, and after he went past I came out from hiding and went home. I left Danny looking for me, and he did not come back for another half an hour after I returned.

We look back now and giggle about what would have happened if the people in the house had looked out of their window and seen this woman in her forties, hiding in their garden under a bush. It is the insanity of infidelity.

Rosie

CHAPTER 44

Journal Entry - August 2007

A Sunday in August 2007

It's been two months since I have been keeping this journal, and I have come so far.

A weird thing happened to me today. A man who used to live in our road came into our garden and stole one of our potted plants. It was as if he wanted to be caught. This is a man who obviously has a good job, and intelligence; so why do it? He didn't pick a particularly nice pot, just one with a boring bush in it.

I ran out after him and confronted him. He gave it back straight away and looked so shocked at what he had done. – As if my shouting at him had jolted him back to reality. All he kept saying was how sorry he was and as I walked away he burst into tears. I walked back to him and put my arms around him. All he kept saying was "What have I done? What have I done? My life is falling apart I have ruined everything."

I felt such an affinity with him; and I said "I do understand, my husband has had an affair. I understand what it feels like, when your life is falling apart." He then went on to tell me that he hadn't had an affair, but that he was losing his job and maybe his house.

I told him that not one of those things was insurmountable, that he could sort them out. He said he was sorry for what Danny had done to me; and did Danny realise just what he had in me because I was great.

I told him that Danny was fighting hard to keep me, but that I was not an easy person to keep; and that he knew just what he had lost.

What I realised was that this man was so stressed with life: with the commute, and the bills, with trying to keep his family happy; that for one blind moment he did something really stupid. I took in the look of loss, bewilderment, and fear on his face, and it suddenly became clear that somebody or something was trying to show me what Danny felt like. Except that there hadn't been anyone there to help Danny.

I told the man to go home to his wife and to talk to her and not to bottle things up and make it a million times worse.

He was so grateful; and it made me feel good.

I just wish someone could have helped me in the same way.

Brilliant day yesterday, struggling today.

NB: Danny gave me one of my anniversary presents early today, my old silver bracelet with the heart on it. He had the heart engraved with "Je taime – Rosie "

He gave it to me on Friday and, yes, it means so much, it helps.

But I still have a broken heart.

Why?

Rosie

Reflections Here & Now

As I was writing my book I was reading my journal again for the first time in an age; and I had forgotten this episode and the conversation that I had with that man.

I had just returned from London after bringing Danny home after his first night shift; and it was very early on a Sunday morning. There was nobody about and the avenue was quiet. I was reading my book and I just happened to look up as I saw a man come into our garden bend down quickly, pick up my pot, and walk away with it.

It touched a nerve because it reminded me that Danny and 'her' had thought that they could do anything to me and that I would put up with it; so I ran out of the door and shouted at him to stop. Initially I was just so angry that this person thought that they could come into my garden and steal something from me: just as 'she' had thought that 'she' could steal Danny.

The man looked a wreck; he clearly hadn't shaved or washed for a while and looked as if he was just falling apart. But despite the situation I was still able to have some empathy with someone who had just stolen from me; able to see that I was not alone with regard to being in pain, that there were so many other people struggling too; and that pain comes in all forms, shapes and sizes.

Although I thought at the time there was no-one there helping 'me in the same way' there clearly was: because that's why this thing had happened. Life had shown me someone else's pain to enable me to see Danny's pain, and understand that I was not alone in this world of despair.

That whole episode was so important for me because that was how I felt: alone. As if I was the only person in the world that had pain to deal with; and what happened reminded me that was not the case: everybody has something that they have to deal with in their life.

Before 'The War' Danny had bought me a silver bracelet with a heart on it for Christmas; it had become a casualty of 'The War': thrown into one of the black plastic bags that contained all of the things that reminded me of Danny. When Danny had gone through his belongings after my sister in law collected them he had hidden the heart in his shoe, so that 'she' would not find it and put it on. When Danny returned he had asked me to put it back on but I refused and told him he would have to make it something 'new' before I would wear it again. So he had it engraved; and I did put it back on; over time it stretched and I was unable to wear it, but I still keep it somewhere safe.

Rosie

A Tuesday in August 2007

I kept crying yesterday. I know that an element of it is my hormones, because the things that normally no-longer get to me do at this time of the month; but aren't they only contributing to the fact that I find it harder to control my head? Doesn't that mean that the thoughts are still there?

Nothing has changed between me and Danny. We don't talk about it every day, in fact in the last week we have only talked about it once; and that was a very brief conversation on Friday. (I can't be bothered to go into what it was about, and what caused it.) But it is still there, always still there; hanging in the air over our heads.

I realised last night that one of the things that makes me sad is that when I feel like this, feel this sad: the person that I used to talk to, needed to talk to, I am not able to talk to anymore. Not about this, because they are the person that caused it; and that makes me cry.

I spoke to Louise last night, and she said that it is still very early with regard to the sadness and the bereavement; that she honestly believes that eventually I will be able to confide in Danny again.

As I am writing this I am thinking about how happy I felt on Saturday and realising that I should have written in here then, to show myself the happiness I can feel when I am with Danny.

I explained to Louise that over the past couple of weeks, because my own head is doing my own head in, I have considered whether I need to go away from Danny for one to two weeks; to see how I feel when I am away from him; especially now, when I have moved on so much, and am in a completely different place to where I was before. Sometimes I wonder whether this will make me realise how much I want to be with him, make Danny realise how much it hurts to not have the person you love with you in some ways; and enable me to realise that being with Danny is the most important thing and move on. I don't know it may be something I may have to consider in the future.

But when I woke up this morning some of what Louise had said had sunk in: Really it is what I have said before – that this is something new. So again there are two issues:

1. The sadness that I feel because of what Danny has done to me, when I trusted him so implicitly; sadness for what I had before. Even now that causes me such pain.
2. The new thing that I have now, where the person who I am with adores me so much; because he nearly lost me. For the new things we can do together, for the new me.

They are positives, all good, so much more than some people will ever have. So why am I crying? Because I have just realised I still have a broken heart.

Rosie

Reflections Here & Now

My poor hormones, they got the blame for everything!

This entry shows the madness that I suffered because Danny had betrayed me: My previous entries had shown that I was getting a grip of my situation; but that didn't mean the reality of my situation did not punch me on the side of the head suddenly every now and again, just to remind me of where I was. That is the aftermath of an affair: everyone's life is a mess; and the whole situation is very sad.

I acquired a saying during 'The War' that I still use today: 'It is what it is, it ain't what it ain't.' I didn't realise at the time that it was in fact a mantra that I used to remind myself that I had to accept it. In fact I didn't realise at this stage just how crucial that acceptance was. But clearly by brain knew because it popped this little mantra into my head for me to use for the rest of my life. Acceptance eventually meant that the punch didn't hurt as much when it came because I knew it was coming.

I remember the feeling of realising that the one person I thought I could always talk to was now the one person that I could no longer talk to about how I really felt. I hate to say it (because she won't let me forget it!) but Louise was right: as time moved on I could confide in Danny again; we confide in each other about everything now. My heart has completely healed (with scars), Danny's heart has not; because he cannot forgive himself. But I help him with that; because the Rosie who wrote this journal has enabled me to. Only today I read Danny someone's blog; a man who had an affair, and even though he was describing how Danny felt, Danny still found it hard to hear because like this poor man he still hates himself a lot of the time.

The Rosie who wrote this journal at the time was right: I should have written in my journal when I was happy to enable me to see a balance. But that is such a difficult thing to do early on because all you feel is pain; all you can see is the negative. It is virtually impossible in the immediate aftermath of an affair to see anything but negativity. My world and all that I believed in had been turned upside down; and the life that I had been living was not going to return.

The irony is that the life that I thought was idyllic and happy was in fact based on a bed of lies and over time I came to realise that I didn't want it back anyway. But in those early months of madness I could only see that rose tinted life that I had lost.

If I had put some space between us I don't think I would have gone back; my pride would have kicked in and it would have been easier to walk away. My sister Louise knew that, so she persuaded me to stay.

I was starting to accept that the Danny was no-longer the Danny who had left me: he was a different person because he too has been going through so much.

It is hard to help someone understand that the person who left you was the person in that moment; and the person who is with you now is a different person.

I often struggled to see the things that Danny was doing to make amends; I was so stuck in what had happened in the past that it was clouding my judgement in the moment I was in and thereby putting our future in jeopardy.

It is the same as some people who are so caught up in the past and the past 'happiness' that they fail to see that the person in the here and now with them is no longer making them happy. It works both ways.

I hung on to the fact that the man who stood in front of me each day was a different man to the one who had left. In fact he changed every day as he learnt more about himself and us, because he had broken his own heart; and as he came to realise that he then realised that he had to understand why he always ran away. I knew that I didn't need to help him destroy himself; I wasn't going to feel any better by doing that. Although there were times, that I still tormented him and played on his fears. Those were the times when the demon in my head told me stories and I listened; those were the times when pride and ego took over, and over time I did untold damage.

Throughout what we went through and even today, I look at Danny: a man who truly adores me, and I could never break the heart of the Danny who is with me now; because he is not that man who left me.

Rosie

A Friday in August 2007

I am writing in my journal today because I have a good feeling about me and Danny.

This journal is meant to be about showing the journey we are taking, the bad and the good; and although I have found it to be extremely therapeutic to write in my journal, I have noticed that I don't tend to write in it when I feel good – which kind of defeats the object.

I cried and cried on Tuesday, I couldn't control it. – My hormones had a lot to do with it. But the incredible hurt and sadness that I feel is immense.

Danny knew from the Monday that I was upset and asked me about it. We talked: I really cried.

I asked Danny if he still cried and he said that he still thinks about it every day, and cried about one or two times a week. That he had cried on Monday night because he knew I was upset. I explained how I felt, and told him what I had talked to Louise about, and I read him what I had written in my journal on Tuesday.

We talked about:

1. Me getting away from him; so Danny offered to go away. But that would not be what I needed, it would have to be me who went away, away from everything. I explained to Danny that this was just an option I may have to consider; not one I was definitely going to take.
2. About selling the house, which would give us more money. I don't want to sell the house as it is my back up, my plan B: because if we didn't survive I would sell the house and take the money and go wherever life took me. (Although as I am writing this I know that wherever life took me I would want Danny with me; I know that now.)

3. I explained to Danny (again) that he must put his arms around me when I cry. That perhaps he needs to say sorry every day. That he has broken my heart so badly; he knows that now. That he has virtually destroyed me.

But even though I was sobbing when I told him, Danny still didn't put his arms around me; and when I pointed out that this was so what I needed he said he was afraid: he thought what I was saying sounded like a goodbye speech. I did point out to Danny that whatever I say, including asking him what he wants for tea, sounds like a goodbye speech to him!

I went upstairs as I find it so hurtful when I cry in front of Danny and he doesn't comfort me. He followed me, he looked so unhappy, his face was as grey as when he had when he first came back home. As I am writing this I am realising that it is killing him, this is killing him: I don't want that.

Danny explained that the main thing he thinks of is how he shouldn't have left me; and how he has broken my heart; he knows that he was running away. He still swears that they never had full sex, I do believe him.

I explained to Danny that it is no good him crying in one place and me crying in another: We need to cry together; to understand and know how we are both feeling, and to not be afraid of it. This will bring us closer together. It has been good since then; I still cried yesterday but I do expect that, and it was only very briefly.

I thought that I would write all of the positives that do come into my mind now:

- How much stronger I am than I was the day I started to write this journal.
- How much more I know: that it was not a long affair. In fact if I detach myself from it I can see that it was nothing at all.
- How much Danny loves me, treasures me; the look in his eyes when he looks at me.
- How far we have come together.
- How sorry Danny is. How, if he could sacrifice anything to change what he did to me he would.

Yesterday we went to my bank and added Danny's name to my account. We also arranged for Danny to have his salary paid into the new joint account. A small thing but Danny was so excited and so pleased that we had done that, it almost made me cry because it was so important to him.

Today I caught sight of Danny looking at me, and it is the way he looks at me: the adoration in his eyes; tell me where do I find that again? I don't!

I am really looking forward to our time off together now; seeing Alison and Peter tonight, everyone coming to our house tomorrow, going to France on Monday. But before we do any of that, I am going to make love with my husband this afternoon.

I can honestly say that today, for the first time, I feel that Danny and I are going to make it, with no doubts.

Footnote:

Today we were talking about buying a fireguard in France and of how we could look at it in the winter and think of France, when Danny said "and watch Strictly Come Dancing, and Match of the Day with my head on your lap." The look on his face told me how much he wanted that, how much he has always wanted that; that he obviously didn't want to let that go in the first place.

It just emphasised how much of this (what has happened) was all about manipulation, circumstances, and fear. It made my eyes fill up with tears, not of sadness but with happiness, because I could see that Danny's love for me is so total, so complete; and how it always has been.

Rosie

Reflections Here & Now

I have read various descriptions of what 'acceptance' is and the Eckhart Tolle version, from 'The Power of Now' describes it as such:

".... acceptance is the "this is it" response to anything occurring in any moment in life….."

I know that we have to accept where we are: accept the moment, accept the weather, and accept the things we cannot change because otherwise we would drive ourselves mad. But I also think that we also have to learn to accept our feelings: that we are sad, angry, afraid, bereft, unsure, insecure, and vulnerable.

This entry in my journal shows that I am starting to accept what has happened. and I couldn't change it, we were where we were.

I knew that I had to accept it: knew that I would cry some days, feel good some days, and then cry the next. I knew that the demon would be waiting for me in my car, and that I had to face what Danny had done. In fact at the end of the entry I say how I had come to expect that I was still going to cry, and it is telling that I only cried for a brief space of time, because I had accepted it was going to happen and therefore it wasn't as bad.

I do feel that to recover fully, understanding the fear that some people who have betrayed feel when they are trying to rebuild a relationship that they broke is essential. It was important that I understood that Danny was afraid. Yes there were still times that I thought he had no entitlement to feel afraid, or have any help or empathy from others; but if I had continued on that vein and not considered Danny's feelings (no matter how hard that was at times) we would not be where we are today.

Although I was heartbroken, and although it hurt so much when I cried in front of Danny and he didn't put his arms around me (despite me previously explaining to him how important this was to my recovery); I knew when I wrote this journal entry that it was because he was afraid. It was important that I understood that to enable me to give Danny the confidence to do it.

Only a year or so ago I read Danny the chapter where I first found out about the affair; the part where he left and didn't come back all night. As I read it to him I didn't expect his response: He just looked at me with immense pain etched on his face; burst into tears and said "I am so sorry." That told me how much pain Danny is still in at times, and it breaks my heart that he feels that way.

It was important to me that Danny was happy about us having a joint back account again because when he had told the counsellor that he thought one of the reasons I was having him back was his money it had broken my heart, and it had made me consider whether I could really stay with Danny. My increased hours at work had meant that I had my own money and as the weeks went by Danny could see that

I was becoming more and more independent of him; the tables were turned and it was Danny who started to feel insecure and wanted us to have a shared bank account again. It seems quite telling that instead of me being added to Danny's bank account I insisted that Danny be added to mine. It was just another small step of me finding me again.

Before 'The War' Danny would sit with his head on my lap whilst we watched TV in the evenings. That had all been destroyed. I have a lingering memory of Danny with his head on my lap as 'she' knocked on the door and how Danny sat up abruptly before Ethan let 'her' in. So after Danny's return I didn't want him to have his head on my lap; and in all honesty we have never gone back to that. Perhaps that is just about making something new.   ·

Rosie

A Tuesday in August 2007

Yes! Can you believe that I have not written in my journal for over a week? And what a brilliant ten days it has been.

After the last time I wrote in my journal I read it to Danny. It made us both cry.

On the Friday that I wrote that entry Danny couldn't 'perform' and when I read him my journal he got upset and said about it (that he couldn't perform) and how he had so wanted to. But I now understand that it was because of his shifts and that at times Danny felt that extra pressure on him; which then made things worse, and this is one of the things that I have come to understand – how much shift work affected Danny.

Anyway we had a brilliant weekend: spent time with Alison and Peter on Friday and all the people from London who came to our house on Saturday. Everybody really gelled together and it made me realise how much we had lost the people that really mattered; and spent too much time with people that not only didn't matter, but who were truly poison for us, especially me. I now realise how different Danny and I are: In that I am always me in whatever circumstances, and Danny becomes the people he is with (that is why I write this journal as it makes things so clear to me sometimes.)

On the Sunday we had a slight blip, because I caught Danny out in another lie about 'The War'. I have lost count how many times I have told Danny not to lie and to confront his fears. The way I changed, immediately I became so hard towards him, it shocked him. But I can do that now; I will always have that ability now to switch off (to a degree); even though I love him. We talked it through and I went upstairs to wrap his anniversary present. I put George Benson on 'The Greatest love of all', and Danny came upstairs because some songs I play frighten him. He said "Sorry" and then sobbed and sobbed, more than ever before, and that was it, done.

We are having a fantastic time in France. We had a brilliant anniversaire de marriage. I am currently sitting in a chair in front of panoramic windows overlooking the sea in a hotel in Varengeville. I will update on France and thoughts later.

Rosie

Reflections Here & Now

I wrote this entry in my journal less than five months after the shit hit the fan; but I had still moved on (of course I would also go backwards again) and what a contrast to the weekend in Le Touquet when I told Danny 'a shag was a shag.'

We were both starting to look at our old life in comparison to our new life, and were able to see that it was not as great as we thought it had been. It was the first tentative steps to us both accepting that what we had could have been better; and that we had the opportunity to learn from our mistakes and make it better now.

From this entry I am reminded of the arguments Danny and I had before 'The War' about his lack of libido. I always had a higher libido than Danny and it really came between us at times. I had come to realise the immense pressure Danny was under with his job; and how all of the overtime that he had taken on to enable us to keep the house and me to work part-time had affected his libido. But it is interesting that I had not even considered for one moment that perhaps some of Danny's problems lay with the fact that he felt so insecure where I was concerned. That voice in his head would tell him that he 'had to perform' otherwise he would not keep me. I can see now that add to that the fact that I would get upset if he could not perform and you can see where we ended up on a hamster wheel going round and round and getting nowhere.

I know that a lot of the insecurities that Danny had were because of me. Not necessarily anything that I consciously did, but one of the things that I didn't do was stop and contemplates and see his insecurities. God knows I had enough wherewithal to help him, but it took me a long while to see the whole picture. At the time I wrote this entry I was too caught up in my own heartbreak to be able to see it: but in my defence it was early days and we both had a lot learning to do.

But I was starting to understand that the underlying day to day mundane things that none of us notice had taken their toll and allowed things to happen. We learnt to respect how the mundane can affect a relationship in such a way it can contribute to problems and over time kill it. We never take our relationship or what either of us contributes to it for granted; if one of us is under pressure we talk about it and put things into place to support each other. I am not talking about dressing up in sexy nightwear, or doing extravagant things I am talking about understanding the small things and helping each other every day.

As you may have guessed we were in France when I wrote this entry where we had celebrated our eighth wedding anniversary and when I read this I was surprised that I had not written an entry then; but I obviously didn't feel the need, and little did I know it at the time, I was moving on.

Rosie

A Saturday in August 2007

Where do I start? I feel the need to write in my journal because I am happy, and because I feel the need to update it. I can truly say that we have come so far. There are also thoughts and things that have happened that I feel need to be logged. So I think that I will start with things that happened in France and let it flow from there.

I also want to write myself a list of the way Danny is, and the things he has done.

I am sitting in my back room at the moment, looking at a picture of Danny and I on holiday, and we truly look happy, our happiness shows, especially in my eyes.

On our wedding anniversary we met a French man (Marc) who took a liking to both Danny and I. He took us to his club and bar and was a truly lovely host. The nature of his business meant that he was very astute, especially about character. When Danny had gone to the bar he turned to me and said "He really loves you so much. You - I am not so sure." It shocked me; as I didn't realise that I gave off that much of a vibe of mixed emotions. I didn't realise how much I was showing that I was not sure if I was doing the right thing where Danny and I were concerned.

It frightened me; and set me thinking about Danny and I, and what he had done. On the following Thursday at Le Crotoy I couldn't get what had happened out of my mind: all of it. But I did get it under control and didn't bring it up to Danny because I couldn't see the point: What is there to talk about regarding it anymore? But as I am writing this I realise that it is still part of the bereavement, and that is why I was feeling sad. But I can also see that it was only for one day this time, not all the time. Also Danny was brilliant: he never said anything but he knew. All he did was cuddle me, kiss me, hug me, adore me; he was the loving husband that I used to have from a couple of years ago; and I knew how hard he was trying, and it was the right thing for him to do, it made it easier, and by the evening it made it better. When we got back to the room Danny was so desperate to make love to me, and it was very lovely and it helped.

What I said about crying together was true: It does help and has brought us closer together. The next day whilst in the car we played 'Just Say, Just Say' by Diana and Marvin and we both started crying at the words; it brought us closer together, united. We had a lovely day in St Valery; we sat by the river with a picnic and watched the boats and people go by.

When we returned to Le Touquet we saw Marc again and had a drink with him. As we said goodbye to him for this year he looked at me, grabbed my hand and said "I will see you next year, see you together, yes? Make sure it is together, do not let it go." It made me want to cry.

I know that he meant 'do not let go' of the love that Danny has for me; and believe me that is what keeps me here; because I know I would be mad to throw it away.

I have realised how far we have come, how much things have changed, how much I have changed. In the second week after Danny came back we went to Bexhill and a man in the pub said to me "You really love him don't you?" Now it has reversed, and although I still really love Danny (trust me) he now gives off a greater vibe of how much he loves me than I do with regard to how much I love him.

On the Sunday in Le Touquet a man in the bar asked me if I had a boyfriend. When I told him that Danny was my husband he apologised to Danny, but then went on to tell him how lucky he was and that I was "magnifique." Sometimes I do feel as if someone, or something, just likes to ram home to Danny what a prat he was!

I sent a text to Nel later in the holiday when she had text me to ask how we were, it said

'Really great; back in love. It was too strong to destroy.'

Nel then replied with 'I was thinking about what my first reaction was when Danny left, that I didn't want you to go through all that crap. But sometimes you have to so that you are reminded of what you have.'

I replied 'absolutely.' And that says it all: I now have what I have wanted for the last couple of years, a husband who adores me and this time always will.'

When I went to Louise's last night we had a big chat and she said that it was true that the' old' Rosie was well and truly back. That she could really see it, especially how I acted with Danny; but that she thought it was better; she asked if I thought that Danny would let me down again and I hesitated so she answered for me and said that she didn't ever think that he would again.

But I also know that what will be, will be; and although it makes me sad: that one day I may feel that I don't want to stay with Danny, I will not be able to change it if that happens. But I also know that we can work on what we have got, to try and prevent that from happening.

Rosie

Reflections Here & Now

Our love affair with France was truly underway.

With regard to Marc he was a very clever man. What I haven't put in my journal is that he had waited until I had gone to the toilet and looked at Danny and said "You have been very stupid; very, very stupid." We hadn't told him what had happened, but he apparently knew.

We both took things away from that encounter that night: things that got us to where we are today. When you meet someone who is so astute, someone who wants you to come back together the following year you have to listen, don't you?

I learnt that recovering after infidelity is small steps. In fact it is everything small: every small gesture, every small encounter with people who make you think about life, every small action, every small conversation, even words: A look, a smile, the look in someone's eyes, their body language. We both learnt (me especially as I was the one who had to be persuaded to stay) to see everything that was sent our way and listen to the message. I now compare all those small things to pieces of a jigsaw; the type with thousands of tiny pieces. Then as I put them all together they mapped out a path and showed me the way to go. I will say here that if you use this analogy it is not just an analogy for staying: they may map out a path that shows people that they need to be brave and move on without that person.

This event in my life taught me that life shows you the way. There is a quote from 'The Road Less Travelled' (A book that changed my life) where M Scott Peck realises that in life you have to let go, because, as he says, 'someone else is doing the driving.' I have always believed that everything happens for a reason and that be they good or bad things you need to listen.

This journal entry was during a ten day holiday in Northern France and we travelled to different villages and towns in Le Somme. Crotoy is a beautiful little town on the Somme opposite the equally pretty harbour town of St Valery; it has a 1920s vintage train that travels between the two towns across the Somme. We hired bikes and got on the vintage train to St Valery for a picnic. I can remember how the thought of what Danny had done was running through my head in beat to the sound of the train on the tracks that day. I don't know if it was because we should have been so happy, looked so happy to others who saw us, but I felt as if it was all a lie, because they didn't know the truth.

At that time no matter how happy I was it also felt like a façade of bullshit. At times I felt as if we were just clinging to each other and I didn't know if we could survive. How could we do all these wonderful things; see all of these wonderful places and still feel so unhappy at times? But I realise now that those people were seeing something that did exist: after all it was in front of them, but it was us who couldn't see it.

It was true that crying together helped because we were appreciating that both of our hearts were broken: so we were then both coming from the same place as we tried to glue them back together. It was the simplest thing that we had in common.

With regard to my fear: of course I was afraid. This was only four months since my husband had turned my world upside down and destroyed my faith in him. Although he was working hard I was terrified of being let down again. But as I say to people I learnt over time not to be afraid because the worst had already happened, and I was stronger and had myself so I had nothing to fear. But it took a long time for me to get there.

Louise was right, Danny has never ever hurt me again, and I know now that he never will.

Rosie

Danny's List August 2007:

Thursday In August – became so emotional because we now have joint bank account again.

Friday In August – Became so emotional when I read him my journal entry.

Saturday In August – Back to normal, really brilliant; Danny got a bit tearful about what he had nearly lost.

Sunday in August – Slight blip, but Danny really sobbed with me. Went out to the pub and Danny was looking adoringly at me across the bar and I knew his eyes were full of tears!

Tuesday in August – Beautiful day, beautiful presents. Danny tried so hard to make it special.

Wednesday in August – Attentive all day, confronted his fears, helped to take the pain away, made love.

Monday in August – Cried together to Diana and Marvin.

The list just goes on and on now.

God haven't we come a long way?!

Rosie

Reflections Here & Now

France had become our place of sanctuary. It was because it was something new, totally new, and somewhere where we could go to find a new normality, away from the house and the memories.

Once again I have written a list of all the things that Danny had done whilst we had been away: small things but they all added up; and when the demon came to call I could go back and read them to keep me going, to give me hope.

I especially love the fact that I had noted that Danny had been attentive all day, and more than anything had confronted his fears. He knew that I was having a really bad day when we went to St Valery but he never gave up, even though he faced rejection at every turn. As I have said before the man was like a limpet.

It surprises me that in both of these entries I didn't mention that during our holiday in France Ethan had called us to ask if his friend Adam could come to live with us, because he had found himself homeless. I think that Danny and I both agreed to it because we felt that we should help someone else in the same way as other people were helping us: As if us getting back together was part of a bigger plan that would help others.

Rosie

CHAPTER 45

Journal Entry - September -2007

A Tuesday in September 2007

I don't know why I feel the need to write in my journal – the dreaded hormones I think.

But they are not anywhere near as bad as they have been. I am having more of the 'pop ups' in my head but again no-where nearly as bad as before. I find that despite the hormones, I am able to get them back under control.

I also feel that sadness again but only occasionally, not all consuming like it was last month.

I think that my promotion has also made me a bit apprehensive. Yesterday I was really tired and so was Danny; too much alcohol over the weekend I think.

I am also worried about Louise, and I haven't spoken to Nel in nearly a month – I will ring her tomorrow.

I don't know what it is; even writing in my journal hasn't helped today.

Just hormones I think.

Rosie

Reflections Here & Now

I was feeling an immense sadness because of what we had lost; we were only five months from when 'The War' had begun and it was still early days.

When I read my journal entries now though, after reading other's stories, it does surprise me how quickly I did start to move forward; and I know now that one of the main reasons for this was that I was not going to let what happened define me. But I can vividly remember how one minute I would feel okay and then the sadness would hit me like a brick. I felt such disappointment and regret for what we had both taken for granted in our relationship; and of course the grief for what we had lost.

When I wrote this I had just been promoted for the first time to a position that was actually two grades above my previous job. But with promotion came challenges and this is what was bothering me, but I didn't realise it at the time. That is why the entry is a short entry: I knew that something was bothering me but I didn't know what, so I assumed that it was because of 'The War'; when it fact it wasn't. It highlights that even when 'life' things get to you there is this automatic assumption that how you feel is because of the betrayal; when in fact it is just the shit that life throws at you on a daily basis, and nothing to do with the fact that your partner has had an affair.

It would be some time before I came to realise that this was the case: that the demon in my head was spinning every small problem around to be about the 'affair'. It took a lot of control to eventually understand that and not listen.

Rosie

A Wednesday in September 2007

Last night Danny and I had a lovely night (which we normally do now) but it ended in a row and I made Danny cry.

I knew my hormones were kicking in, but I was surprised by how much I could keep them under control.

Last night towards the end of the evening Danny quite innocently showed me a photo that he had taken of me when I was asleep last Thursday. I hated it! I looked really fat in it, although in my head I looked really fat, because I bought myself a size 12 top yesterday. But you see prior to the 'The War' during the months of deceit, my weight was one of the things that 'she' used against me; and, although Danny didn't actually say the words it was one of the things he was complicit in.

I never realised until Danny showed me the photo just how much my weight now affects me: in that I will never give anyone that ammunition again, especially Danny. Really sad I know, but something that I have been landed with through no actions of my own; and something that I can do nothing about.

I didn't get angry or upset but I did say I hated it and wanted Danny to delete it. Danny got really arsy and defensive. He couldn't understand why I would react like that to a picture. I tried to explain to Danny how he sometimes seems to have no comprehension of the damage that has been done; doesn't want to as he is too afraid of it. But because he got arsy I got arsy. He deleted the photo, threw the camera on the floor and stormed outside. I informed him not to expect me to come after him because I wouldn't, and not to hold his breath waiting because he would suffocate!

After he had a cigarette he tentatively came back, slow steps, kept stopping because he thought I was going to tell him to "fuck off!" But I was not angry, determined, but not angry. I had also thought about how to try and explain it calmly. Although it would still be uncomfortable for Danny to hear, that is his problem, a problem that he created!

So I did explain it to him, and with that Danny burst into tears and said that he loved the photo, that he loves looking at me when I am sleeping, thinks I am beautiful all the time, and that is what he was trying to show me; but that he had realised that he could never do that again.

That made me really sad, I still feel that now, writing this.

This morning I lay in bed watching Danny sleeping, and realised it is something I also love to do.

You see, it is the trust thing with Danny, and sometimes still not knowing if I know him. Although I understand some of the thought processes now – about why it happened – I still don't understand how Danny could have been so complicit in making an idiot of me.

I am sure that over time I will.

But now I am happy for him to take any picture of me, because I know now: it's because he loves me...... so much.

Rosie

Reflections Here & Now

I have often said since 'The War' that pride was my deadly sin. I realised fairly quickly that the name of the demon in my head was Pride. I realise now that it was actually Pride and Ego.

As I have explained I know now that I was angrier with how they had made a fool of me, lied to me, and laughed at me than I was about the sex or the intimacy. As the years have gone by I have come to realise that to live a peaceful happy life it really is best if you can let your ego go; and I only came to this realisation because of the path I have followed as a result of Danny leaving me and breaking my heart.

During the build up to 'The War' 'she' would often find a way to compare us: how 'she' was taller than me, how 'she' was thinner than me; and 'she' would bring the issue up whenever 'she' could: how 'she' was a size fourteen for the first time since 'she' could remember; whilst I was piling the weight on. By the time war broke out I was nearly a size twenty. Even after Danny returned I still got on my stepper and I always made sure that I looked good.

When I saw the photo that Danny had taken of me I hated it because I thought that he would have something of me that he may be able to use against me in the future. This was only four months after 'The War' and I was no-where near to trusting Danny in any way; even if sometimes I said I did. Because of what had happened to me I needed to like my own image so when I looked at that photo it reminded me of the person that I used to be.

The saddest thing was that Danny cried because he thought I was beautiful no matter what; and one of the biggest things for him to come to terms with and then work on was that I no longer trusted him where that was concerned. Before 'The War' I knew that he thought I was beautiful but what he did during 'The War' including the cruel games that he played with 'her' destroyed all that; and it was one of the things that he really had to work on for years after before I would believe him again when he told me I was beautiful.

To rebuild that trust he used to say every day that I was "his beautiful wife." Yes, I have used the words 'used to' because he doesn't have to say them every day now. I know that is the way he thinks by the way he looks at me.

Both Danny and I always knew that we had something, even when Danny was not with me I knew that I hadn't imagined what we had. Because of that it was worth putting my pride demon to one side to see if we could build something new. I think that when the counsellor told Danny and I that we had an 'inner spark' that indicated we would survive, she actually told us to give us hope in what we had. We held on tight to what she said for a long while but looking back now perhaps she says it to everyone just because she knows one of the essential things they will need is 'hope'.

Rosie

A Tuesday in September 2007 – Early in the morning after Danny had left for work

I am really struggling and I don't understand why; and I have to be honest, it is doing my head in!

I know my hormones have kicked in but this time it seems to be not in a massively huge flood, like the past few months, but on a continuous 'high 'state that has lasted about a week now, just under. I have blamed the way I have felt since Friday (perhaps Tuesday) on them; but if am being honest, although they are contributory factor, I don't think it is all my hormones; and that frightens me.

I am writing my journal to try and make some sense of why I have so many thoughts in my head; because more than anything that is the thing that gets to me now: I just don't want those thoughts in my head anymore. The idea that they will be there forever just does my head in, as I know that I cannot live with that, not forever.

Over the last week my sister has had a major operation and my dear friend Jacquie, who has always been there to support me over the past twenty five years, rang me to say that her brain tumour had returned. Yes, all those things got to me and Danny got the brunt of it on Friday night; because these people love me and are suffering, and he had just let me down.

Danny often sees himself as a 'cancer' that I need to get rid of. But he is not the 'cancer' what he did is; and I rely on Danny being the cure, along with time; and I hope that together they will heal my broken heart.

I realised last night, whilst sitting having a glass of wine before I went to bed, that one of the things that drives a wedge between Danny and I is the totally different experiences that we have had from this. As I am writing this I realise that although Danny has told me how he felt during the actual 'War', his experience was nothing like mine. I am crying now because Danny has never really wanted to hear what I was like when he wasn't here for those three weeks: he has wanted to run away from it, and never wanted (I know it is because he finds it so painful) to know the mess that I was in.

As a result of that he doesn't, cannot, understand why at times I swing from high to low with him. It has changed me so profoundly in all aspects of my life, but where Danny is concerned more than any other.

But now Danny is getting sensitive to it all: picking up on things that even I don't pick up on. Last Thursday I gave a photo to Susan of us; I should have asked Danny because I took it of our 'Journey by the Sea' board that we had bought to commemorate our holiday in France, but I didn't. On Friday Danny told me it had really upset him that I was not on the board anymore, that there were no pictures of me; and that Danny took from that that I didn't want to be involved in it, and that is why he had not put the board up on the wall. I realised from the conversation that I had not even thought of Danny when I gave the photo away. That I hadn't even realised the message I had sent out.

On Sunday we discussed the possibility of Danny's leaving 'do' because he had applied for a new job. We both admitted that neither of us would feel comfortable with the other one going out without them: Danny especially; he couldn't handle me going out for the night with my friends. I understand that, so we agreed that we would go out together.

During the conversation Danny also picked up on the fact that I keep calling him 'my friend'. I do keep saying to him "Can I talk to you as a friend." I realised that. He said that he felt that eventually that is all he will be: a friend. I said that it was because an important part of our relationship was/is based on friendship.

But I have been thinking: I notice now that when bad thoughts are in my head I stop myself, and remind myself that the Danny who did all of those things to me has gone and that this is a new Danny; and then I make myself look at our relationship as a friendship first, something that we can then build on, because we have to build something new.

As I am writing this I am realising that over the past month or so Danny and I have started to go back to the intenseness that we had before: back to the old Danny and Rosie. I now understand why all the thoughts are back in my head, because although we had such a lovely time in France we have started to go too quickly; and I am afraid of that intensity.

I just need to slow down a little bit.

Hopefully this will work.

Rosie

Reflections Here & Now

When I read the word 'profoundly' in my journal, I knew that I couldn't have picked a better word to describe the change that I went through. It was intense, deep rooted, heartfelt, and at times overwhelming; and the most frightening thing of all was that I had no control over it. But now I know that it needs to be this way for you to survive whether with your partner or without them

This journal entry highlights the thing that those who have been betrayed know, (because I think it is safe to say it is the thing that drives you mad): it is the constant highs and lows that you go through when you are suffering from a broken heart, from a loss, grieving for the thing that you had that you don't have any more, all the emotions that make you wonder if you can stay. For me at times it felt so unbearable (two steps forward, four steps back) that I thought that if I left I wouldn't suffer any more. I know I felt like that when I wrote this entry; I couldn't bear the thought that Danny having had an affair would be in my head forever. Of course it happened it would never go away completely; but I know now that eventually it just becomes something that is there (a bit like an old wash-stand) and you just walk round it, or ignore it, or use what you have learnt from it when you need to; the key thing is you don't fear it anymore. It's just there in the background.

Over time I learnt that even if I walked away from Danny I would still feel bereaved, betrayed, unable to trust, and heartbroken; the only difference would be that I would not be with Danny anymore. Because Danny was trying so hard, there were so many things he did that kept me there during the many times that I thought about leaving, and because of those small things I stayed. If Danny had not shown how sorry he was and worked so hard every day I would not have stayed; and Danny knew that too.

Louise's operation and Jacqui's situation were also pertinent because they were contributing factors to how I was feeling; but what I did was turn that feeling around and blame it all on what had happened to Danny and I. I found whenever the crap of life hit the fan my brain always blamed it on 'The War'.

I was right though: Danny was the cure not the cancer.

It is true that we had different experiences; which means that we hadn't always followed the same path, and may not always be able to relate to things in the same way (still). Although over the years we have talked about how I was when Danny wasn't with me, he still finds it so painful to listen to and cries because he cannot change it; what's done is done.

Danny becoming so sensitive to things is one of the things that made me fall in love with him all over again; and still makes me love him today: Because now he faces his emotions, recognises them, talks to me about them instead of burying his head in the sand and pretending they are not there.

We had bought a shabby chic board whilst in France and we had added various mementoes of our holiday in the summer with photos, postcards, and little things like the tickets for the train. Danny was starting to become highly sensitive to the smallest of things and by me giving that picture to Susan it was as if I was removing myself from our life together; the fact that he raised the issue helped me to stop and see what I was doing and made me think about it.

I was right by calling Danny my friend because we learned that was first and foremost the most important thing in our relationship. I learned that before 'The War' I had expected Danny to be my 'hero'; to make everything okay and that in fact I had set him an impossible task. Because we were 'in love' my expectation of that love was to provide me with all of my security: emotional, financial, everything. Now I know that in fact we needed to be friends first; I don't expect a magical relationship from my friends I expect something real.

Rosie

A Tuesday in September 2007 – 7.20pm

I felt better after writing in my journal and I have had a good day at work – normal, which it is every day now.

I gave Sherri a lift home and as we chatted she went to say something but hesitated. I knew what she was going to say, because I had already thought it today: she doesn't know if Danny is the right person for me now; or if staying with him is the right thing to-do. I finished what she was trying to say for her: "When I could leave and be happy with someone else who, yes, I know I would meet." I know what she is saying, pretty much what Susan tries to say. I understand where they are coming from; it didn't upset me.

But when I came home, I found myself having one of those chats that people have with themselves in the mirror; and for the first time in a long time I really cried. Because all of my life I have believed in that 'love affair', that 'special love; and although I said earlier in this journal that I no-longer believed in it that was a lie. It is what I want; I can't settle for second best, because I will always wonder if I have done the right thing. I want that all time 'love affair' and I don't know if Danny can give me that now.

I was totally honest with myself in the mirror: that is what I want.

That is why I keep calling Danny my friend; because we have to start with something new and build on that if he is to have any chance. I don't want the 'old' Danny back.

The reasons for this and for going slowly, are because when Danny tells me he loves me, has always loved me, it doesn't mean as much anymore, because I immediately think 'Oh yeah, right! So why did you do what you did then?!'

Now my dilemma is that I know that Danny worships the ground I walk on, loves me so much, adores me; gives me now all that I want. So how do I walk away from that; break my own heart to do it; and search for it with someone else?

But at the same time, how do I keep staying if it is forever going to be tarnished? Which stops it fulfilling my heeds?

I know that only time will tell me the answers; and I also know that I have been wrong to get caught up in the emotion and tell Danny that there are no deadlines and that I am one hundred per cent happy. I need to start being honest with myself all the time, and when I think of what Danny has done I am not happy.

I have to give Danny that chance for the total love he has for me; and because I still love him. But I also have to set a time limit – funny this was something Louise said and agreed with me about a long time ago.

Realistically I have to go through every anniversary and milestone to know if the decision I make is the right one. So I will give it a year from today, September 11th 2008.

Rosie

Reflections here & now

This second journal entry for the same day made me cry because I know just how much I was struggling every minute of every hour of every day.

As I type this at my desk I have a mirror in front of me and I looked at myself today and cried because I do have that 'love affair' with Danny. I know that some people will not understand this; how I can say this when he broke my heart? But you see the person who broke my heart is not the Danny who is with me today: The Danny of today is not the person who left, the person who was cruel to me. The Danny today is the person who worked so hard to keep me, took everything I threw at him and came back for more; he is the person who changed and evolved and enabled me to fall back in love with him all over again. And I thank God that I gave him that chance.

Even when I wrote this entry the Danny then was not the person who left; as I have said in the entry: Danny 'worships the ground I walk on, loves me so much, and adores me.' I could see that even then.

I haven't settled for second best, I have the best: it is real, it is flawed, it has cracks in it but it is strong. For me that is 'real love.' As I have said in my previous entry our love was based on friendship first which, for me, makes it real.

The definition of 'Love Affair' is either a romantic or sexual liaison between two people who are not married to each other (bit of irony there!) or an intense passion or enthusiasm for something.

So if we go with the second definition it is clear that nothing intense can last; it must, by its definition burn itself out; whereas when I look at something that is 'real' which is 'actually existing and not fiction', then I know would go with real over love affair every day.

I love that in this entry I realise that I had to try, despite thinking that I would always wonder if I could have met someone new, and had something untarnished. I also knew that I had a man who loved and adored me, and that I should not, and could not, just walk away from that.

Louise had pointed out to me that I could meet someone new, but they may be someone who refused to change their underwear for a week, and insisted on wearing their socks when we had sex!

More importantly who was to say they would love me as much as Danny did at the time I had written this entry? Who was to say that they wouldn't hurt me in the future just as Danny had done? At least we had something on which we could rebuild and make it stronger.

It's interesting that despite the fact that I have written in my journal twice in one day, and felt such despair, I had also extended the deadline from January to September. Clearly my sub-conscious was in play in helping me stay.

Rosie

A Friday in September 2007

I wasn't going to write in my journal today, even though it has been 10 days since I last wrote in it. But I have the opportunity and I feel the need to update.

On Thursday we went to Brighton for Danny's interview for a new role on the railway. I went to support Danny. We had a nice day and stopped in a lovely pub near Smugglers Cove that we had seen before. In fact we are going there tonight for a meal.

When we came home there were no teenagers and we went to bed; but Danny couldn't perform. We had a good talk and I asked him why? He said that he knew there was something on my mind, and that he had been picking up the vibe for about a week (he is getting like the dog!).

I explained to Danny how I had been feeling; what kind of thoughts go through my head:

Did they have a laugh when they were together about me being fat?

Did Danny say how he didn't fancy me?

The types of thing that I wouldn't know about, because they would have been things between Danny and 'her'.

Danny got upset, but he listened which was important for me to be able to tell him how I feel; and for him to understand the difference in 'us' now. I said about the different experiences we have had, and how that now makes 'us' different; we both got upset together.

Danny said again how he sees himself as the 'cancer' that will destroy me; he is afraid of it affecting my mind, and feels that if he was not in the equation I would be alright. I went back to what Josh had said many moons ago: that even if Danny were not here those thoughts would still be there. They would not go away; and that Danny is the 'cure', what he did is the 'cancer'.

In my mind as I am writing this I can see that the 'cure' for me may mean that eventually I can move on from Danny. That I get stronger every minute of every day, but sometimes as I get stronger, I also see myself leaving.

This week I have been out with Nel and her friend Gemma, not on the pull, but just having a good laugh. I have started my new job and as always have come up against new obstacles, but nothing that I can't handle. I have on my credit score alone credit available to me and that has made me feel good. It made me realise what a nonentity I had become. This also made Danny cry because his credit is crap! And I suppose it just reinforced the fact that I am moving on at a fast rate of knots, and Danny thinks he cannot keep up with me. This week I have felt good.

But yesterday it all went shit shaped. I approached Danny for sex, but he obviously wasn't up for it, no problem there as we have discussed the issues of shift work and I have a cold and didn't feel well etc. But then, as I was doing my stepping, I realised that Danny had in fact had a wank. I am not bothered by that at all, but when I asked him he denied it. Why?

It took me right back to how we used to be: Danny not being honest and embarrassed about sex and I don't want to go back there. Don't want to go back to those two people who we were. It upset me. The last time we had a conversation about Danny not wanting sex was on the Wednesday before 'The War'; and it brought it all back to me.

Danny asked me what was the matter and I told him; we cuddled (eventually, I didn't want to at first.) Danny said he would never masturbate again; but that is not what it was about. It is about the honesty in our sex lives; not just Danny hoping I will stop making a move on him and making me feel like shit and unattractive.

I spoke to Nel about it, but it has put my barriers back up. I honestly don't know where I will be in five years' time.

The world is my oyster.

Rosie

Reflections here & now

I will start with how I felt that day in Brighton:

How common it must be for every person who has been betrayed to wonder what their partner had said to the other person when they had been together; and how common is it that the person who has been betrayed convinces themselves that it must have been about them?

I have come to realise that everything was the hardest thing for me; and over time I dealt with each issue on its own merit meaning that the next issue became 'the 'hardest thing'. This was one of those issues: wondering what they had talked about, and convincing myself that all they had talked about was me. I wondered what they did together, where they went together, who they spent time with, and on this particular day that I am writing about, when the weather was glorious and the drive through the English countryside wonderful, that was all I could think about.

Here we were five months down the line, and still the anger and embarrassment I felt about Danny colluding with someone else to ridicule me was so raw. But what is important in this entry is that Danny listened: we had to understand each other to be able to move forward and Danny had to be able to listen without wanting to run away. But he didn't dismiss the way I felt, in fact I think he felt more pain than I felt because he had caused it, and he couldn't take it away.

We went to the pub we had found that night for a meal. I wore a new woollen dress I had bought and I felt good. When we got to the pub we met a man we knew from in town and he watched me walk to the bar and looked at Danny and said how lucky he was to have me; Danny said he knew he was lucky but then told him what he had done. When I came back the man laughed looked at Danny and said "you're some sort of idiot, because there is no way you are going to keep her!" This was one of the worst things he could have said to Danny, but I wasn't thinking of Danny, I was more concerned that Danny had told him and that the man was laughing at me – or so I felt at the time. The evening was ruined and I just wanted to go home.

The sex issue was a big one:

In the past, prior to 'The War' Danny had often rejected me and made me feel like shit where sex was concerned; he had made me feel unattractive and undesirable. So when he rejected me the emotions of how I used to feel just flooded over me. But as I have said it was not the rejection it was the fact that he had lied about why he was not in the mood for sex; lied again about sex this time with himself, and not someone else. I have never had a problem with masturbation but when it is 'instead of' or someone lies about it then it causes a problem. It was the lack of honesty, again; with the added complexity of the knowledge that Danny had been intimate and had sex with someone else.

It was only by talking it through, that we were able to move forward and we still talk today if either of us feel rejected or insecure about our sex life. That is one of the biggest things to come out of this: we learnt to talk and listen.

Rosie

A Friday in September 2007

I have a husband who adores me, worships the ground I walk on. Last night in bed he just said "You are beautiful." And now I am welling up with tears because I feel so sorry for Danny. I know that if he could change anything (all of it) he would; give anything to be able to undo it. I wish he could.

But I have those awful thoughts in my head everyday – still. I am conscious of the counsellor saying about the six month rule - that after six months you should have one day when it doesn't come up. I know you cannot be rigid about that, and must be flexible, but I do doubt whether that day will ever come for me; and whether I can live with that fact.

Then I think about Danny; about walking away from him, leaving him to his own devices – of how he will destroy himself. I really don't want that to happen, I care about him too much.

Yesterday I asked myself, 'if I won the lottery what would I do?' (I know that earlier in this journal I said I didn't know or that I would leave). The answer this time was that I would take Danny with me; that says so much.

On Monday we were talking and Danny said that I ask him the same questions – as if I am looking for a different answer, one that will enable me to walk away; I can understand where he is coming from. So how hard is it for him never knowing, and so afraid of losing me?

Last Friday I got drunk, and arsy, (as a result of Thursday, when Danny couldn't perform) Danny said he was going to go but he never, because he knew that I would not beg or ask him to stay again. I won't; and as I write this I am realising that he has a point: It is as if I am trying to destroy it, us; to enable me to leave that demon behind.

I know I am at the last hurdle now, the highest hurdle; so now I imagine a beautiful angel, with full wings, everything an angel should have; and when these thoughts get hold of me I imagine that angel pulling me away from the past and into the present and the future.

Today, before my husband left for work, he looked at me and said "I love you." It is the way he said it.......

I know he does.

Rosie

Reflections Here & Now

How long? How long until I don't think about it anymore? The age old question from all those people in immense pain who have been betrayed by the one they love. For me the answer to the question was this:

There will never be a time when it is not there. It will always be there because it is something that happened. But as time goes by you can get to a stage where you don't consciously think about it every day. I found that there is no timeframe because it depends on so many things: how you deal with things, whether you let bitterness take over, whether you listen, whether they listen; whether you're stubborn; whether their stubborn; how they behave.

The counsellor had told us that as a general bench mark at six months there will be some days when you don't think about what has happened. I focused on that and I realise now that I shouldn't have; because I now know that at this stage I was a long way off from when I didn't think about the affair every day. If Danny were honest he still thinks about it every day, because it is he who carries the burden now not me;

Visualisation is something that I used often throughout the early stages of our story; I cannot begin to tell you how much it helped me. I love this analogy of the angel pulling me up into the present and away from the past. I also love my optimism that this will be the final hurdle; of course it wasn't! But it was just hope again, that every present companion that I needed with me to survive. By having that it enabled me to believe that I was moving on and that every hurdle was the 'last hurdle'. If I had sat and thought about all of the hurdles that were ahead of me and us then I don't know if we would have survived. It is the age old analogy: One step at a time.

When people ask me how long I use this analogy:

You start by carrying it like a rucksack full of bricks on your back until eventually the rucksack starts to become lighter as you leave behind the things that you realise are not important. Eventually you lose the rucksack, because you realise that it becomes so small you can carry it in your pocket. But you also accept that it will always be with you, because it made you the person that you are today. It happened it can never 'un-happen'. If you can understand that then it cannot fall out of your pocket like a bloody great rock and hurt you again, because you have accepted it. When it came into my mind I learned to say 'Oh it's you!' and then put it back in my pocket: out of sight and at the back of my mind. I no longer if it has come into my mind. I have just learned that it is part of my life, so I don't even notice it.

Rosie

CHAPTER 46

Journal Entry – October 2007

A Tuesday in October 2007

I am writing in my journal as an update, an important update.

On Friday Danny and I had a lovely evening: lit the fire in the snug, had a mellow drink; in fact didn't even put the telly or any music on; we just chatted. But from that came the following:

Danny is still frightened to text me, ring me, or email me because he is afraid I won't ring him back or reply. That shocked me because I left that feeling behind a long time ago. Now when I text Danny I don't worry whether he texts me back or not. I have moved on from that.

Danny also said that he doesn't feel like he belongs anywhere now; which is really sad. But as I am writing this I am thinking where do I belong? As a result of what has happened I don't feel the same about my house, and I am unsure that I can depend on Danny. But I also know that I belong to myself – I am not afraid of that.

Danny still expects to come home and his bags to be packed, or for me to ring and say that I have gone to Louise's house to stay. I don't want him to feel like that. I do love him.

On Sunday I read Nel the card that I had bought Danny a couple of weeks ago. It was meant to be a positive card but I knew that the card had upset him – although that was not my intention. But Nel said that it did sound like a 'goodbye' card. So I have put it away at the back of my journal.

On Sunday Danny cried when we lit the fire in the front room, cried for the lovely roast dinner I had made; because in his words "I never thought I would be able to do this again."

I am relishing my new job, my new found me. Getting that credit card is so important to me because it shows that I have an identity again.

Yesterday, when I gave Sherri a lift home from work we chatted and she admitted that both she and Hanna don't think that being with Danny is what I really want now. That in two or three years' time I won't be with him. That didn't shock me; and I can understand how Danny must pick up that vibe. I realised when I drove away after dropping Sherri off just how much stronger (perhaps harder) I had got. During the talk with Sherri some things had started to make sense.

On the way home I put the track by Nelly Furtado 'Back in God's hands' on; the very track that I had sobbed to on the kitchen floor all those months ago. That track has always been too painful for me to listen to; but I know now that I can listen to it and be quite hard about it – it's a piece of my past, about a different person, not me now. I never cried. I cannot stress what a big thing that is for me.

I listened to it twice and the second time I sat outside our house until it had finished. When I came in Danny seemed edgy – anyway cut to the chase:

When I got in Danny got the hump and I answered him. Eventually we got into an in depth conversation and Danny said it was the way I spoke to him. I said it wasn't it was because I didn't always agree with him now; and that I wasn't always going to agree with him now. I am entitled to have my own opinions – something that I didn't always do before; that I am a different person. It makes me ask myself: is Danny sure he wants to be with this Rosie, as he has never known her before?

As always Danny took that as me telling him to sod off!

I explained to Danny (very well I thought) the things that I had realised when I was chatting to Sherri:

That I believe that Danny still wants back what we had before; that total all-consuming love. The Rosie who put him on a pedestal – which is something nobody else has ever done to Danny.

But that he can't have that back, it is gone! I don't love him in the same way as I did before.

What Danny is finding hard is that he destroyed it; and he doesn't want to admit it has gone because he would have to face the fact that it's his fault; and Danny just wants to bury his head in the sand. But Danny must face that fact to move on: The thing we have now is better, and healthier in a lot of ways.

I believe that Danny has hit that bereavement stage, he is fighting to pretend that it hasn't gone and he is grieving for it; because he knows in his heart of hearts that it is true, it has gone. That is why Danny feels so insecure and he is crying all the time because all the things we do are not what they were before and he knows it. Yes this is sad; he is feeling the same emotions that I felt when I visualised the bath of despair. But I have moved on, although I am still sad at times every day I get stronger.

Only when you accept responsibility for what you have done and recognise it, can you move on from it. But Danny has never been like that; he has always buried his head in the sand.

The conversation opened everything: the pain on Danny's face was so intense that he couldn't cry properly; I held him, I am stronger than him, but I do still love him.

I told Danny that he must now start to look for that thing that I see in him; to help him keep me.

I have come a long way.

Rosie

Reflections Here & Now

I was right I had come a long, long way. In fact I was starting to fly with regards to becoming a 'new' me. It is hardly any wonder that Danny felt as he did: wondering if I would have left him when he got home from work, expecting to find a note, or all my things gone; because I was still so angry with him.

Whilst I was getting stronger with regards to my life, work, exercise and other things besides, I still had a broken heart; I was still reeling and I was still so bloody angry. So I would text Danny to say that I was leaving work and then go and sit on the Downs for two hours before I went home; I would switch my phone off so that Danny couldn't find me because I was punishing him for those three weeks when he did that to me.

Knowing what I now know, watching my darling husband cry to records even now, I can see that I was so caught up in my own grief, and it was all about me. But the entries are changing and they show that I was supporting Danny and trying to help him more and more. I loved him you see, I always have; and I knew that despite it all, we had something good and I didn't want to let him go.

Where we were concerned we both had to accept responsibility for our actions and acknowledge them to be able to move forward. If only one of us recognised our responsibility then what would have stopped either one of us from making the same mistakes again? We had both made mistakes, we had taken each other for granted and we had not looked after what we had. It makes it quite pertinent that I had listened to the Nelly Furtado record 'Back in God's hands', because in it she says it all:

> 'We didn't respect it, we went and neglected it
> We didn't deserve it, but I never expected this'

> **Back in God's Hands**
> **Nelly Furtado Rick Nowles**

Rosie

The message on Danny's card Read:

> 'We cannot change yesterday, that is quite clear;
> Nor begin on tomorrow until it is here.
> So all that is left, for you and for me
> Is to make today as sweet as can be......'

I had written in it.

To my Darling Husband Danny
I thought that this card said it all. And if we live our lives like this, where can we go wrong?

Sometimes when I hurt I want to hurt you too. But I do truly love you, perhaps in a different way, but just as strong, and even better.

I love you darling

Here is to every day

Rosie xxxx

I shared this to highlight how so often when an affair takes place the couple who try and reconcile are coming at the relationship from completely different angles:

I could see the positivity in this card, Danny could only see negativity.

Rosie

A Sunday in October 2007

Hormones! I swore that this time I would not let them get the better of me; and I haven't as much, but they have had a helping hand.

On Tuesday it came out that Danny did get a hard on with 'her'. That he did stick his cock insider 'her', and then he lost his erection. So in my mind that is defined as full sex! Something that Danny swore he had not done. Something on which I have based everything we have done since the July is that Danny did not have 'full sex' with 'her' because in July he told me he couldn't keep an erection with 'her'. Another lie!!

I just read back over some of my journal; read how many times I believed Danny, how I know when he is lying to me; but I obviously don't! As he lied to me quite often and I didn't see it.

So now I am back, right back as far as Danny and I am concerned: me on my own because I am still much stronger as an individual. I wonder whether Danny can ever face the truth, can ever stop lying because he thinks lying makes things easier. From Danny's point of view I understand why the counsellor told him that I don't need to know everything, because Danny had told 'her' that he was so afraid of losing me, and was afraid that if I knew everything then he would lose me. But from my point of view it was the worst piece of advice she could have given him! It makes me wonder what it is that he is hiding from me that would make me walk away – when everything that has happened so far hasn't!

What is the point of building us up again only to find that that it has all been based on a lie again? Yes, my pride, my self-esteem comes into it; but that is all part of the person that I am. What is going to come and bite me on the arse in the future, like Tuesday's revelation did? I am so afraid of that, so afraid that I will work hard to try and rebuild our relationship only to find that it has all been based on Danny lying to me again. Making a fool of me again!

I know that we cannot have what we had before, and it obviously wasn't as good as I thought it was, or I would not be where I am now, so I don't want it anyway! But I do want to try and make us work; but to do that it must ALL be based on honesty and the truth. If Danny wants to keep me, as he says he does, then he must be honest. If one more lie comes up he will harden my heart more than he realises. Because of this these are the things that I imagine he is lying about:

How many times they had sex. He has already lied about this and said the following:

1. Ten times
2. Five times (which he actually counted on his fucking fingers one night!)
3. Now a handful – he is not sure how many.

Why not? He counted them on his fucking fingers remember?!

1. How many times he met her in Essex; really, how long the relationship had been going on for?
2. Whether they had sex in our bed – Is that why Danny wants to get rid of the mattress?
3. Whether he did ring and text 'her' for the whole eight months, because Danny was adamant that they were not texting each other until the March before he left.

Basically what is it that I don't need to know about?

I do want us to work; I think that for us to break up would be a waste and incredibly sad; a catastrophe for Danny.

But if Danny really loves me, as he says he does, he must be honest with me now. Let this new relationship be built on the truth; lying is no good, hiding things is no good. In Shakespeare's words "The truth will out."

The other thing is when Danny doesn't comfort me when I am upset. I have written in this journal so many times how I <u>need</u> him to do that, and he doesn't! I need to know that when it comes to the crunch Danny will not let me down again.

I think that it would be best for Danny to read this entry without seeing my emotions and that should make it easier.

Rosie

Reflections Here & Now

After reading this entry I had to give myself a couple of days to think about my reflection, because I thought that some people reading this would be thinking 'Oh my God it is never going to get better, because she has gone back to square one!' It certainly looks that way and whilst at that moment in time I had gone backwards the important thing is that I didn't stay there for long. I had started to find that as each day, week and month went past the lows didn't last as long and I was able to fight my way out of them.

Some people who haven't experienced this type of betrayal do not understand that it is more than the immense pain of a broken heart; it is a broken life. They say things such as 'You should be moving on by now.' or 'you need to start to get over it.' Get over what?

- Your life is no longer the life as you knew it, or realising that what you had was not what you thought you had at all. Sometimes for some people that reality has been going on for years.
- Get over the grief? What in a matter of months?
- Or the fact that you are unsure of your own instincts, or yourself, of how you look, of who you are?
- Or do you need to get over the fact that you are starting again, wherever you are in this sad soap opera; having to build something new, in whatever format: staying or leaving.

So there is nothing to 'get over'; all there was available to me was acceptance: if I wanted to recover then I had to accept where I was and move on from there. I had to decide whether to move forward or get stuck on the spiral of bitterness and despair and I used my contempt for 'her' to make sure that I didn't do that.

Stubbornness stopped me from getting caught up in that spiral. I was not going to let 'her' ruin my life any more than 'she' already had. They say that stubbornness is a deadly sin, as it is linked with pride and we all know that was my deadly sin. But this was a double edged sword because if I not been stubborn with regard to letting 'her' beat me then we would not be here today.

I had to decide (and it is important to add here at that moment in time) to consider what I wanted my new relationship to be based on. At the time I wrote this entry I believed that knowing everything was paramount to our survival. But I know now that I was not strong enough at that time to know everything, I would have walked if I had. Then as time wore on and other things came into play knowing everything became less important and I realised that there are many facets to 'the truth'. That is why I call 'the truth' a unicorn: it's only true if you believe it.

I used to say to Danny that if I ever found out that he had lied to me about how long it had been going on for; or how long they had been making a fool of me: then, irrespective of what we had or where we had got to in our relationship, irrespective of how good it was, I would leave; because it would all have been based on a bed of lies. I probably said that for about the first six years after we had got back together.

Now I know that I had to make my mind up about what I believed to have been the truth and go with that because I will never know the truth. It doesn't matter what Danny says I will never fully believe him. If 'she' should come back out from under a stone to say that they had flown to the moon and back on a unicorn I won't know whether it is the truth or not!(perhaps the unicorn bit!)

I made up my mind to believe that the 'worst thing' was the truth, the things that I found so painful: (that they had been seeing each other and having sex for well over a year before I found out.) and I realise now that by doing that it put me back in control of something that I had no control over.

I learnt that the only truth was what was here in front of me now. I would never really know what had happened in the past; and looking back there are some things that I didn't need to know. But if I thought something was off, if all my instincts were screaming at me about something, then I would listen to them irrespective of how painful it was, or how much Danny denied it, and I would tell Danny that I needed to know and he would tell me. And then I still didn't believe him! (See how you just drive yourself insane?)

At the time of this entry I was angry with myself for believing what was obviously a heap of bullshit. Oh come on, they never had full sex? They rented a house together did I really believe that they lay in bed not touching?

But I had to come to the realisation that it was a lie over time. I couldn't do it at the beginning because I knew that I would leave and I didn't want to leave: I loved Danny, and I wanted to stay. So I lied to myself; just like I lied to myself during the affair, but this time it was because I was afraid that I would leave and not Danny.

But as I got stronger I could face the truth and be honest with myself. This entry was the start of that lesson: I had to let go of whatever little candyfloss story I had told myself, and it was a hard lesson to learn. I knew that I should decide on the truth based on the facts that were in front of me:

- They kissed in the July of the previous year
- Danny had text 'her' after looking up 'her' number on my phone.
- They met to have sex in the October of the previous year
- What happened at the Halloween party
- How distant Danny was in the New Year; and horrible to me on my birthday.
- What 'she' had said to 'her' friend about my bedroom.
- That my gut had told me to look for blonde hairs in my bed.

By not ignoring all of these facts it enabled me to paint my own picture; and as it got less painful as the years wore on, and I got stronger, I was able to look back and add other incidents to the scenario to see the even bigger picture. Even today Danny denies what I now believe, but that is up to him; whether he is telling me the truth or not I don't believe him and it no-longer impacts on my life today. I made my mind up and I went with my story in the end.

But I also realised that our future could only be built on what we started to build after we got back together, and whilst whatever happened in the past was significant, future honesty about the here and now was the most important thing.

It was also a lesson for Danny in understanding how hurtful it is to continue to lie when you are asked. How will you gain the trust of someone if you continue to lie to them as you did before? Danny had lied already, and I was asking him to tell the truth and he learnt that he had to face all his fears in knowing that I don't believe him even now.

Over time my lesson in understanding was this:

- That sometimes people who have made such terrible mistakes and hurt someone so badly just don't want to hurt them anymore; so they lie about the things that they cannot change.
- That sometimes people are afraid of what they have done; so they try to bury their head in the sand and pretend that it never happened.
- Understanding that no matter what you are told you will never know if it is true and that sometimes the truth will hurt you more. In the end I would ask myself if I really wanted to know the answer and more importantly what I was going to do with it. I had already established that I loved Danny, and that I wanted to try and make it work so what would I do with more information about the past?

I now know why the counsellor told Danny I didn't need to know everything: because I didn't; as the old proverb says 'What you don't know can't hurt you.' But at that time my bruised ego didn't agree with the counsellor. Now I understand that the information would have probably destroyed us. If Danny had been honest and told me everything, it would have led to us splitting up. I would question if I would feel better today? Would that information have made a wonderful difference to my life or a catastrophic one? Would I still be wondering if it all was true anyway?

The counsellor knew that as time passed I would be able to deal with information more rationally than I could at the beginning. Although I could be more rational as I got stronger and became my own person, it didn't mean that I would still not leave. Only the actions that Danny took after we got back together kept me there when I found out more and more. But I believe that the counsellor knew that if Danny put in the work then that would be the outcome: I would stay. I have to say that it was a clever tactic.

Rosie

CHAPTER 47

Stories to tell - October 2007

One evening in the October after 'The War' Danny and I had been out for the evening; we had enjoyed ourselves, actually been able to have time where we didn't talk about 'The War', and we felt tentatively happy. But as we walked home in the cold and rain 'The War' raised its ugly head, as it so often did. We had turned into our Avenue which was covered with autumn leaves and it hit me – I was back to that night when Danny walked down the road towards me crying, back to the night he left with 'her'. I just changed immediately, and Danny, who by now was finely attuned to coldness when 'The War' was back on the agenda, went quiet because he was terrified.

Danny said he couldn't understand why I was bringing 'The War' up now, when we had been having such a lovely evening. That pissed me off even more, he couldn't understand! Why couldn't he understand? He just seemed to want to run away all the time from how much he had broken my heart.

By now we were halfway up the avenue and the leaves were piled high in the gutters, soaking wet and clinging together. I screamed at Danny that if he felt that I shouldn't get upset anymore then he had no idea how I felt. How it was 'alright for him' he had gone off, fucked someone else, had a good time and here I was left with the aftermath. I told him I couldn't do it, I didn't want to stay and I took my wedding and engagement rings off and offered them to him. But Danny wouldn't take them, and by now I was in a rage, so I threw them at him! Off they bounced, tinkling as they went across the road, the road strewn with wet autumn leaves, and they disappeared.

Now you have to bear in mind that the entire street knew what had happened between Danny and I so for Danny to do what he did in this story is all the more poignant.

Danny couldn't believe I had thrown my rings away. I remember he turned and looked at me with disbelief and asked me why I had done it and with that he started to cry. Then (and this is the video that lives in my head and is with me even today) Danny got on his hands and knees in the dark dimly lit street, and proceeded to scrabble about amongst the leaves, sobbing all the time whilst trying to find my rings. He was like a man possessed and the more he looked the more frenetic he became: crawling around in the puddles and mud, not caring who could see him, determined to find my rings.

I remember how I just stood there watching this big tall man crawling about in the rain and mud, sobbing, and refusing to give up; even though I thought that the chances of finding my rings in the October fall was useless. After twenty minutes I said that I was going indoors (we were only about two houses from our own front door) I didn't give a shit if my rings were lost: we were lost! But I couldn't leave him; because as I watched him I thought 'What the fuck am I doing? What is this going to achieve?'

The voice in my head, the voice of reason, told me to look at the man who was crawling about in the gutter for me. It asked me 'did I really want to throw that kind of love away, that kind of commitment?' That voice at that moment told me to look at the here and now, at the man who clearly loved me from his actions. It pointed out how he didn't care who saw him because he loved me so much; and it asked me if I was just going to throw that away.

I realised that this Danny, the Danny at that moment, was not the man who had left me for someone else; this Danny was a new man and I had to remember that and not keep seeing the man from the past. I had to stop ignoring all of the things he was doing now to try to make this better, or we would never survive.

Danny found both of my rings after about an hour, with the help of fate who made my vintage engagement ring twinkle in the dim light where it lay under the wheel of a car. When he got up from the road he walked over to me and said 'put these back on your fucking finger and don't ever take them off again. 'I did put them back on my finger and I never took my wedding ring off again; and my engagement ring is firmly on a ring tree if not on my finger.

I am sharing this story with you because I know that this small thing was in fact a huge thing with regard to us surviving and getting to where we are today; because I would remind myself of this (and so many other things) when my head told me to leave.

It is important that I say that this happened only six months in from Dday (no time at all) it was at a time when our relationship was at its most fragile, but not the time when it was most at risk, that was much later: as I found myself.

Danny's actions on this night are one of the many small things that made me fall in love with my husband all over again.

Rosie

CHAPTER 48

Journal Entries - November 2007

Friday November 2007

Obviously the first thing I need to write is five weeks!!! This is the longest I have gone without writing in my journal, and the good thing is that I haven't felt the need.

Danny read what I had written in my last entry and it was hard. He read it when I was there and it all got very emotional. But what really surprised me was that he read it again the following Thursday on his own. He got a lot from it and said it was really good.

Since then, when I now look back, Danny has tried even harder – Jesus couldn't try harder than him!!

We had a beautiful time in France; Danny is fantastic on his days off: lights the fires, lights the candles, does the shopping, all the mundane things that I used to be taken for granted for. He wants so much to please me. Over the last month he did become very tearful for what he had done to me; I think he now has a sense of disbelief.

I have been asked to work full time, at two grades higher than my current grade. Everything is changing at work and I am so excited about the challenge - something that I haven't felt for ten years. It really made me realise what a drudge I had become. I said yes to the full time post; but only short term until March, without consulting Danny. I think it's because I am still acutely aware that I have to look after myself and can never put myself in that vulnerable position again; so that's why I don't consult him. And perhaps, as always as I am writing this, things come to mind and I know that I subconsciously keep that small distance between us.

Danny, as always, and as I knew he would, thought that this was all part of my escape plan (the tunnel he thinks I am digging!) But I don't have an escape plan; I will however always have a plan B. And again that is a change in me and our relationship. Perhaps I should write a list!

My life is better. We have more money now than we have ever had (because I am back, and back to my full earnings capacity!) I must fulfil my career now.

My husband treasures me. I use this word deliberately because it means 'something so valuable, to be looked after and handled carefully. Something that you would not want to lose, that you value so much. 'I know this is how Danny feels about me but…..

This makes me cry. I have decided to write in my journal because (although I have had the best month I have ever had with my hormones) I feel sad. Because I still have a broken heart, and I have come to realise that I always will have. I thought that Danny could fix it, but he can't. I never thought that Danny would let me down, and he has. Everyone in my life who I have loved has let me down and hurt me; and I realise that I am on my own. As always I am crying my eyes out now because I have written it down, been honest; but I am hoping that by acknowledging it and confronting it, as I know you always have to do to move on, I will move on.

I look at all the things that are better in my life: I am thinner, have more money, have 'me' back. These are all things that I have done, not anybody else. But Danny is also better, in fairness: he is confronting his fears, more loving, adores me, and, yes, that is better. But undermining that is that he broke my heart, and did what he did; and that will never go away. If I stay with Danny I will have to live with that forever; I know that is now a wedge between us. I tried to explain this to Danny last night. but he just thought that this was me giving a 'goodbye speech'. To me this just highlights that we can't share everything anymore; another wedge between us. After Danny had his defensive tantrum I explained this to him again:

That perhaps when Danny gets upset and says "I can't believe what I did to you" instead of comforting him I say "neither can I!!" That Danny needs to confront what he has done and part of that is opening his eyes and seeing, really seeing, the damage he has done to me. Because only by really understanding that and recognising that can we move on to wherever we are going.

My strength that everyone keeps telling me about is also the thing that keeps making me wonder if I can live the rest of my life with this in the back of my head, or whether I should walk away; but to what? The thing that keeps me here is Danny's love, his adoration. I could meet someone else, but I don't think that they will be able to give me that love and adoration like Danny does. They won't be Danny.

I did say to Danny that I don't believe half the things he has told me. I do still think he is lying, but I am bored with going down that road now, I have made my decision on that.

I have just read this again and sobbed. Because although we have had the best month we have ever had, this does look like a goodbye speech. I am afraid that I am not going to stay. But I have said that I will give it a year from September and I will.

I have also come to realise over the past month how selfish people have become; I have been guilty of it myself. How we are all 'entitled' to pursue what we want because it is 'our lives'. But we get so caught up on this fixation that we don't think about the people that we trample on, or hurt. I have a responsibility to Ethan, to Snowy the dog, to the kittens, and even to Adam who now lives with us; and yes, despite what Danny has done, and because he has put himself through this hell, I have a responsibility to Danny. If I walked away I would be one of those selfish, 'it's all about my life', people. In fact I realise that Danny has already realised that and stopped being one of those people. He has stepped up to the line, and I need to join him there.

Rosie

Reflections Here & Now

There are many things that I love about this entry: it's positivity, and because I had finally started to realise that it was not all about me.

But the most important part of this entry is that I acknowledge that I don't believe what Danny had told me, and that I still thought that he was lying but that I was 'bored with it now'. So many people ask me when the time does come that you stop asking questions, the only answer I can give you is: when you decide to stop.

To not have written in my journal for over five weeks was immense (every small thing counts remember?). It meant that 'The War' was no longer dominating my life for every minute of every hour of every day. I had found myself again in the way I looked and also in my career; but I didn't know it at the time that I still had a long way to go to find myself as a person.

I had started to see the small and good things that Danny did and appreciate them. But the important thing was that I had started to understand just how much Danny both loved me and adored me. His actions had spurred me on to look up the definition of 'treasured' because I knew how important it was to give Danny the acknowledgement he deserved.

I still think that when someone you loved and trusted has turned your world upside down then it is necessary to have a plan B: to keep a little of yourself back is in some ways only natural. It was only as time passed that I stopped doing that because I started to trust Danny again; and this only happened when I trusted myself enough to feel really safe in my own hands, knowing that no-matter what happened I would always be able to take care of myself. Which leads me back to: 'if you don't have yourself you have nothing.'

It's hardly any wonder that I cried when I wrote this entry because I thought that I would always have what had happened in the back of my head, knowing that Danny had broken my heart; as I have said would 'have to live with that forever'. I can honestly say to you that I no longer have a broken heart. Yes it has scars but I do not live with what happened to us every day; I live with what we have now. There is no wedge between us, because what we have is based on things and actions after 'The War' and therefore the 'wedge' Rosie felt existed has dissipated.

Just before this entry I had been to see a friend who loved Danny and I and what we represented to her: true love, the perfect love, people who adored each other. We had given her kudos that the knight in the shining armour did exist and because of that we gave her hope that she would find the same as we had. And then the knight left me; and in so doing he destroyed her hope of finding that all-encompassing 'perfect love.' So when I went to see her she sat and sobbed for the whole two hours I was there: sobbed at the sadness of it all, sobbed because it had destroyed her dream. When I came away I realised how our selfish actions can impact on so many, like ripples on a pond.

I told Danny what had happened when I got home: of how she had cried and as a result Danny then cried because he believed that he had ruined not only my life with his actions but so many others as well.

I cried then; I cried for him because I didn't want him to feel such a responsibility. Looking back now I understand that this was one of the many things that Danny did that enabled me to stay; because I had such respect for his ability to recognise, acknowledge and regret his actions.

As a result I acknowledged that if I was going to make a commitment to our recovery I too had to step up to the plate and I did. But it was Danny who put out his hand and pulled me up there with him; and here I am many years later only realising that now.

Rosie

A Sunday in November 2007

On Friday night Danny and I had one of our big, but constructive, and also calm talks.

I had sent him a text on Friday that said:

"I thought that I would send you a message that you could read on your own throughout the day. I know that I upset you last night and I understand why. But I did need to say it. You were someone I could always talk to and I am trying to get that back, but if it means that I can't, then it means that it is something we can't have and I know that you would not want that any more than me.

I wrote in my journal today that you 'treasure me'; that I am really something that is so precious and important to you that you have to take extra special care of it because you would not want to lose it. I know that you feel like that about me, trust me, that means so much, and I love you so much for it. – Please don't stop. See you tonight darling. Love you Rosie xx"

I knew when I got home that Danny was not happy; and eventually when I called Danny's bluff by not doing all the talking – which then makes Danny talk – he admitted that he was upset, that the text had really upset him. I was shocked because I actually meant for it to cheer him up!

We went through the text together it was the part at the beginning – it made Danny realise the damage he had done, that it is still there, that we don't have everything back; and maybe never will. But he didn't look at the part after; just saw the negative, and not the positive.

We talked and Danny said about what had happened. I have decided to draw my own conclusions; and I told Danny that because he is not open about things this is all I can do. That given the way his family behaved he had been seeing 'her' for the eight months at least, that he did think that he was in love with 'her' and that I only wanted him back for the house. Now I have admitted the worst to myself I am able to deal with it. If Danny will not talk to me about it then this is what I must do; and Danny will reap the consequences.

I also said that common sense dictates that he would not have met 'her' in London if he had not been talking to 'her' on the phone or texting her. But now I have said it I can analyse it: I think 'she' told his family all those things. I think that Danny just walked around in a state of shock when they were together. I think that his family reacted in the way that they did because part of them was happy to see the 'perfect life' that Danny had come crashing down around him; because it made them feel better about where they were in their own lives. I have been on the receiving end of that myself.

I had a big long chat with Nel yesterday and as I talked I came to these conclusions myself:

No I don't think Danny ever thought he was in love with 'her'. He told other people that he was to shut them up and get them off his back (for what he had done.) Danny told me he loved 'her' because I had hurt him with the 'wedding speech' when I had spoken to him on the phone that day, when I had told him I was too good for him. Danny always thought that anyway so I was really sticking the knife in that day.

Part of me wants Danny to carry on thinking that what I said on Friday night: about making my own mind up about what happened was because I want to hurt him, and pay him back, like he hurt me. But I am not going to do that, I do need to make my own mind up, I cannot wait for Danny to tell me the truth any more.

Ethan went to London with Danny yesterday, the road was closed and Danny got stressed; but Ethan was so worried about him he rang me later because he knew Danny was really stressed about the possibility of losing me. Ethan told me I must help Danny and reassure him. That he was going to stick up for Danny from now on.

When Danny came home (after ringing me five times in the day) I gave him a big kiss and told him what Ethan had said to me. We had a lovely evening; but during it Danny reminded me that he had a panic attack in the night. That he had dreamt that he had woken up in a strange place, alone and I wasn't there. That he had sat up in bed calling out for me and looking for me. I don't remember – I must have been asleep – but he said that I comforted him and told him to wake up.

I love Danny; I don't want him to feel like this. I am achieving nothing.

I realised that on balance I keep my guard up, and hardly ever ring Danny. I do make gestures but my guard is up all the time. I must try now to help him. I know it will take time, but I need to start to lower that guard or Danny will die, because this is what will happen if he believes he doesn't have me. I don't want that; I love him ……. So much.

Rosie

Reflections Here & Now

There it is, the time when I finally realised that to think the worst and confront it meant that it could no longer bite me on the arse!

The worse that I was thinking was that it had started in the June of the year before: Our boiler had broken down and we had visited 'her' house to use 'her' shower. 'She' had been there and we had gone across separately; but when Danny had gone across he was there a long time. My sub-conscious in 2007 after 'The War' had known that this was the case; and I had clearly said it to Danny on the Friday before this entry.

Now despite the fact that I say we should never lie to ourselves again; on this occasion, and on others, I did. I have written in my journal that I only said it to hurt Danny; that's not true: I said it because that is really what was in the back of my mind. If I had acknowledged this at the time I wrote this entry I would not have stayed. Now I can acknowledge it because I am in a safe place, where I am concerned and where Danny and I are concerned. I am also applying what I have learnt and I don't lie to myself.

In this entry I also believed Danny when he told me that he had only said he loved 'her' to get me back because I had said about the wedding speech. But this was also a lie; Danny had told me he loved 'her' before I said about the wedding speech; in fact he had told me he loved 'her' on the Thursday after he left when we spoke about the house and they laughed at me. But I believed him then because I had to, so that I could stay.

As part of writing this book I have been researching other's stories and the length of time that the affair had been going on is of course, one of the main issues that just keeps coming up again and again; it was for me because one of the biggest things was how long they had been making a fool out of me.

Over the years I have gone through the timeline in my head including the time we went to their house before we left for our holidays and Danny commented on her 'new pyjamas': how did he know they were new? I look back to an afternoon we spent on the beach with them, or to the time in the September when Danny said how he felt sorry for 'her' and how we should invite 'her' and 'her' partner out for a drink. I think of all the times on our holiday that Danny was on the balcony with his phone and all of it indicates that they had been seeing each other since the June. That's what I believe now; and even a polygraph wouldn't change my mind.

I actually raised this issue with Danny as I was writing this book. I wasn't seeking clarification, because I wouldn't believe whatever he said, but the topic did come up in conversation. The reason I am telling you is that when I raised it, even now all these years later, it still terrified him; he looked at me and said "I am frightened that by writing this book it will bring it all back and you will leave me."

I left it there and put the demon back in its place at the back of my mind because I know that there is no point in going back there when we are in the here and now. It was so many years ago now and, as then, it doesn't matter when it started, it started. The only important thing is that I don't lie to myself about it.

Having read back what I sent to Danny all those years ago in that text I can understand why he thought it was a goodbye speech. Although the end of the speech was really positive Danny felt that he deserved a goodbye speech and was always therefore, looking for it. In fairness I do say to him that he was someone I could always talk to and at that time I didn't think that I would ever trust Danny enough for him to be the 'go to' person that we all need in our lives.

But Danny is my 'go to' person now, as well as my sister. Because of what we have been through he understands me better than anyone else ever can; better than I understand myself sometimes.

I had forgotten the conversation with Ethan. Our son was at times more intuitive than the adults in his life, even though he was only seventeen.

I was clearly falling in love with Danny all over again: the new Danny. Despite this, I would at times still turn my phone off so he didn't know where I was; and I know that part of the reason for that was because I was afraid of falling in love with him again, and being vulnerable.

Rosie

A Monday in November 2007

So I don't write in my journal for five weeks and now I have written in it three times in five days!!

It is because I feel so down. Originally I put it down to the dreaded hormones but I don't think it is just that; I cannot put my finger on what it is, and I am frightened. ~

As I have written this my have eyes filled up with tears; so being frightened must be part of it: I am frightened I will not stay. I am frightened I cannot stay. I am frightened that if do stay this will not go away; I am frightened I am getting depressed and will not be able to control it. I am frightened I will waste what I have with Danny. I am frightened I will give 'her' what she wants, because by walking away and leaving Danny I will be giving 'her' just that. I am frightened for Danny.

I have stopped crying now.

When I watch Danny sometimes I realise that I am so lucky that I have these coping mechanisms in place; because they do work. But I also realise that not everyone can do that.

Last night I read Danny my entry from yesterday because it was very positive. He then said that he had cried at work in front of the new bloke that had started to work on his team. We started to talk; I knew that he had cried at work on Saturday and that is why Don had sent him home early. He said that the way Ethan had seen him in the car was how he was with people all the time: sharp and sarcastic. That he is really horrible to another bloke on his team.

From what I read and what he said we got talking about 'The War'; a hard, very hard, talk. I am finding it hard to write about it now. Danny just finds it all so hard.

I found it difficult to hear that they sat snogging in the car in Lowly; and that Danny would do that to me. But that was Danny then, not the Danny that is here in front of me now; but I do struggle to deal with that. I know I must for my own sanity (I am crying again) but I know I must go through this to climb over the hurdle and move on.

Danny went from the beginning and told me his story: he finds it hard to say what he thought because he is so horrified by it all that it is obvious that he blocks it out. Danny gets all the dates and days muddled up and it is obvious that he has dealt with it by blanking it from his mind. (The ostrich syndrome that Danny so favours!) But that is Danny and I have to accept that; and do you know as I am writing this, I realise that I love him for it.

Danny was so manipulated because he was so weak; but I truly believe that Danny will never be manipulated again. He has learnt from this, got stronger. He said how 'she' used to continuously say how I was horrible to him; and then he said how 'she' told him I had told 'her' I had an affair. The pain on Danny's face as he said this reflected my pain: he started to cry and said "I cannot tell you the devastation I felt, the devastation that I have now caused to you."

I am okay now; this was the hardest thing. We have done it! I don't want to know anymore, or talk about it anymore. Moving on...

My guard is back up, but I will work on that now.

Moving forward.

Done!!

Rosie

Reflections Here & Now

I was frightened! I now know that it was because somewhere deep inside of me I knew that I could possibly throw something that was ultimately so good away. I just didn't know that the fear was because of that; because the pain I felt would not allow me to see the good that I had; not fully.

I felt confusion, mistrust, betrayal and I understand that part of that was also my ego telling me that I was worth more. I also felt frightened of letting my guard down and being vulnerable again; and that terrified me as I know it terrifies others. That is why I say that if you have yourself, like the way you are, like the way you look, earn enough to survive without them (sorry but we have to be realistic and this does come into the equation) then you can face that fear because you know you have yourself, that you are not as vulnerable as you were.

I know that if I had still been dependent on Danny: relying on him to be part of what defined me, needing him for money, being afraid to be on my own, then we would not have survived. I know that vulnerability at that time for me would have made me walk away because I would have been afraid of it.

I cannot stress enough that I believe that finding yourself is paramount to survival. I was afraid of it because I knew that it may mean that I may walk away. That I may find myself to such a degree that I no-longer liked Danny; and I was really afraid that I would not like him because of the person that he was and not because he had broken my heart.

The positivity of this entry shines through because we really talked about what each other had been through; and until I read this today I had forgotten this talk. But as soon as I read it I could remember the pain on Danny's face: a pain so immense it made me realise that I was not the only one in pain, I was not the only one who had suffered heartbreak. At that time that was difficult to understand but I learned that when someone is remorseful and works so hard to make amends the chances are they have a broken heart too. They broke their own heart.

One of the other important things that I say in this entry is that Danny had 'The Ostrich Syndrome', as in he buried his head in the sand. But it was important that I recognised that Danny got dates, times and even parts of the story mixed up because he was trying to box it up and not think about it because it was too painful. This stopped me from being angry with him and thinking that he was just hiding and lying about things. I realised that the reasons for not telling me everything were multi-faceted.

Rosie

A Wednesday in November 2007

I am not getting any better. That is how I feel. I have cried every day for about a week now and I don't understand how I have gone back to that.

I have tried to look at the positives but it just makes me think why? Why should I be doing this? Why am I in the position that I have to do this? I know I am going into a depression. I don't want to go to the doctors; that is not me and it will not help. I know that looking at the positives is the only thing I can do.

Last night, for the first time more than any other, when Danny and I had sex I had to close my eyes and think of England. I couldn't get out of my head what he had done and I didn't want to be there; didn't want to come, didn't want to cuddle after. I have never felt that way. I cannot believe that Danny didn't notice or will he just bury his head in the sand and pretend it is not happening?!!

I couldn't sleep properly and eventually when I woke up, I asked God for help. I started to think of all the positives that I get from Danny now; and also the commitment I have made to the boys and the animals (the 'not all about me' commitment!)

When I fell asleep I had the weirdest dreams. I cannot fully remember the first one, but the second one was me in New York, with David Cameron and his entourage (weird!). But the point was I was in this lovely hotel room alone; I went down to the bar with David Cameron and his entourage and we got the plane home. I left everything behind in the room. I forgot to pack let alone collect it: my glasses, contact lenses, clothes, everything. When I got home (to mum, dad and Louise) I realised my mistake and tried to ring the hotel to get them to forward my stuff on to me. But for some reason the woman couldn't understand me, and it was really hard. She couldn't understand why I would leave it all behind and spoke to me as if I was stupid. And I so desperately wanted the stuff back.

I understand.

I woke up and my immediate thoughts were that I should be looking at all the positives from Danny. (Not the ones I have achieved for myself.) Just yesterday he:

1. Rang me (I would not answer the phone. One of the things he is afraid of and I did it!!)
2. Text me (I didn't reply, same as above, I reinforced one of the things he is terrified of.)
3. Fixed my hairdryer.
4. Cooked our dinner – had it all ready with the candles alight and the fire lit.
5. Did all the ironing that was left to be done.
6. Hoovered through downstairs.

7. Did as much washing and drying of the laundry as he could and put it all away.
8. Made sure the kitchen table was clear of crap, because he knows it winds me up!!
9. Made the tea to have in bed when we went to bed.
10. Even took his bloody pants off because I commented on him wearing them in bed and not wanting to be naked with me.

He can't do anymore. My dream symbolises my life: I feel like I want to run away from it, I am not taking care of it; and when I am away from it and have left it behind I will realise how desperately I want to keep it; and how stupid I was to throw it away.

Mirrors what happened to Danny really!

Rosie

Reflections Here & Now

I fully understand that dream now. The fact that I was with David Cameron as part of his entourage represented my new life, with my work and promotion; and leaving my belongings behind: everything that was important to me at that time (it included my glasses and my contact lenses things I cannot live without), represented me walking away from Danny and everything that I had in my life. When I called the receptionist she spoke to me as if I was stupid for walking away from what I had; she couldn't understand what I was saying to her because it was incomprehensible that I would walk away. Very telling is that in the dream I felt the strong emotion of so desperately wanting it all back: my subconscious way of telling me not to walk away.

I went home to my mum, dad and Louise, which would never have been possible because my mum and dad had died; perhaps that was the message – it was impossible to walk away, and it was impossible to go back; that even if I had walked away it would not be what I wanted; and where Danny and I were concerned I couldn't go back to what we had, and I didn't want to even though I may have thought I did. The only way I could go was forward. The woman speaking to me as if I was stupid was my brain saying to me that I would be stupid to walk away, and it was asking me why I couldn't see that

We were getting better; I just couldn't see it at the time. I think that what I wanted was for it all to go away, and although I had accepted that things were never going to be the way they were before I thought that by this point when I wrote this entry, the thoughts of it would have gone.

As I have said what happened will always be with me because it exists but it is like a mist in the back of my mind because I learned to accept it. When we try to fight something and don't accept what is happening then it won't go away: because your own thoughts keep bringing it back.

Does what happened define me? No. But this chapter of my life led me to be the person that I am today: someone who looks at the psychology of things, who reads philosophies and someone who now changes every week, if not every day, because of the things that life shows her. I learnt that change is the only constant in life and understanding and acceptance of that and what it entails is actually all you need.

As ever there are so many positives in this entry, even though I was struggling; and that is what I love: that the Rosie and Danny of then never, ever gave up!

There were times during intimacy when the thoughts in my head were defeating me and I would have to 'close my eyes and think of England.' Looking back it was the fact that I had not felt like that in the months previously that was making me feel as if I was being sucked backwards again. Danny knew what I was doing; and even now if I close my eyes Danny's demon sometimes gets the better of him and he thinks that I don't want to be there.

I found it so useful to write lists of the positives that had happened in our life because then it helped me to focus on the positive when a trigger hit, or a wave of despair: I couldn't lie to myself if I had written it down, I could revisit the positives when my brain was only telling me negatives.

Rosie

CHAPTER 49

Journal Entries – December 2007

A Friday in December 2007

I am writing to update my journal, but this time not because I feel the need, I just want to update it. I went to my sister Louise's house on the Friday after my last entry and cried. I said that I thought I need to go back to the counsellor. Louise and her friend Lettie gave this advice for both me and Danny:

- Stop trying to get back what you had because you will never get that back. If that is what you want you need to find someone else because you will never get it back with Danny. Instead of trying to recover something make something new and better.
- Stop thinking that whenever you are fed up it is always because of what happened. It may just be because you're tired, have got the arsehole with work, whatever. But because what happened is always foremost in your mind you always take your feelings back to that: in the same way as Danny always assumes you're going to leave him. STOP doing it!
- Forget things that were said when you both got back together initially as you were both mental! You both said things you didn't mean Danny said things just because he didn't know the answer himself. (Danny and I talked about this and why

I started this journal. He is mortified by what he said about being flattered that two women were fighting over him; and he does not find it an ego boost in any way now.)

- Danny has to understand that my barriers are up; and may well be up for a couple of years. But whilst I have my barriers up I should still be me, which I had not been when I was writing in my journal over the last three to four entries. I had created distance between us as well: was not being tactile, was not being me. By doing this (to punish Danny in a way) I was making myself miserable.

I took all of this advice on board and my head is sorted. I had a blip of four days, but no-where near as bad as before, and I could control it.

We have been to France again and had the most fantastic time. Danny breaks up from work today for Christmas and we have eleven days off together. I am so looking forward to it. We are having a shindig for Ethan's eighteenth birthday tomorrow and Danny is so excited to be part of it. I think that says it all.

Rosie

Reflections Here & Now

The first thing I thought when I read this entry was that I had completely forgotten the conversation with my sister and Lettie; which surprised me because it was a very important one and helped me massively in dealing with things in the future: they were both so right.

Danny was the one that had to let go of what we had; as you know from what I have written in this book, I had come to realise that a long time before this entry. But for me the most important piece of advice they gave me was to stop thinking that everything revolved around what had happened to us. Whenever I had a problem in life I would immediately link it to what had happened, to what Danny had done to me, and therefore everything had to be his fault. Quite simply it wasn't!

I could have felt pissed off because I had a bad day at work, or because someone had upset me or something had gone wrong, as things do in life. But when anything happened I would get in the car and the 'demon' (oh yes he was still there it would take a long while before he no longer existed. I sold him with my car!!) would get into my head and turn my upset around and tell me it was all because of what Danny had done to me. It was all about 'The War'!

Understanding that it wasn't all about 'The War' was a huge thing for me because as soon as I understood what I was doing I was able to tell that demon to shut up. But I also started to realise that 'The War' didn't define me: it was not the total of my life: and I had to stop letting it be that. Although it influenced my life greatly and made me the person that I am today it is a contributing factor, but only one of many.

For a long time after 'The War' Danny would think that anything that went wrong was his fault. He would take sole responsibility for every little thing: from the boiler going wrong to someone upsetting me at work. Sometimes he still does that even now, and I just stop and say to him "What are you saying sorry for?" He normally laughs then and says he doesn't know.

The advice about forgetting what was said when we first got back together was also good advice because we were insane, and certainly not thinking in any way rationally. I know that most people struggle with this because we all crave to be 'normal' again, to 'think straight' again; when in actual fact our lives have been turned upside down and shook about, so why do we expect that of ourselves? It has actually been recognised that when something like this happens to you then you are actually suffering from a form of PTSD; so that explains why I did some of the insane things that I did, because I was insane.

I love the quote 'I thought I was going mad, but the unicorn in the kitchen told me I was okay.' That pretty much sums up how I felt in the first year of our recovery.

When we initially got back together Danny did say things to me that weren't true, things that contradicted themselves because he just didn't want to hurt me any more than he had already. After a while he did start to talk about it and tried to explain himself to me, but he found it so difficult because he was at a loss as to why he had done it himself: he would ask himself the question why, and couldn't even answer himself. Then he progressed to berating himself for what he had done, what he had said and in the end he totally lost himself; and as you will see later in our story all of this eventually had massive impact on his mental health.

A good example of our madness is when I started this journal: because Danny had said that he found it a compliment that two women were fighting over him. By the time I had come to write this entry in my journal he was mortified that he not only said it but that he thought it at the time. He still feels that way today: he shakes his head and says 'I cannot believe what an arsehole I was.'

Ethan's birthday was on Christmas Eve, so we held a surprise eighteenth birthday party on the weekend before, and it was a great success. I look at the photos now and see how thrilled Danny was that he was there involved in the celebrations. On Christmas Eve we all went out including Adam, and took Ethan to the pub, an English tradition. Danny was so chuffed that he was there to be able to give Ethan some money and send him to the bar so that he could order his first drink legally. We left the boys in town after that and made our way home to prepare the meal for Christmas day. It was something so normal, and I kept my head under control because I felt a responsibility to the other people around me to make sure that this festivity was not marked with tears.

That Christmas was wonderful; we had gone overboard to make it special: with a Christmas tree on the balcony as well as in the house. After dinner we all opened a present and my present from Danny was the most beautiful watch, but the most beautiful thing for me were the tears in Danny's eyes when I opened it. I knew he was so sorry and that in itself was the best gift he could give me.

It was important to us that we could make it special for many reasons but not least because at one point in the year we had both thought that we would never celebrate Christmas together in our beautiful house again, so it was another small thing: to make new Christmas memories that we could look back on that were not 'tainted' with the affair.

Things like this are all steps that you take to make things something new, a 'new normal'

Rosie

2008

CHAPTER 50

Journal Entries – January 2008

A Sunday in January 2008

> *"You face a new future, with time to brood, your realise it is not the future you imagined. Your resulting sadness and lethargy come from a sense of loss – and what many people do not realise is that there can be a feeling of grief for a way of life which has been changed utterly. It can happen at the end of a marriage, or at retirement, or when somebody realises the script of her life has been re-written, and there is nothing she can do about it."*

Bel Mooney
Writing for The Daily Mail

I have felt very sad all week, in fact I am just acknowledging the sadness that is always there; but it sometimes feels stronger than at other times. I read this quote in an advice column of the newspaper (The wonderful Bel Mooney) and I realised that it applied to me; and enabled me to put a tag, a reason if you like, to my feelings.

I know I am bereaved, that I am grieving. Kate at work explained that I am in the second stage of grief. She explained that it has the same emotions as the first but without the shock and disbelief; that this stage is about accepting what has happened and accepting that your life will never be the same again.

I thought in Danny, that I had found someone who would always support me and never let me down. I have to now accept that was never the case. That Danny was never that person and that for the last ten years I had been living a lie –to a degree of my own making. I know now that Danny is so desperate to be that person and make it up to me; but I don't think he can, he is not like me, he cannot be the person that I thought he was (I am crying now).

I thought that I had found the love that everybody searches for; I thought I was so lucky. But it wasn't what I thought it was at all. I really feel that the last ten years were just a heap of shit!

I know that Danny is so desperate for us to have that 'love affair' back, but we never really had it in the first place!

Through no fault of my own my world has been turned upside down; and no matter what we do, no matter how hard we try, they are the facts and I have to face them to move on. That is why I say about the other things I have to consider Ethan, Adam, the dog, cats, house, lifestyle; because those things do keep me here now, not just my love for Danny. Before it would have only been my love for Danny!

I have moved forward with my life: thinner, promotion, regular exercise; in those things my life is better and I would not want to go back; and, yes, I have only achieved those things because what happened kick started me to achieve them. But I have achieved all the things that are better in my new life on my own. Yes I go to France with Danny and I really enjoy it, but I could do that on my own. Yes Ethan's party was brilliant and Danny worked so hard to contribute because it was so important to him, but I could have done it on my own.

Christmas was lovely; and no I couldn't have done that on my own because Danny being here made it lovely. He is so loving now, I never actually realised how much of an arsehole he had become before 'The War'; and I ask myself can I not fall in love with the person I have now? I don't know. Danny will have always had sex with someone else, kissed someone else, set up home with someone else, so only time will tell.

I asked myself today would I be able to, or want to stay if Ethan and Adam were not here? The honest answer is I don't know. But I know that time will change everything again and when that time comes I will be in a different place; and then I look at Danny (I am crying again now) he is so desperate to keep me. I know he is living his life constantly striving: worships me, adores me, all the things I have always wanted, thought that I had with him once; but it cannot change the way that I feel – alone.

I loved Danny so much, I thought he was my soulmate; but he is not now and I find that so sad because he so wants to be; and because of his weakness he threw it all away and that too makes me sad.

I know I have to face the future and not be afraid of where it will take me. I have to stop worrying about Danny and let it take its course. When I started writing this journal I was afraid, and I realise as I am writing this now that I have moved on from that, I am not afraid, I am just incredibly sad.

Rosie

Reflections Here & Now

By this time I had changed my life so much; as I have said in this entry I had been promoted by two pay bands, had gone back to work full time, was really fit and really thin and I didn't feel the need to write in my journal every day, or even every week!

Even today I love this piece of advice that I quote at the beginning of this entry; from Bel Mooney's column in The Daily Mail. At the time it touched such a chord with me that I included it in my journal so that I could read it and remember it when times were hard; because that is exactly what had happened to me: the future I had imagined was gone, through no fault of my own; and the start of the new year had highlighted that to me. I was on a new journey now, one that I would never have imagined I would be on the previous year, and I just had to go with it.

I know the person who wrote this journal entry felt so sad, and I feel sad now reading her thoughts. But over the years I have learnt that everything we go through is a lesson, and that more often than not those lessons are soul destroying hard lessons. But I now know that if we learn from those lessons and work through them, as Danny and I were doing and continued to do for a long time, then it wasn't all 'shit' it was just part of the lesson. – I know that's hard to hear if you're world has just fallen apart – but I have to tell it like it is, I can only tell you my story.

The lady I worked with was right when she told me I was still grieving; only the shock had subsided; the grief was still there and the waves of grief would still be there for a long time to come.

At that time I hung onto anything to keep me there; anything that would enable me to stay with Danny and try and make it work; because every day the demon in my head told me I shouldn't stay.

I have listed all the things that 'made my life better', and at the time they did; because my heart was broken. I had to use them to keep me there; I had a responsibility to others as well as myself. But If Danny had not been contrite, if Danny had not worked hard every day to keep me and show me how sorry he was, I would have left (or he would have left because I wasn't giving up the house!) I was right I could have taken care of all the others anyway. They were just a tool that I used, I reminded myself of the upset that they would go through if I called time; I then added them to Danny's actions in trying to make it work; this enabled me to stay and quiet the demon.

I knew that when I wrote this entry at the beginning of the year there was a chance that by the end of that year (a high chance) that I would no longer be with Danny: that I would have left him behind and gone on without him. I knew that by rebuilding my life with all the things that Danny was not included in (the way I looked, my career) I was effectively building a life without him; and although I did it I was really scared at the same time of what the outcome would be. But I also knew that I had no choice; and I know even now that if I had not done that we would not be here today. I had to take that chance; I had to be me.

But actually the most important thing I had then, although I didn't realise it at the time, was that Danny was so loving and so sorry. As I have said a man who 'adored me, worshipped me', a man who was constantly striving to keep me; and yet at that time I didn't see that as a contributing thing that defined me – because I was afraid to. I didn't see that as the most important thing to me; although somewhere I knew, or I wouldn't have written it down. At the time I wrote this journal entry I didn't feel that Danny would ever be counted as something important to me, I felt that I couldn't allow myself to be vulnerable, where Danny was concerned, ever again. And look at where I am now.

Although I have said that it was all 'such a needless waste of all that love and devotion' I now see it differently: What happened to us enabled us to be the people that we are today.

Rosie

CHAPTER 51

Journal Entries – February 2008

A Sunday in February 2008

It now seems to be about a month's duration before I write in my journal. Even now I deliberated whether to write in it, but I feel that I do need to update it. I notice it is the same sort of time of the month and I do notice now that my hormones seem to be affecting me but I can honestly say that this is the best I have felt.

A month has gone by and I feel very different to how I did when I wrote my last entry.

I spoke to Aunty Joyce that day and she said that I was brooding, thinking too much. That I should just let things take their course and see where life took me. She was worried about me and rang Louise who then rang me. Louise said the same old same old "it is too soon to make a decision; it is still too raw"; and that I was/ am expecting to be over it when I cannot be. On the day of that entry I became irrational – signed up to get Danny's phone details and check his phone – he has never contacted 'her'.

Since then my darling friend Jacqui has become terminally ill; she is an ally who has been there for me from the beginning of 'The War', someone who has always been there for me. I am losing another person who I could always rely on.

Danny has been fantastic; whilst he would have been there before in situations such as these, he would have stayed in the background. This time he hasn't, he has been there for me 'full on.' But he is afraid that this will make me re-evaluate my life and decide not to include him in it.

On Tuesday I was hormonal and had a cry on my way home from work; but when I got home Danny had bought me roses and a Valentines present which is all wrapped up on the mantelpiece as I write this. (We had stopped buying each other gifts for Valentine's Day years ago.) All the candles were lit and my dinner was ready; it totally undid how I had been feeling in the car.

After going to see Jacqui on Wednesday we had a drink on the Thursday evening and were quite drunk. I told Danny that I had been thinking all day and that I realised how much Danny now lives his life walking on eggshells. That I couldn't guarantee I would ever get over it, and how I felt that we cannot go on living our lives forever like we are now. That I cannot see how Danny can continue to live his life like he is; and if I walked away we would both be able to get over it, eventually. But Danny grabbed me like he was never going to let go and said that he would take whatever was available, anything he could get, to carry on living his life with me; that anything is better than not having me at all. That said so much.

Over the last month I have come to realise that Danny could become my soulmate again; a different one, a better one; that I could love him so deeply, in a different way, in a better way.

I asked Danny on Thursday (when he said that I didn't understand how much he loved me; had always loved me) why did he do it? He said that if he understood and could answer that question he would be a millionaire; that he asked himself that question every day.

If I ever do send this to print, then understand this: for a moment of selfishness, or excitement if you like, from the normalities of life, you will let off a nuclear bomb into your life. I cannot explain how much devastation you will unintentionally cause that will last forever.

Rosie

Reflections Here & Now

The first thing about this entry is what Danny said when I asked him why he had done it: that if he had the answer to that question he would be a millionaire, I understand that answer today.

I do believe that people cannot tell you for a host of reasons: including denial and fear. Even today I know that question ruminates around Danny's brain; if he could undo it he would, if I could undo it I wouldn't (but that is for another discussion another day)

This entry highlights the highs and lows that you experience because it is such a stark contrast to the previous entry; and that is the thing that drove me mad, the thing that I did not think I would be able to cope with for the rest of my life: the highs and lows; feeling one way one day and completely the opposite the next. It was probably one of the biggest things that would have made me walk away. But of course now I know that it does pass, but I have to add the caveat here: If you let it. Only I was in control of my emotions and only I would be able to get them back under control. This is why I urge people not to get caught up in bitterness and vitriol; if I had then for me it would have been a poison.

When I wrote this journal entry I was considering the fact that Danny could be my soul mate: a better stronger one. This was only ten months on from Danny coming back, but I could see it. Now don't get me wrong there was still a long, long, way to go on our journey - we hadn't even hit the anniversary of D-day yet; and despite what I wrote in my journal I would still consider leaving Danny every day; every single day, for a long time to come. That is the joy of a broken heart caused by adultery.

In this entry I have considered leaving Danny for his own sake. I was making him walk on eggshells and, at times, I enjoyed doing it: enjoyed punishing him for what he had done to me. But ultimately the fact that I loved him was why I didn't want him to suffer every day; and despite not wanting Danny to feel the way that he was I honestly didn't know if I could get past what had happened or stop punishing him. Even though the anger and rage didn't burn as intensely as they had, the fire was still there inside me: a small flame that could ignite at any moment. Trust me ten months is no time at all.

Danny did the best thing he could when he grabbed me by arms (I can still picture it today) and said that he would take anything that I offered, just to stay with me. Even today I think that is the sad side of infidelity; that some of the people who have committed the adultery will often berate themselves every day when they are truly sorry; but there will never be anything that they can do, or we can say, to take that pain away.

As part of the process of writing my book I have become part of a community. It was something that I never envisaged, although I had always intended that my book would help other people one day. (In fact I had even written in this journal entry all those years ago) The community that I now find myself in is supportive of others, and gives them strength at times when they need it; and it is evidence that out of something so destructive good can still come.

I came to realise that I was the one who held all the cards. I was the person who had been lied to and manipulated, shamed and destroyed because of the infidelity. But I was the one who had to let things go to enable recovery for both of us. I was the one who held all the 'power' (and I use that word carefully). The power to make things right for myself and the power to take whoever I wanted along with me.

My beautiful friend being terminally ill did make me consider life and how we should make the most of every moment. Yes it did make me question what I was doing by staying (including destroying Danny in the process) but it also made me see what I had at that moment in time, and could have in the future. The past had gone and I couldn't get it back; I realised that looking back over phone records was not going to change anything; because life is quite simply too short to keep going backwards.

I loved that I was finally starting to see that it was not all about me. I was clearly falling in love with this Danny because I cared that he was walking on eggshells all the time. But my husband never, ever gave up. He took all that was dished out and still kept trying.

Rosie

CHAPTER 52

Journal Entries – March 2008

A Friday / Saturday in March 2008

Hormones again! But my God how much better am I than the ramblings of the mad woman back in July?

But although I am sad the only difference now is that I understand that it is normal for me to feel sad. I am grieving for a life I had lost- even though I would not want that actual life back now. But what I would take from that life is the total trust that I had in Danny: that feeling that he loved me so totally; in a way that no-one else would. I am sad because I now know that is not/was not true. In fact he probably loves me in that way more now than ever before......I had to stop writing this yesterday because Danny came in and have to write this alone; I also know that it freaks Danny out when I write in my journal.

Since then we had a massive row, a combination of drink and hormones, but something that makes the truth come out sometimes. It was so stupid: I said to Danny that I know he gets upset every day and he said he didn't, and I got angry about that.

Why would I want Danny to get upset very day?

I think that it was because the implication from Danny is that he doesn't get upset when I know that he is upset, and it is as if he is being arrogant again. But now I look at it it's not that; it's that he is still so afraid. I am smiling now because I didn't know I was going to write that word. But it is the word that Danny continuously used at the beginning of this awful journey – that he is so 'afraid'. And now I have written this down I understand why Danny appears upset all the time.

I went to London last week to a course for bereavement training. I learnt so much: that batting between feelings is the normal thing to do when you are grieving; and I know how much better I am now and understand that if you try to move on and change things, and make a new life, time can ease the pain.

After the row last night I still wonder if we would be better calling it a day to enable us to move on completely. I don't know if being together is like picking at the scabs and never allowing them to heal; but then I think of Danny: of never coming home to him again, or never going shopping with him again, never holding his hand as we walk along the road; and I would miss it all too much. I also know it would destroy him, and I would get no satisfaction from that.

When I went on the course I realised how much further down the road I am than Danny and that I need to help him. I forgive Danny for what he has done; I truly do. I know he is so sorry, that it is time to forgive; I want to move on with my life and I cannot if I am consumed by bitterness. I told Danny and he thought it was because I had been drinking that I was saying this, but it wasn't.

The next day, when I hadn't had a drink he said that I didn't mean it because this week I have been distant. I haven't been as distant as before and I really have tried to help Danny, with all the problems at work and Don his close colleague getting the sack.

But sometimes I still get down and I am trying to explain to Danny that this is all part of the process: That one day you will be happy and then bounce back to being down, upset, afraid, whatever, only to bounce back to being happy.

I am going to try to help Danny understand for me and for him.
Rosie

Rosie's List:

Bereavement feelings:
Loss, Shock, bewilderment, anger, fear, vengefulness, depression, sadness, loneliness, isolation, wanting to run away, doubt, numb, sick.

Danny's list: Bereavement feelings:
Frightened, upset, shocked, embarrassed, depressed, anger, disbelief, bewilderment, dismay, dislike for himself.

Rosie's List: New Life/Moving on
Changed job, lost weight, more confidence, inner confidence, mellow, new friends, exercise, family contact, France, more money, loved more by Danny, adored by Danny, better family life, more team working, happiness (at times) contentment (at times)

Danny List: New/moving on
Got Rosie back, France, more money, no overtime, spends more time at home, cooking, having the courage of his convictions, supportive in-laws, more understanding.

Note: Danny didn't say happiness or contentment because he felt as if he was on borrowed time.

Reflections Here & Now

I remember that training so well. It was when I finally came to realise exactly what the grieving process entailed: going backwards and forwards between your emotions; feeling as if you are moving forward one day and then back to square one the next.

I learned that we grieve for what we have lost: death, love, our career, children growing up and moving on, a life we once had. But I realised that whilst I was grieving Danny was also grieving for what he had lost, and that I had struggled at times to allow Danny to grieve; or to show him empathy for his feelings; after all hadn't he brought them all on himself?

Where infidelity is concerned I do think that it is similar to death: you have lost the life you had and the person you loved; you feel immeasurable pain and it drives you insane with grief; but the additional element in this type of grief is having to deal with the deception: the lies they told you, the trust you have lost and the lies that you told yourself; all of which make you feel that everything that went before was a lie; and you grieve for the loss of what you thought you had.

With regard to forgiveness: I did truly feel for Danny when I wrote this and I did forgive him in essence. But I ask even today what forgiveness is; does anyone know? I know that I didn't when I wrote this entry. Now I believe that forgiveness is not the same for everyone because it is tied in with too many different emotions: so what may have been a strong emotion for me may not be a strong emotion for another.

Having researched the various definitions of forgiveness they include: pardoning someone, granting absolution, even exonerating them. Over time the word that defined it for me was: 'understanding'. It was only when I started to understand why; and the things that had contributed to what had happened that I was able to move forward and accept what had happened.

It was important to me that Danny stopped 'burying his head in the sand'; pretending that it had never happened; important that he understood that if I kept asking him the same questions that he had to answer me honestly, whether I went on to believe him or not. If he hadn't talked to me, no matter how painful it was at the time, then I could not understand what had happened. So Danny talked to me, showed me what he was afraid of and this enabled us to move forward and ultimately I could forgive him.

Some other definitions of forgiveness include mercy and clemency and these are the ones that resonated with me because they both mean to show compassion. As the years went on I came to realise that for me forgiveness was acceptance: to stop feeling anger and to stop blaming Danny for everything and especially for what had happened. This then enabled me to allow Danny to build something new for me. As I write this now I can see that I often had compassion for Danny, I began to be sympathetic to his suffering; and I didn't want him to suffer because I loved him.

One of the things that helped me get to that point was that I didn't want to be destroyed by bitterness, because it meant that 'she' would have won; and at that time I was not prepared to let 'her' beat me in any way.

I used what I had learnt on the course to help Danny, and I drew him a table that showed all the things he had in his old life on one side, and all the things he had in his new life on the other side. Danny studied that table and took it all on board.

Rosie

CHAPTER 53

The First Dday Anniversary

March & April 2008

This section of the book is my memory of the first anniversary after 'The War'. Dday as it has come to be known (how apt!) I was so surprised that I hadn't written about it in my journal. But having reflected on that I realise that it was because it was such a painful time and I was probably afraid to write in my journal what I was feeling at that time. In addition I was trying to move forward and I was starting to feel as if my journal, and constantly writing about 'The War', was holding me back.

In this section it will show things that you have already read about; but I have written in such a way as to show how the memories and triggers came back into my head and did build to a crescendo. Despite that I did keep my emotions under control during this time, because, as the year passed, I had learned not to let them control me. I had learned that I could control them, I had to.

This was how I felt that first year....

March 2008

In the month leading up to 'The War' Danny had been meeting 'her' nearly every day and the affair had escalated. So in March 2008 I ran through my head every day where Danny would have been the year before: what shift he had been working, what days he would have been able to meet up with 'her'. I looked at his phone logs (yes a year later) and I thought of all the things we had done in that month. I thought about how all the signals had been there and how I had just ignored them.

When my beloved mum died someone once gave me some good advice: 'Get through the first year and then they will get easier, because you have done it once already!' It was true. In that case they meant birthdays, Easter, Christmas, anniversaries, Halloween. When someone you love has died all of those things are the things you dread, because they were happy times and now that person was not going to be there, and this time they were going to be sad times. But once the first anniversary of each celebration has passed you know that you can do it without them and the special times will be happy and poignant all at the same time.

When an affair blows your world apart you do suffer grief; but the difference is you struggle through the first year in a blur and each celebration becomes something else, because you look back at the previous celebration and think how you were being lied to; how you were being gas lighted; you wonder if everything that you had ever known was a lie. It is the same as when someone dies: that you do have to make new memories, in fact even more so because all of the old memories are tainted. I found I had to do something completely different to stop me looking back at all the other times, to give me something different to focus on.

Then after the first year you hit the new anniversary known as Dday but for me it was not just Dday. I had memories of all the times I had been lied to, of the weeks leading up to Dday as the affair had escalated, and I had to process them. I had no choice. That is the difference to when a person you love has died: it takes more than a year to be able to face all those 'happy' times again. I could not look back on what I had before; as far as I was concerned it was all crap. I had to get through the first year and then get through the second year before I had happy memories to reflect on.

I won't say it gets easier because we are all different and for it to get easier it will depend on your attitude and whether you want to keep picking that scab. I did pick that scab for a number of years when this time of year came round, but I found that it only started to get easier when I decided to take control of the situation and move forward.

So back to our first year anniversary, and the lead up to it: I had begun to resent Danny in a big way. Despite all the work we had done, that old friend anger and rage came back during the month of March when I thought, every day, about what Danny may (or may not) have been doing the year before. What I did know was this:

That Danny had come to the Doctors with me when I was ill and feigned concern (that was how I felt when I looked back on it.) I thought about how worried he had been and then I thought how he had brought me home and left to go to work on a late shift. I thought of how he had left early because he had a 'meeting'; and I now knew that the meeting had actually been with her'; and as I thought of that I wanted to punch him.

I thought back to how I had found 'her' and Danny talking (almost arguing) in the kitchen. Over the year since 'The War' broke out Danny had told me of how he had been trying to get away from 'her' and how he had been angry with 'her' because she kept coming to our house, and he had started to see how she was ridiculing me by coming to our house all the time knowing that 'she' was seeing my husband behind my back. Sadly the fact that he had been furious with 'her' didn't help him when the month of March came round leading up to Dday, because I just thought back to that time and of how he had still continued to meet 'her', of how by doing that he, himself, had ridiculed me and had allowed 'her' to. Whether he was scared or not the new 'me' felt that he should have had the courage of his fucking convictions!

I thought of the night the year before when 'she' sent the text to our house; of how when I contacted Danny he had been so soothing and denied everything. When in fact, as I had learned over the year since 'The War', he had been ringing 'her' in between ringing me to try and placate me. He had told me he had to take a call for work when in fact he was shitting himself and calling 'her' to ask 'her' what the fuck 'she' was doing. I thought of how he had sat at our breakfast bar (that had now been taken down because of that memory) and lied to my face when he had said 'do you really think that I would leave you for her?'

Well by the time March 2008 came round I knew the answer to that didn't I?!

I thought back to the meal we had in a restaurant to celebrate being together nine years, and how aloof Danny had been: He didn't like the meal, he didn't like the restaurant, and he didn't want to be there when I looked back. Of course in March 2008 I knew the truth - 'she' had been texting him all the time asking him why he was celebrating with me when he really wanted to be with 'her'.

And of course the piece de resistance was the night we had gone over to 'her' house and 'she' had constantly filled my glass up and I got pissed. The night that I knew, the night that I had lied to myself, the night that they had made me look like a cunt, the night that I have written about before.

I thought of all the times his phone was on silent.

Needless to say by the end of March 2008 I was raging.......

April 2008

By the time Dday loomed I didn't care what had happened over the last year or care about all the work that Danny had put in. At that time I thought that my rage was directed at Danny; but looking back now I know that really my rage was with myself: I was really seeing the person that I had become: the person who had allowed herself to be lied to, and gas lighted; and it was her that I was angry with.

Danny was, understandably, terrified: He knew I didn't need him and that if I put my mind to it I could walk away. I knew that as well, but all the work and trauma and despair we had gone through had also shown me that we had something and that I had something in the person who was with me in the here and now of that moment.

After getting back together I had originally given it until January; now January had been and gone and I was still there; not for money, not for the house, not for the fact that it meant that I had a man (because I still felt that people pitied me: poor Rosie the person whose husband cheated, bless her!)

I was there because I had a man who loved me; he was not arrogant, he was not argumentative, he was not defensive, he was not simply sorry; he was bereft. How do you walk away from that?

So I stayed because I loved this gentle man, I loved him for his tenacity in staying with me: for facing his fears every day. After all every day I got stronger he was reminded that I could leave at any time, and he had to fight to keep me every day. Little did I know that as I got stronger he actually got weaker where his opinion of himself was concerned (But that is for later in our story. I can say that I should have paid attention to that.)

On the anniversary of Dday we had both decided that neither of us wanted to be at home. Our house, our beautiful house, still felt contaminated by 'her' everywhere we went. There were way too many memories and triggers, so we both decided to go to a place where we felt safe: France.

To prove a point I told Danny that he had to sort it all out and he did. He booked us a flat in the small seaside town of Varengeville right in the centre. We had booked it for the whole three weeks that coincided with the three weeks that Danny had not lived with me, the three weeks Danny had lived with 'her'. In fact we had arranged to come back on the 4th of May so that it was past the anniversary of when Danny had come home, and it would be a new date that we could focus on instead of the date of when Danny returned.

Because 'The War' had started over two days we booked to stay in a pretty hotel on the front of the port town where we would be sailing from the following day. This would have been the anniversary of the dreaded BBQ the year before, when 'her' partner decided to inform me that Danny had been seeing 'her'; the BBQ where Danny had been kissing 'her' in my pantry; the BBQ where I nearly pushed 'her' off our balcony.

It was a good decision I couldn't have stepped a foot in our garden that day; it would have been as if a video was running through my head: too many memories.

On the morning that we came to leave it was bright and sunny; pretty much as it had been the year before. I was quiet and Danny just kept quiet, because he was afraid of what would happen if he said anything. I was stronger, I knew that I was not in the vulnerable position I had been in the year before and that in itself gave me the composure to keep it all together.

I have a resounding memory: We were walking out of the front door when Danny turned to me, with tears in his eyes, and said 'I am so sorry'. My eyes filled with tears and I said 'I know you are.' But I couldn't say any more, it was all too painful and I just wanted to get out.

When we booked into the hotel; we arranged to have a sauna together and it was then that I started to realise just how insecure Danny had become: he had never had a sauna, something at which I was amazed, and it made me realise just how little I had actually known the man I had lived with for ten years. I can remember how Danny followed my lead like a puppy. It was as if he had no confidence unless he was with me, and even then I didn't want him to feel like that.

We had a beautiful day, and had a meal in the hotel restaurant that evening. You would never have known to look at us that we were running away from painful memories and still clinging on by the skin of our teeth.

April 2007 – springtime in France

When we arrived in France the first stop was the pretty seaside town of Wimereaux. We had stayed there the first time we had visited France; it had good memories of us trying to heal each other just under a year ago. So we chose to stay in the same hotel, a small select hotel; and we ate in the same restaurant; we even ordered the same food to relive the memory of when we first got back together, the memory of us trying to survive. Despite the pain and despair that we had been in, were still in some of the time, the memories of our first trip to France were good ones.

The next day as I woke I immediately thought back to the year before: when I had woken at my sister's house to a missed call from Danny. I thought back to how I had come home to clear all of Danny's stuff out of our house, I thought back to being on my own. I knew that I should put those thoughts out of my mind, knew that we were in France to make new memories; but something inside me also knew that I had to do it; I had to process it or I would never be able to file it away and move on.

We travelled on to the bustling town of Le Touquet; where we had spent so many weekends since 'The War'. A place where we had French friends and mostly good memories. We visited our dear friend Michel and met up with Marc, who the summer before had made me consider my position with regard to Danny and I. It was telling that they were so pleased to see us, and so pleased we were together.

As we journeyed further into France I would actually think back to each hour of each of each day from the year before: this time last year I was with Jacqui, this time last year I threw Danny's stuff out, this time last year Danny came home and collected his stuff and left, this time last year I didn't know what was going to happen to me. And then I would think 'this time last year I was alone, but I'm not now; this time last year I didn't know how Ethan and I were going to survive, but I do now; this time last year I worked part time, I was fat; this time last year I was afraid. And then I would remind myself that I was not any of those things now; I was stronger and my own person.

It was true that at times when I thought back to times and places I could feel the anger bubble up inside me; it was like picking at a scab and I just couldn't stop myself. But when it happened I got on the stepper, or I put music on and danced, or I just went away from Danny and gave myself some space for half an hour or so.

We left for Varengeville on the Saturday and when I awoke that morning I thought back to the day a year ago when Danny had finally returned my call, and laughed at me, of when he asked me how I was ever going to keep the house, when he told me that he loved 'her'.

On the journey down to Varengeville I was outwardly happy and smiling, but inside I was dying, thinking about the year before. I knew that Danny was terrified because I was quiet, and anyone who knows me knows that when I am quiet then that is when I am at my most deadly. But I had to process it, I had no choice: I knew even then that if I faced up to it then one day it wouldn't be able to bite me on the arse any more.

So I focused on the French countryside, on where we were going, and reminded myself again of where I was now, not then.

But then the memories would come back again: I ruminated about where I was at this time the year before: sitting on my back step crying, sitting in the snug in my house, crying, crying, crying, crying.

I just knew that there was no point in fighting them: I had to let them come; I had to face them and accept them.

When we arrived at the flat it was in the centre square of Varengeville with all the shops and cafes and bars close by; it was small but more than we needed, and Danny was so nervous that I wouldn't like it. But it was perfect for us, because it just wasn't our home.

During those three weeks we shagged like rabbits, I know now that this is actually natural, it's called hysterical bonding: you are desperately trying to rebuild a connection. It was strange, how I could fuck the arse off Danny and not care about what he had done with 'her', but if I was honest at that time I was not 'making love with him.' Danny was to me, but I wasn't to him.

This was the thing you see: although I was with Danny, although I wanted us to work; I was still keeping a part of me back, keeping a part of me safe. I couldn't trust Danny with all of me anymore, so I had a barrier up. I was with Danny, I was married to Danny, I loved Danny, I shagged Danny but I was my own person all the time: that was the barrier - I was the barrier. I would listen to music on my own; I would insist that I did some things on my own, simple things like going to the Boulangerie. I read copious amounts of books whilst we were away because I could exclude Danny from those activities. By doing this it enabled me to keep my distance and allow me to keep one foot out of the door ready to run.

The weather was warm and we travelled out to pretty little towns, we did lots of activities together: cooked food in the small galley kitchen, played music, visited the markets, had aperitifs in the little Tabac just on the corner. I made sure I looked good all the time; to make myself feel better, and to remind Danny of what he might lose.

Little did I know that this trip was actually going to be a major turning point for me because as the weeks went by I started to see the damage that had actually been done to my husband.......

April 2008 – Varengeville

We continued to enjoy France: went for picnics, found beautiful little French villages and beaches. Our favourite village was just outside Varengeville it was called Veules Les Roses. It had a river running all around it that led past old washer women's houses, and led down to the sea. It was so peaceful and one of those places that just filled you with a feeling of tranquillity and calm.

As we walked around the village one day I remember watching Danny: he looked so on edge. I was relaxed and enjoying the atmosphere but Danny wasn't. Although he was trying to relax, he just looked so agitated. I thought to myself 'Is this how I want him to feel?' I knew it was me that was making him feel this way, I knew that although I was with him he wondered every day if I would stay and I realised as I sat in that beautiful village in France that I didn't want him to feel that way.

As we drove back to our little flat that evening Michael Buble's 'Lost' was playing in the car and as the line 'that you were crying' played I was crying and I knew that Danny was too. The whole song summed up how we felt.

There were two key things during this time that made me start to change toward Danny, and made me realise that I couldn't keep punishing him, that I didn't want to hurt him anymore. I could see that I was starting to make him ill:

The first was when I was in the bathroom of our rented flat one morning. Danny was having a cigarette and looking out of the open window. I heard the seagulls cry out and suddenly realised that every time they cried out Danny also cried out mimicking the seagulls cry. Then a moped went past with its distinctive high pitched sound; and Danny made the sound of the moped. I stood in the bathroom as he imitated every sound he heard and I knew that he didn't even know that he was doing it. When I came out of the bathroom I made a joke of it, because I didn't want to freak him out, and said that he sounded as if he had 'Tourette's'. He looked at me as if he didn't know what I was talking about, because he hadn't even known that he was mimicking the noises that he heard. Then we both laughed but I had realised that he had been doing this for some time. Over the next few months I would watch out for it and bring it to his attention (he imitated the sound of a loader in a well-known hardware store once - going beep, beep, beep, until I poked him) and eventually he managed to bring it back under control.

From this incident I realised that the affair, and our trying to recover, was having an impact on Danny's mental health: he was living in a state of high alert every day; and it was this type of thing that had contributed to the affair in the first place. I knew that if we were going to survive I had to change my approach and cut Danny some slack so that he could stop permanently running on adrenalin.

The other instance was our expedition to the large swimming pool situated right on the beach in Varengeville: It was an indoor pool with a heated outside lido and Jacuzzi's. We decided to visit it for the day, but when we got there Danny was told that he couldn't wear his Bermuda shorts; it is the law in France that you cannot wear baggy swimming shorts in their communal pools, you have to wear speedos. Oh my! That was a major thing for my husband who thought that he was too fat, and too unattractive to be with me. The demon in his head told him that everyone was going to laugh at him and wonder what the hell I was doing with him; and as a result Danny said he didn't want to go in swimming.

I bought the speedos that they had available and took Danny to the window looking over the pool and I showed him how many men were in there in exactly the same trunks: some shorter than him, older than him, fatter than him. I asked him why he thought that he would stand out from the crowd, and assured him that nobody would be looking at him; assured him that I loved him in whatever he wore, I saw him naked every day for Christ's sake.

We went to the communal changing room, where there were large cubicles where you could change, if you didn't want to let it 'all hang out' in front of others. I went into one of the cubicles only to find Danny was right behind me, literally right up my arse, terrified that I would shut him out. I realised then just how insecure my husband really was. He was worried about the speedos and he needed to be with me to give him confidence. My heart could have broken all over again, only this time for the man stood in front of me. I just got changed with him and told him it would all be okay.

We had a great time in the pool, and eventually Danny got out of the water and walked to other parts of the pool and finally relaxed. I realised that he wouldn't have done that without me; realised how I gave Danny the confidence he needed to move forward in life, and that without me he was lost. It was only then that I understood how lost Danny had felt when he thought he had lost me; and I fully realised just how gentle and insecure Danny was; for the first time in over nine years.

Rosie

CHAPTER 54

Journal Entries- May 2008

A Monday in May 2008

When I came to write this today I was shocked at how long ago it had been since I last wrote in it. Now I am even more shocked when I realise I have been writing it for nearly a year!

I don't feel the need to write everything down word for word anymore. I don't always feel like writing in this journal. In fact I have been so happy I have almost felt afraid of writing in it, of bringing everything back. But I have come to realise over the last couple of days that it has not fully gone away. Never will. Time will ease it but it won't ever go away completely.

I have felt weird over the past week, nothing I can put my finger on, other than time is kicking in and things are changing, without any effort or control on my part.

I am happy. I have had a fantastic holiday in France, at a time when it should have been awful. I learnt how terribly bullied Danny was when he was younger (thanks to Susan); and what I have realised as a result of our conversations, was that Danny wasn't leaving me, he was running away, the only thing he had been taught to do.

I gave Danny a 'bye' in France, and promised that if he told me the truth I would not leave as a result of it.

The Truth:

Danny never met 'her' in the October before 'The War' at 'her' sister's house. He told me that because that is what 'she' put on the divorce papers. Danny was so terrified I would see them he made up a lie and it was this information that he had told the counsellor; and it was this information that the counsellor told him to not tell me the truth about. They had decided that I didn't need to know. But the problem was Danny's story then did not add up and that just led to Danny telling one lie after another and digging a deeper and deeper hole – running away again!

At first I was elated that it had been proved to me that I couldn't have got it so wrong, but I have also come to realise how different Danny and I are; always have been. I have just read my first entry in this journal today, a year later; in it I had written that I didn't know Danny at all; and now I know that I was right: I didn't!

All these years and I never realised how Danny is afraid of everything. I can look back and see so many instances of it over the past ten years; I am so me again; and so not like Danny! It makes me wonder what I was doing here in the first place. It makes me wonder if I can ever have any respect for Danny. I can now see what everybody else could see: he was an arsehole and not good enough for me. I am now sad, but in a resigned sort of way, not in an all-consuming way anymore.

I asked myself a question – What is the most important thing that I would like to keep in the near future? And the answer was 'my job'. I can never ever give up my independence again.

I think I will be writing some more of this – a new phase now – I need to analyse me.

Rosie

Reflections Here & Now

I know that many people want to understand how to just put one foot in front of the other; get through another day; they ask me often how I did it. I can only explain that the biggest lesson that I learnt was acceptance. It was in fact a gift that I took forward in all aspects of my life: when we are afraid of something, when we want something to be different we often fight 'what is' tooth and nail; but there is no point because what has happened has happened, where you are is where you are: 'what is' is 'what is', it exists and there is no good in trying to pretend that it doesn't.

There is no going back. What you have is what you have; if something is playing on your mind do you know what? It's playing on your mind! Accept it. If your heart is broken your heart is broken; if you feel better one day and then shit the next then accept that is a fact of life at that moment. I found that by accepting 'what is' the things that were bothering me started to lose their power. I knew what they were, I accepted that they existed, I accepted that I could not change them; and by doing that the 'spin doctor' in my head could no longer bring them up to taunt me. I was no longer fighting something that could not be beaten.

If you read back over the last year I have written about how I learnt so many things: to get in the car and say hello to the demon who was waiting to torment me on my drive home with what had happened. I learnt that (and would continue to learn as you will see) I could feel great and then within seconds I could be in tears. I learnt to say to my head when it became so down 'Oh there you are, I wondered when you were going to appear!' I literally used to say that.

In this journal entry I say how happy I am; that I had not written in my journal because I was happy; and then by the end of this very entry I say what an arsehole Danny was and how he was not good enough for me! I say that if I had to choose something in life I didn't want to lose it would be my job! Clearly I was really happy!

Looking back I can say I was happier; but I was still destroyed; and I know that you all understand that. It does get better but only with acceptance and time.

With regard to Danny telling me 'the 'truth' about what had happened, as I have said before, what is the truth? Whatever you want to believe; because you will only believe what you want to anyway.

I don't believe Danny, even today. I believe that the original story that he told me the night he wanted to come home was probably as near to the truth as I was ever going to get. I believe that Danny told me a year later whilst in France that it was all a lie was because he was so desperate to keep me; and he could see that I was becoming stronger and stronger; independent of him both financially and personally; and that I had got 'me' back again. Danny knew that the possibility of me leaving him actually grew greater every day and he did what he could to keep me: he lied.

Now I know that this is a massive thing for all those who have been betrayed. But here is my take on it many, many years later:

Even today Danny is adamant that it is the truth; but for me there are too many things that add together to make the original story more feasible; and I will never lie to myself again. But I can forgive Danny that lie, and probably many others, because I understand that he was terrified of losing me; which in itself showed how much he loved me.

I have now come to realise that it doesn't matter how long it went on; it happened. It doesn't matter what he lied to me about; he lied. It doesn't matter how many times they had sex; they had sex; how many times they spoke on the phone; how many places they visited together; how many times he met 'her' when he was supposed to be at work and on and on and on: He had an affair; he broke my heart, he lied to me, he laughed at me, he said he loved someone else, that's all I need to know. Only I could make up my mind whether to stay and what to base that decision on; and it wasn't going to be the past but the here and now: the man who came back and worked so hard; the man in France who stood in front of me, and the man who stands in front of me now.

Danny made a massive fucking mistake and his urge was to run away and he did; then he came back and he stayed; he put up with every piece of shit I threw at him (and trust me he was covered). Even today the demon in his head tells him I will leave one day; but he stays anyway because although he is terrified of losing me, he loves me and will take every day with me, living in fear or not.

One of the things that I see now is how harsh I was: I never considered, even a year later that Danny's heart was as broken as it was. I learnt that over the years, and I know that it is still broken today. The sad thing is that Danny broke his own heart and no matter what I say to him now to make it better I cannot help him fix it. It will be broken forever. But when I wrote this entry I had failed to see all the hard work that Danny had put in to keep us there – At that time, where I was concerned, I was a selfish cow and it really was 'it's all about me.com.'

Danny had been bullied throughout his years at secondary school, and, yes his answer had always been to run away; but when I wrote this entry I had failed to see that although Danny had run away from me, this time he had come back. Even though I had said in my journal many times that Danny had stepped up to the line, in fact pulled me up there with him, when I wrote this entry I had forgotten all of that because I had become selfish; I felt that I was the only one to have a broken heart, the only one to be upset, the only person that had been damaged. But I could see that acting that way and not considering Danny meant that I was at risk of becoming bitter and I was not prepared to do that.

Rosie

CHAPTER 55

Stories to Tell - June 2008

Everything was changing

After returning from France in May I was advised that a permanent promotion was coming up and to apply for the post. I can remember preparing my presentation for that interview and how nervous I was; but I sailed through everything and was offered the post.

Danny was so pleased for me, but looking back now I can see that he was also terrified because every promotion, and increase in salary I achieved, was another stepping-stone away from him.

To celebrate I went out with Sherrie and Hannah from work to a new chic bar that had opened in Hastings. Looking back I was still making Danny pay: I didn't go out to celebrate with him.

Whilst Danny's job was going well, he was getting to the point where he hated it, and hated the journey because it all reminded him of what he had done. Every time he drove down that motorway for over an hour he would remember talking to 'her' on the phone. He had also suggested that we sell our house and move because he couldn't bear the memories that were in it. But I was not prepared to sell the house; not after all the hard work that I had put into renovating it. I felt as if we would be giving in to 'her' and giving up what we had worked so hard for. I knew a lot of what had happened and 'her' actions were aimed directly at me: 'she' had seen someone who appeared to have it all and 'she' had set out to destroy it. So to sell the house I loved was, to me, like letting 'her' win which was something I was never prepared to do.

But on reflection I can see that the house, whilst still stunningly beautiful, had been tainted with all that had gone on. It was still a happy home; we had made it so with both of the boys living with us: we had made new memories; and although I didn't walk around the house remembering things, ironically Danny did and he hated that, and the fact that the street knew what had happened.

But I insisted so we stayed. ......

Rosie

CHAPTER 56

Journal entries – July 2008

Journal Entry – July 2008 – final entry for this journal

The End
  Of this section!!
  The next journal will be for me.
  I am right. I need to analyse me now, to always understand where I am. Years ago I used to keep a diary, this will be the same, I am going to keep a journal about me now.
  The 'drama' of me and Danny is now over for me, The scars are there but the immediate thought is "I am bored with it now!!".
  Rosie

Reflections Here & Now

I had written this entry because I had been in town one day and seen a journal in a shop, it had a picture of cherry blossom and handbags, a dress and shoes and it called out to me, because at that time it represented to me the 'new me', the person that had evolved since 'The War'. So I bought it and decided to stop writing in my 'mad journal' as it had become known. Although at times I was still mad.
  When I read what I wrote at the end of my 'mad journal' it made me smile because I can assure you that it was not over; we still had a long, long way to go and had a lot of learning to do. But I understand

why I needed to start a new journal: I felt as if 'The War' was defining me and I didn't want it to. As I have said I needed to keep a journal to understand myself, not to understand what someone else had done to me.

But of course 'The War' would be written about because it was a defining episode in my life; although this time the entries in the many journals that I have gone on to keep showed less of the aftermath of infidelity and more of the recovery and how we moved forward.

Rosie

ROSIE'S JOURNAL
FINDING MYSELF
2008

'Be honest with yourself and take responsibility for your actions.'

'Be tough on yourself and analyse your own involvement
in something before you blame' others

Journal Entries – July 2008

A Saturday in July 2008

After the last sixteen months of my life I no longer feel the need to keep my old journal. But so much has changed for me and I have changed so much; mainly by going back to the personality that I had before my mum died. I feel the need to analyse myself and I hope that by writing this journal, a new journal, I will be able to understand who I am and why I have some of the thoughts that I have.

Also, I have a very strong personality, and I have learnt that this can intimidate some people (their problem, not mine!) But I am also aware that I need to slow down for some of the people I love; for the people who try to undermine me, criticise me or humiliate me I don't.

I am hoping that by writing this journal I will be able to deal with those negative people assertively, not aggressively; whilst not allowing myself to be brow beaten by them in a manipulative way. Too many people have done that to me in my life and I have let them; not anymore!

What I have come to understand over the last year, more than ever before, is that I can always stand on my own two feet. I am very lucky that I have the ability to up my game -to go from a part time job paying me a low wage to a full time job paying me over double what I had been earning, with the possibility of further promotions. I am proud of myself and I will not let anyone make me feel as if I shouldn't be. I only want me to be in control of 'me' now.

With regard to Danny and I: I think that people have had enough of listening about it now; and as I am writing this I am asking myself if I need them to. Isn't it something that I need to sort through in my own head? If I really needed to run something past someone then I can. But if I am being honest I don't really know what it is I am trying to say. That is why I am writing this journal, to find myself again.

For the last ten years I was not myself until last year; I didn't realise how much I had not got over my mum dying. That I had become only three quarters of myself. But because of everything:

being a single parent of a young child, mum and dad becoming ill and dying, I think I was just worn out. I needed to re-charge my batteries and wanted someone who would take care of me. I met Danny who was gentle, kind, and needed someone in his life; and I thought that he could provide me with what I needed. I ignored all of the warning signs; put everything into Danny and never fully recovered that quarter that I was missing of myself.

I look back now at how angry I used to become; because somewhere my mind was screaming at me and asking me what I was doing. I wasn't truly happy. I look at the times I spent with Danny's family, and realise that although I was made 'welcome' I never really felt as if I was part of it; never really felt as if I belonged there; because really I didn't. Perhaps they could see that more than I could!

But as I am writing this I know that my feelings for Danny are more complex, and I have realised in just these few short pages that I am writing this to find out what they really are.

Rosie

Reflections Here & Now

All of this is relevant; because the fallout from what happens during and after an affair impacts on everyone; in our case this included Danny's family (as it does with so many stories). Whilst I understand some of the actions that some of them took, they are still actions that I would not have taken. So it highlighted to me that in fact I had never really 'fitted in' and that we were very different. That's the thing with traumatic occurrences they ripple out and affect so many aspects of our lives. Perhaps it is because they make us see things that we chose to overlook.

At the time that I wrote this entry some people still listened to me talk about 'us': mainly my sister and very close friends; but others felt that we should have just 'moved on' with our lives. It never ceases to surprise me that people fail to see the utmost significance of a broken heart, of broken lives. Perhaps they feel too uncomfortable because it reminds them of just how vulnerable they are.

It is interesting that I have commented how I had never 'got over my mum dying'. You never 'get over' someone dying, you just have to come to terms with it and live your life in a different way than you did before; because your life is different, it will never be the same again. Sound familiar? Yes I found it to be exactly the same with infidelity in fact it was this episode in my life that enabled me to consider so much more than I had considered before. I learned that to rebuild our relationship I had to accept what had happened and learn to live with it in my life; in the same way I had to learn to live my life without my parents. It was a life changing event for me that contributed to the person that I am today.

If you asked Danny, he would say the same to you, but it took him a while longer to come to realise it; and despite knowing that what happened to us did make us stronger, he still struggles with the idea of the pain he put me through.

I was right when I wrote that I didn't know what I was trying to say, or even where I was going. When I started this new journal I thought that all of the aftermath of 'The War' was behind us. Of course it wasn't; we still had a long way to go. I was on a path of discovery: finding 'me' again.

When infidelity entered my life I was lost. What I thought I had was broken and what I had worked hard to build was no more. I questioned whether it had ever been what I thought it was in the first place. As part of building our relationship at the beginning I gave myself to it and then when it was destroyed I was lost. I did not know who I was or trust where I was. I had to find myself all over again, and in doing that I changed again, because life, and what had happened, changed me.

I knew when this happened to me that if I truly found myself and held on to myself (which I did) it carried a high risk that I wouldn't stay; that I would become so strong that Danny would not mean anything in my life, and I wouldn't want to stay and carry the burden of what had happened anymore. At this point when I wrote in my journal I was becoming stronger every day, and the chance of me leaving Danny grew every day, irrespective of how much work we put into the relationship. The idea of that really terrified me, but I knew that I could not and should not resist that change; it was all part of the process, but I was afraid never the less.

Reflecting on our lives was essential to enable us to get to where we are today: it meant being honest with ourselves, and acknowledging things that were incredibly painful. I have come to understand that if we hadn't done this then the chances of problems arising again were high. We were on a new shore and we had to decide what parts of our life to take with us (if we could) and what parts we should leave behind; and we could only do this by reflecting on our past behaviours and considering what we had in the here and now on a day to day basis; and to not look too far into the future.

I have said how I understood that I was the type of person that is capable of seeing things so quickly: understanding things and quickly taking them forward, sometimes at a hundred miles an hour. When Danny and I first got back together my sister said to me that I needed to understand this about myself; because most people were not able to pick things up as quickly as me. I listened to her, and sometimes I listen to me, even now, and say to myself 'You need to slow down Rosie'

Rosie

A Wednesday in July 2008

I wasn't going to write this tonight; but my hormones are raging, and I have had a stressful day, so I thought that it would help to reflect.

Someone at work pissed me off! But having read my previous entry I realise that he is like one of the people I have mentioned – people who try and undermine me. But I have got myself together and from tomorrow it will be professional and business-like.

As I drove home from work I was constantly thinking about Danny, and analysing what I think; and for the first time I wondered if I was falling out of love with Danny.

I know I am on a journey, and that I don't know where that will take me, or where my life is going. When I think that I realise how sad that it is: although I am with Danny I am on my own. I suppose I feel like that because I was left on my own by Danny, he let me down in the worst way possible. (I was going to put so badly but that doesn't cut it!) So I am back to being 'always stands on her own two feet Rosie.'

Danny picks up on the vibes I give off, but I can't do anything about that; I don't want to do anything about that. Coming home part of me thought why should I? I don't owe Danny anything.

I know I am still licking my wounds, I realised that driving home. I realised that I am still fighting my own head; and that shocked me. I suppose that is why I am writing this.

Rosie

Reflections Here & Now

When I read this entry I could immediately see that I had forgotten the advice my sister and her friend had given me the December before: that not everything was about what had happened between Danny and I; that sometimes in life shit happens which is nothing to do with the affair!

I do understand why I was always taking everything back to what had happened between Danny and I: because I didn't feel that I had a solid enough relationship to feel safe in when the normal day to day shit hit the fan. Therefore every time something happened my mind reminded me that I had no safety net; I only had me, and that would then lead me back to 'The War' and how all of my feelings were because of it.

Home is meant to be the 'safe place': the place where you feel nobody or nothing can hurt you. I no longer felt that: 'she' had invaded my beautiful home, and contaminated it. Danny had let me down and although he was trying so hard, I couldn't count on him; I was afraid to let my guard down.

Even fifteen months later, and despite all we had achieved, there was still a high risk that I would leave Danny behind – something that Sherrie had predicted months before. But the thing that kept me there was Danny, who was fighting tooth and nail to keep me; and the fact that he would not give up kept me there. How could I leave a man who when I came home had made the dinner, cleaned the house, left me a note to say how much he loved me before he left for his late shift?

This was not the man who had left me sixteen months earlier; this was a different man and I had to keep reminding myself of that.

The 'back to being always stands on her own two feet Rosie' was a reference to how people have always told me throughout my life, that because I have such a strong personality I would always be alright. Of course it was true I am resilient, but it didn't mean that I didn't want someone to look after me; someone that would be able to support me rather than me always having to support myself because no-body else could. I was sick of people thinking that saying that to me was okay, that just because I could didn't mean I wasn't struggling.

I do have that person now, his name is Danny. It took a long while for me to find him again, and a long while for him to show me he would never let me down again. So although I have written here that I was falling out of love with Danny, I didn't, because he wouldn't let me.

Rosie

CHAPTER 57

Stories to tell – July 2008

Small Things

One balmy evening during this month of July Danny and I were sitting in the garden, drinking wine and playing music. I had bought Neil Diamond's greatest hits and 'Heart light' started to play. Danny stood in the kitchen singing the lyrics to himself, I was watching him. When the words

'He's lookin' for home,
'Cos everyone needs a place,
And home's the most excellent place of all
And I'll be right here if you should call me'

played, Danny started to sing them and as he closed his eyes the look of pain on his face was palpable.

As I watched him I realised how I was so consumed by what had happened to me that I didn't always consider that when Danny left me he had lost everything that was important to him: me, Ethan, the dog and cats, our house, his home. I had been so caught up in thinking about me, and just me; of how Danny had deserved all he had got, that I kept forgetting that he felt pain and that he was afraid. I didn't give any credence to the pain and fear that he had felt when he had not been with us, because, after all, he had put himself there. As I watched Danny singing that song to himself I could have cried with him and for him; a small thing, but an important one just the same.

Rosie

CHAPTER 58

Journal Entries – August 2008

A Wednesday in August 2008

Still fighting!! I feel like a split personality when my mind goes like this.

I had a lovely weekend, I have a lovely home; everyone is to come down to us and have another lovely weekend. We have booked to go to Cornwall and Salisbury, and the new forest, and I will have a lovely time. I am not unhappy in that side of my life.

But when I am on my own I feel so down. The 'stand on her own two feet Rosie' comment just shook a nerve again. Made me cry; and I wonder why – why are the two contrasts so great?

Even when I am doing things with just Danny I enjoy them. I have a lovely time; but I can also have the same time with friends. It doesn't have to be Danny I suppose.

Or is it that more than anything Danny is my friend. But the part of my mind that I am fighting to keep under control is the essence of me; and winning. Slowly through my sub conscious I am switching off that powerful love I had for Danny, making him just my friend.

The other day coming home from work I thought about what Danny had done and that sacred thing between us that we no longer have: making love. When I thought about Danny with 'her' I felt physically sick at the thought of having sex with Danny. Where did that come from? I have been having sex with Danny for eighteen months now! Why has that bitten me on the arse in such a strong way now?

But as I am writing this I am realising that my need for sex with Danny has slowly been getting less and less since our last visit to France. I think some of that is that I seem to be the person making the move a lot (or have been) and I don't want to do that again. I know Danny has insecurities, but deal with them. Don't keep putting them all on me!!

I think about all the times people including me in the past, say 'poor Danny, he needs more counselling, he is insecure' (I am starting to cry now I am hitting the nail on the head.) It is as if they are saying I am the strong one so I can deal with it. If they could look inside my head they would be shocked because I just want to scream sometimes.

I am letting time do its thing. It has in the past eased off. But I cannot, will not, don't want to pander to Danny and his emotions while I feel like this.

One of my phrases has been 'Just seeing where life takes me' and that is true. Life is an adventure, and ultimately I am the most free that I have been in the last twenty years. But right now I feel like I have gone backwards, as if I am acting a part again; just as I had in previous relationships before I got out of them.

It will be interesting to see where I am at the end of this journal. I thought about going back to the counsellor; perhaps this is just another wave hitting me and all part of the process.

Rosie

Reflections Here & Now

I was struggling when I wrote this journal entry because really life should have been good: I had achieved another promotion at work; we were both earning good money, our friends and family were coming down to celebrate our ninth wedding anniversary; which was, importantly, the second one we had managed to achieve since 'The War'. Life should have been good; but it wasn't. I was still thinking about everything that had happened and I clearly thought that at this stage we should have been in a different place.

I was struggling with the fact that I had gone backwards and had forgotten my own advice from my earlier journal: that it was bereavement that we had suffered, and that you can still bounce backwards in your emotions with regards to grief. We were sixteen months down the line, but that means nothing when you are bereaved.

It is clear from this entry that what I was struggling with was the fact that everyone seemed to think that I was okay; and that I would be okay; when in fact, I was far from okay. Of course I felt pain; I felt pain every single day. I felt as if I had let myself down by staying with Danny. I got in that fucking car every night and that demon already had the CD player on!

Then I would come home to a gentle man who was bereft for what he had done and what he lost; and mostly for the pain that he had caused me; and when I looked at him I couldn't hurt him: not this big, broken man who was standing in front of me.

In fairness Danny knew that I was struggling and so did my sister. I fought it tooth and nail but read the next story: the shit does hit the fan, and it frightened the life out of both of us to such a degree that it made us realise that we could still lose what we had at any moment. But more importantly that we didn't want to.

Rosie

CHAPTER 59 - AUGUST 2008

Stories to Tell

We stepped backwards

It was the 14th of August 2008 and our ninth wedding anniversary. We had decided to walk along the seafront to the pretty quintessential seaside town of Bexhill. It was a warm sunny day and we were excited about what lay ahead.

But as I was getting ready Ethan came upstairs to tell me that he had failed all of his exams at college (again). It was only the year before his father and I had come together and gone to the college to ask if they would allow Ethan to stay; even though he had failed all of his exams and was not putting the work in. The college had relented and agreed, and yet now here was Ethan, eighteen years of age and back in the same place. I was so annoyed with him and Danny was annoyed with him that he had chosen this moment to come up to tell me. Add to that his father then called and was shouting at me and telling me it was my fault and it was not a good start to our holidays.

By the time we finally left the house the late lunch we had planned was long gone and the evening was starting to fall. All was good and even walking through the town of Lowly didn't affect my mood. We decided to go on a pub crawl and visit all of the little quirky pubs in the town and finish off at the Indian restaurant I had walked out of over a year ago. Perhaps this time we would get to eat some food!

At our second pub Danny said that he had noticed that some drug dealing had been going on in the toilet. I am totally anti-drugs and we decided we should leave because Danny said that he thought the bar-man was in with the drug dealing. We had just ordered our second round of drinks (we were now on our third round, and had hardly eaten anything.) All was okay until we left the pub and the air hit us: it was as if we had drunk twenty drinks, had been spiked.

But, of course, when intoxicating substances come in to play your control goes out of the window: the control that you have put into place to stop all of the monsters from coming back out from the shadows in your brain; the control and resolve you have to answer the demon in your head; and the demon takes control. And then it started: I started to question Danny about some of the things he had told me; some of the things that I knew were not accurate; some of the things that I knew that he was lying about. Because of my lack of control I was unable to reason that we were sixteen months down the line; unable to see all the things that Danny had done in those sixteen months; and I was unable to lie to myself. I knew the truth and I was angry because of what it really was; and I didn't really need Danny to confirm it because the demon reminded me that I had lied to myself once too often.

Danny was terrified: I had reverted back to the woman all those months ago who had attacked him; and here we were in the same town and I had lost it again. But I was terrified too: although my drink had been spiked and although I couldn't stop what I was doing or thinking; there was another part of me looking on and wondering how the hell I had got here again; wondering whether it was ever really going to go away.

Danny just stood looking at me and would not answer me; rightly so because no matter what he said he couldn't undo what he had done; and I didn't know if I could stay. That was the thing: I didn't know if I could stay because it was all back and I knew that no matter what it was never going to go away. I didn't know if I wanted to live my life like that. So I just walked away from Danny down towards the beach. He, of course, came running after me.

It was pitch black by now and I felt an overwhelming need to be alone. I can remember turning to Danny and screaming at him why?

Why did he do it? Why did he throw away the total all-consuming love I had for him? Why did he break my heart? Danny just looked at me and said 'I don't know if I can do all this again; I don't think I will ever be able to make you happy.' That just hit me and I started to sob.

I asked him to go and leave me on my own; said that I needed some alone time to think; told him that when I got home I didn't know if I wanted to leave the house. Danny said he would leave and that just made me scream at him again: he had left once already why the fuck did he think that it was always his right to walk away and leave me with the mess to clear up?

I was sobbing now uncontrollably. I can remember desperately wanting Danny to walk away and leave me. I was not afraid of the long walk home in the dark because I knew at that moment in time God help anyone who tried to attack me.

I walked away from Danny but he wouldn't leave me and although he kept his distance he was always within running distance from me. At one point he overtook me as I was sitting on the sea wall crying; he said nothing as he passed by, just walked past like a stranger and that is exactly what he felt like: a stranger.

I just felt numb with shock that all of the emotions were back as strong as they had been sixteen months before; and the thought of this feeling being with me for the rest of my life was overwhelming. I sat on that sea wall and thought about how my life had changed, realised that what we had was well and truly dead, and I howled, literally howled with grief. I was grieving for the love I had for Danny that had been so strong, but was now lost, and I was grieving for the waste of it. I knew that my strong personality was shutting my emotions down and I honestly didn't think I could stay.

When we eventually got home (Danny only a few minutes before me) we both said nothing and just went to bed.

The next morning we both got up feeling shell shocked, knowing that despite all the things we had done, and all the things that we had learnt, it could still come back as strong as ever and destroy us.

We decided to go out for lunch and went to a pub nearby. Neither of us had mentioned the night before but we started to talk, and we both knew that what it had showed us was how terrified we both were of losing each other; terrified that it would never go away and that we would not survive; and although we didn't say it out loud I know that we both made a silent commitment to ourselves not to let it beat us, and we stuck to that.

I have respect for those two people.

But this was a wakeup call: because what we both realised was that no matter what, the fact that we feared losing each other, couldn't imagine life without each other, meant that we had to make a decision about moving forward and trying; and if we decided to stay with each other we had to accept that times like these may happen again.

As a result of that we went on our holiday and I kept to myself the knowledge that the only person who could destroy us in the here and now was me. Despite my commitment, despite all that I have just said I still didn't know if I could stay. I wanted to, but didn't know if I could.

As time went on life sent a series of events my way to make me think and made me live in the here and now. But, at that moment in time, I am not going to lie I was afraid.

August 2008
Small things - The Old Man

Two days after our relapse into hell we left for our holiday in Cornwall.

We decided to make a road trip of it and stop in a little town near Stonehenge. We stayed in a quintessential pub with wood panelling and swirly carpets and a large bar. After booking in to our room we went down to the bar for some food and drink. It was mid-afternoon and the quaint country bar was empty apart from an elderly, dapper, gentleman in the corner. We got chatting to him and he told us how his wife of over forty years had become ill the previous year; and how he had looked after her but was now heartbroken and lost because she had recently died. His eyes filled with tears as he spoke, and it was clear that he had loved her very much.

As he talked to us he looked at us and said "You need to enjoy what you have today; even if you have troubles and problems, because all you have is today; and one day one of you will be left behind without the other. Remember there no happy endings: just endings.'

What had made him say that to us I don't know, perhaps he had picked up a vibe from us; but he clearly knew that he had to tell us to enjoy each other now; and I realised that because of 'The War' we were not doing that. Every day was consumed or tainted by what had happened before; by something that we couldn't change. I understood that even if Danny and I survived the old man was right: one day we would be on our own because the other would have died.

I realised that I was wasting all the opportunities that we had to make our life better, and I took the old man's advice to heart, using it often when I found myself falling back into that dark place with the demon; or during the times when I struggled to clear my head of the thoughts that polluted it. I would think of that old man and remind myself that I was wasting what I had today, and it may be the last day to enjoy my life with Danny. In fact I still use that advice in my life even now.

But that is not the end of the story....

Small things - The things we do not to see. ...

After the old man had left we stayed in the hotel bar and as the night wore on we got chatting to the barmaid; she was telling us all about her life and her boyfriend and kids. When Danny went to the toilet she turned to me and said "He fucking loves you, don't he, you're husband?"

I was surprised that she thought that given everything that had happened and I said "Really? Do you think so?"

She just looked at me and said "I fucking know so! The way he looks at you, I would give anything for a man to look at me like that!"

I said "Well he fucked off with another woman last year and set up home with 'her' for three weeks!" She looked shocked and taken aback; but then she thought about it and said "I don't fucking care! I wouldn't care what he had done. I have never had a man look at me like that in my life; and would give anything for someone to look at me and to love me the way that he loves you!"

I suddenly realised that here I was with someone who loved me so much that other people could see it on his face, and in the way he looked at me. But I was so caught up in what had happened to me (not us, remember it was all about me) that I couldn't see what I actually had in front of me at that moment.

I shut up. What could I say? I sounded so spoilt, like a woman who just took things for granted because it was all about her, what had happened to her; and she didn't think twice about poor Danny!

I cannot begin to tell you what a massive impact this had on me, and our relationship; these two encounters with two people in the same place on the same day, and the messages they delivered were paramount in us being here today. Perhaps they were sent to us because of what had happened the week before; as they say where there is bad there is good, everything goes in a circle.

I listened to the messages that life sent my way, I realised that I was throwing away what I had got: something that some people search for all their life and never find, because of my ego, because of my pride. I had something with Danny that I would never find with someone else: he loved me so much because of what we had been through, yes: 'We'.

I understood that Danny had lost things as well, because of the mistake he had made; I didn't have to make him pay, he was paying every day because he had lost that unconditional love that I had for him. But more importantly I was taking for granted what I had and letting each day slip away when in fact that is all any of us ever have, that particular day; and I was not appreciating or enjoying the unconditional love that Danny had for me.

August 2008 was a big month for us. We learnt that we didn't want to split up; we learnt that we had too much to lose, and we learnt to start to look forwards and not backwards all the time – still did some of the time, but this was a start.

Rosie

CHAPTER 60

Journal Entries – September 2008

A Monday in September 2008

I note that I don't feel the need to write in this very often; and when I do it is always around the same sort of time – when my hormones kick in and it is harder to keep my 'demon' (small d) under control.

I read with interest what I wrote last time. I had forgotten it! I do not feel that strongly about some of it now. – Time the great healer. – But some of it rang so true.

Before I read my last entry I was going to put in my journal how I felt like a split personality: Sometimes I feel like two completely different people.

I have had such a lovely time since my last entry. A fantastic time in Cornwall, and Salisbury; and we got a kitten.

I enjoy Danny's company; I have such a laugh with him; he has made me fall in love with him all over again: the person who I have lived with for the past seventeen months.

I don't love the 'Old Danny' anymore. I have tried to look back at our old life with fondness; but I hate it! I hate the person Danny encouraged me to become. I really did go down quite a few notches and crawled around people that I really don't give a fuck about. Danny was not the person that I gave him credit for. It was all a lie.

It makes me sad that I am not interested in my wedding day. The day that I thought was the best day of my life. No, it wasn't.

But when I am with Danny I enjoy myself; I do relax. But I still feel as if I am on my own.

A few things happened; a few sayings were given to me, which make perfect sense.

'If you keep doing what you are doing, you are always going to get what you have got.'

'Happiness is not a destination; it is the journey along the way.'

They are both good ideals to live your life by.

Tonie and Nel have said how lucky I am to have Danny. I understand exactly what they mean: the man I have adores me, and would do anything to make me happy.

In Salisbury someone called Monica, who we met in the pub, said how lucky I was because of the way that Danny looked at me; that he loved me so much. When I said what had happened she said that she didn't care, she would give anything for a man to look at her the way that Danny looked at me. I understand. I truly understand what I have got.

But when I am on my own, normally in the car, I feel so alone. Even though I know all of the above I feel hardened to Danny. I am happy; but another me has a broken heart. So many awful memories that I suppose I still have to deal with. I know that the 'real' me, is the one that I am fighting; and I don't know if the happiness is enough to stop me going mad.

Time will tell.

"There are no happy endings."

Old Man in his 80's near Salisbury

Rosie

Reflections Here & Now

I am often surprised by what I wrote all those years ago because I had moved, we had moved, onto the next stage in our lives.

I no longer feel that pain, I no longer think back to things that happened day on day. In fact, as I have said before, it does exist but is now only a mist in the back of my mind. That is why when I read my journals now it seems as if I am reading about someone else: a woman who got me to where I am today. So when I read this entry I hadn't remembered what I had written; I just knew that the sea of despair was in fact a seemingly never ending ocean.

We had a lovely holiday; I had taken on board what the old man and the barmaid had said to me. But for me the importance of this entry is that I felt as if I was two different people: I was happy, had a wonderful holiday, and was with a man I loved; but I felt so alone.

I did want to be there; I did love Danny; as I have said I was 'falling in love with him all over again.' I was falling in love with a different man, he had changed so much: faced his fears and worked hard to keep me, and that is why I fell back in love with him: because he made something new. He adored me and he showed me every day. I wasn't putting on an act for him when I was with him, I wanted to be there.

But I always felt alone. This was where the realisation that actually the only person any one of us has in life is ourselves finally came home to me. It took me a long while to realise that this was in fact a good place to be.

When I was alone it was like being trapped in a parallel universe with the demon! My ego would tell me to leave. It would tell me that I didn't need Danny for anything: that I earnt as much as him now, I could pay my own way, I was thinner, looked good, and could meet someone else and more importantly someone who had not fucked someone else! Oh the list goes on and on. Why do you think I wrote all those lists in my journal or in Danny's cards? To keep me there, to give me something to shut my ego up!

When I was in my car I would get angry: I would think of all the things that had happened and wonder whether the demon was right: I was better off alone. One of my favourite all times songs (even now) was 'Stronger' by the Sugababes. The lines made me cry then and still do today because you see I will always be the one 'who stands here longer than the rest'. I used those words in that song to make myself stronger, whether I was going to stay or go.

Over the years as I have written this book and my blog there has been much discussion around the fact that we are all so afraid to be alone; when in fact we are alone whether we realise it or not. It is a very difficult thing to come to terms with, especially if you are broken hearted. You see what 'the demon' didn't tell me, when he whispered in my head, was that I was alone: that you come into life alone and you leave life alone; it was lying by omission. Leaving Danny was not going to make one ounce of difference to my happiness. I was still going to have to deal with what had happened.

But Danny had a role to play in our story: as I have said he never gave up (I repeat that often for the people who betrayed and who are reading this book or my blog). Every day Danny would face his fear knowing that I often thought about leaving it all behind. He would not get defensive, he would just keep going: making me laugh, crying at records, showing he loved me by lighting candles, cooking the dinner, hoovering the house; it wasn't buying me flowers, I didn't need material things, I needed small day to day things. So now although I will still be 'the one who stands here longer than rest, as my landscape changes, rearranges' I will take Danny with me. (Stronger by the Sugababes.)

You see my heart wanted to stay (and the Tao tells you to always listen to your heart) but my ego wanted me to leave (and the Tao tells you to let your ego go because it is your enemy!) I mention the Tao because I have read it, but it could be any other philosophy. In fact what happened to Danny and I set me on a path of reading psychology and philosophy books, something for which I am always grateful.

I say in this entry that it 'was the real me', my strong personality; but I was wrong: my strong personality is what got us here today; it was my ego that I had to learn to control.

It was one of the hardest things in this journey (or perhaps one of the most frightening things) that for many years no matter how happy I was it never seemed enough. I still felt blindsided every time I felt happy and then found myself so sad, angry, and destroyed. I learnt that only I could fix it because only I could manage my emotions; Danny could only do so much because ultimately the choice to stay or go lay with me; and I had a broken heart, for many years.

I was right though when I said that 'time will tell', because, along with the all of the other things, it was time that eventually allowed me to manage my emotions and become truly happy again.

Rosie

CHAPTER 61

Journal Entries – October 2008

A Saturday in October 2008

Same time – same hormones!

But I did mean to write in this journal before now, as I have had lots of thoughts and understandings:

I was listening to Justin T the other day; a song about a man who loses everything; loses his way. I lost my way when my mum died. It took me ten years to find my way again; and I will never lost it again. I have a new life; I have got back the old me: the strong person I was before I met Danny; and I would never want to go back to the person that I was before 'The War'. (As always I read my last entry before writing this and I see that the same theme keeps coming up. I hate the person that I became, and I do blame some of that on Danny.)

I realised as I was listening to the Justin T song that Danny has lost more than anyone. His life is not the same, but it is not better: his 'goes around, comes around' is that he will fear losing me now more than he ever did before. I find that sad.

My darling friend Jacqui died on Tuesday 16th September (RIP) I will remember her as always being there for me.

I loved Jacqui and I had great respect for her. I know that it was my strength that Jacqui loved, the same as it was my strength that my mum loved; because it was not always something that they could do. For them I must never lose my strength again.

Another thing is that Danny and I had words about him not contacting his family. One of the things I have learnt is that Danny does not have the same relationship with them that I had with my parents, and that's why I cannot compare my experiences to his. But it also reminds me that we now have that wedge between us: three weeks that we lived different lives; I will never know the truth about them because even if I was told the truth I wouldn't believe it. It was a 'no win' situation.

As part of the row Danny said that I had got what I wanted – the house!

Now I know this is what he used to think; that it was something that 'she' used to tell him: that I was only with him for the money that he earnt so that it would pay for the house. That was an issue that was used against me in the past.

What a fucking cheek!! Does he not remember that I had it all in place to keep this house anyway? I did point out 'ditto'. I will never be convinced otherwise that one of the reasons he came back is because they realised they would not get this house – Wonder what would have happened if I had just walked away and gave it to them!

The other thing about this is that Danny still thinks it: that I only wanted him for the house. So is it all going to happen again?

It won't be the same for me now; but it makes me take a step back. My barrier will always be up. It's the same when Danny constantly says how I think he is thick. That is his perception because of his insecurities which are, again, still there. But he tries to reflect it back onto me and blame me. I am not having that.

As James Blunt sings 'You can't break my spirit, it's my dreams you take.'

That is how I feel. I don't believe what I had been searching for exists; I don't follow that dream anymore. But I do still have spirit – my greatest asset.

Rosie

Songs referenced: Justin Timberlake 'Losing my way' from 'Future Sex/Love sounds and James Blunt 'Goodbye my Lover' from 'Back to Bedlam'.

Reflections Here & Now

I reference words to music so often in this book because quite simply Danny and I would not have survived without music. (There is a playlist at the end of the book.)

As you know the car was the place where the demon waited for me every day for many years; and to counteract that demon I played music all the time. I listened to the words of every song and I cried to so many of them; but they helped to keep me sane. Then I would go home and share some of those songs with Danny; in fact we spent hours and hours listening to music in our snug, crying together.

Justin Timberlake was one of the first albums I bought in the twenty one days that Danny was gone; it was one of the albums that I played constantly in the car and this song resonated with me and this is why:

When Danny left he decided that he was such an idiot that he had nothing to lose and went back to his old ways before he ever met me: he tried to get some cocaine and just give up. But although he got in touch with a dealer he never went and collected the drugs because, as he said to me after coming back, he knew that he would never ever get back with me if he had. I hate drugs, I always have; Danny knew that would be the final nail in his coffin if he collected those drugs and used them. But what he hadn't realised was that even then he had hope because by not collecting those drugs it meant that in the back of his mind he hoped that he would get me back.

I can remember an incident after our reconciliation: we were sitting in a traffic jam in Hastings when a tramp shuffled past, with a bottle in his hand and cans of beer in a carrier bag. I was driving and Danny was watching him; Danny suddenly looked at me with tears in his eyes and said 'That would have been me wouldn't it, if you hadn't had me back?"

So when I listened to the song I have referenced: about someone just giving up, losing everything, it made me think of Danny; because I knew that although he was with me he had lost so much; and that is so clear in this journal entry.

It was true that Danny and I had three weeks of our lives together where we lived separate lives. Those experiences during that time did shape the people that we are today; and when I wrote this entry I still found the idea of that so upsetting; so did Danny. But now I know that if we had not had that experience then we would not be the people that we are today; and if you asked me if I would go back and stop it happening the answer would be no because I wouldn't be here writing this book to help others. I wouldn't have experienced my adventure in France as I am now; and over the years, as we have talked about what happened to us, even Danny can see that if the affair had not happened we may well have not stayed together anyway because of the people we were becoming before 'The War'.

I have not articulated in this journal entry just how sharp the edge of my tongue was when Danny said that I had only had him back to keep the house. I didn't need Danny to keep the house; I knew by then that I was more than capable of doing anything if I set my mind to it; and I told him so. I also told him how I wondered if we would be together if I had been the type of person to walk away. I still do; I don't think they would have survived as a couple because of the nature of the 'beast' 'she' was; but I don't know if Danny would have come back: because it would have been much easier to stay with 'her' in my house. That was never happening.

I remember that when I told Danny the blunt truth he got upset; but I then pointed out to him that it meant that I stayed because I wanted him and not the fucking house. I still have to remind Danny of that even today: I am here because I want to be, no one material thing keeps me here only my love for Danny, and the person that he is today.

James Blunt's line is a classic.' You can't break my spirit, it's my dreams you take.'

You can't break my spirit. I did allow myself to get lost again in my career (another story) but since living in France I have truly found myself again; mainly through writing this book. I read back at the strength of Rosie then and I see the strength that I have now and I know that my spirit and strength are blessings.

With regard to dreams: I have learnt that although the dreams I had were taken from me, dreams are ephemeral and I feel that we should be open to changing them, going with the flow and allowing them to evolve, who knows what life has planned.

Now I have different dreams, and the ones I had then don't matter to me anymore, because that is just what they were: dreams. I don't believe you should hold on tightly to dreams because then you will stop new and better ones coming your way.

Rosie

A Sunday in October 2008

On the Beach

During this week I have come to realise that the urge inside me to run away (an interesting choice of words!) is still there. I am going to analyse that further on.

This week I had an argument with Ethan about the rent that he had to pay me; he thought that I was charging him too much. It made me realise that for the past twenty years I have always put other people first; even last year when Danny left my immediate thought was that I had to keep a roof over Ethan's head. Now, as in so many other aspects of my life, I know where I stand: On my own!

As well as feeling upset by it, I can also see that it is another part of my freedom that I have been given back. Understanding that now I need to put myself first. I know that it is all these things combined that have given me a strong feeling of freedom, not knowing where life will take me; not knowing if I will stay.

So to my interesting choice of words: do I want to run away? Or do I just want to change what I have always done, and now become a bit selfish for myself? Just be me, and not have to think about anyone?

I have realised that perhaps this is why I keep encouraging Danny to keep in contact with his family so that he would have someone if I left. Perhaps that is why he does not want to keep in touch with them, because he thinks that will make me stay if he were on his own.

I think that the switch is switching off; but I am not sure that I want it to.

Rosie

Reflections Here & Now

How lost was I? Everything that had happened made me look at my whole life, not just Danny and I; and consider where I needed to go, and what I wanted.

It was true I had always put other people first and now I was starting to think about me first; I don't think that is always a bad thing.

What happened had given me freedom; it had made me look at my life; the safe, secure (conform and do what everyone does) life that I had, and ask if that was really what I wanted. I know now that it had set me on a path of discovery; a path that eventually led me to question everything.

I thought that running away was the answer because at the time I believed that it was all about what had happened to Danny and I; when in fact it was just life making me question everything. Ethan moaning about his rent had nothing to do with what had happened to Danny and I. I thought that running away was going to be the answer to all of my problems when in fact there would still be problems, just different ones. That voice in our heads causes mischief whether infidelity is in the mix or not; in fact it was the voice in Danny's head that had caused him to leave in the first place, and we were 'happy' then!

My friends used to say that I was one of those people who once the switch had switched (meaning that I had decided to move on from someone) that was it; and I never went back. They were right, I never did. But this lesson in my life was all about doing something different to what I had done before; and Danny was putting up such a fight to keep me he was winning – more than he or I knew at the time. For me the difference this time was that I fought what I was feeling; because I knew that I had something that I should not throw away easily.

The messages that life was sending me were getting through!
Rosie

CHAPTER 62

Journal Entries - December 2008

New Years Eve December 2008

I was surprised when I looked at the last time that I wrote in my journal. But I do know it is mainly because I have really got my head together over the last few months.

I read a counselling book that just explained so much to me. I learnt about myself and about other people and the way they react to me; and what it has enabled me to do is understand, but not necessarily agree with, their actions; and understand why they have acted in the way that they have: thereby enabling me to deal with it.

Most of the time I am okay: happy with myself and happy in my own skin; but a lot of other people aren't happy, and me being okay intimidates them and they therefore turn their unhappiness on me and try to stop me being okay, thinking it will make them feel better.

But I am now able to look at the reasons they're not okay and understand why without letting them bring me down. Where before I would try and help people, if I understood, now I don't. I just assertively and constructively stop them bringing me down by simply letting them know that this is me, and I am okay – I hope that this makes sense¬

Reading this particular book has helped me understand why people feel the need to do that to bring me down, when I don't feel the need to do it to them. Before their actions would have upset me, and I would feel that it was my fault. Now I know it is not my fault, I know that it is their problem.

I have had a brilliant Christmas and when I look back a brilliant year so I thought that it was appropriate to finish the year off in my journal.

However, I do feel like crying; and although I know I am hormonal, it is the first time I have felt like this for a long time; perhaps because it is the end of the year: a time for reflection.

I am happy. I have a good life, and so much more than other people have. But I wish I didn't have to carry with me something that I have to suppress: a burden that I carry through no fault of my own; and as next year progresses I wonder whether that burden will eventually make me decide to put it down, and walk away from it.

I realised during a conversation with Danny the night before last that Danny does not really know or understand me at all. It made me wonder if I do still dumb down for him. I do not want to do that anymore; I will not do that anymore.

I am looking forward to next year, and all that it may hold.

Happy New Year.

Rosie

Reflections Here & Now

I was really starting to find myself. With regard to Danny not understanding me: trust me, he understood me more than I ever realised; that is why he continued to fight for me, and had to face his fears every day.

How awful that I felt that I had dumbed down for Danny; how arrogant of me: because I know now that he was the cleverer one of the two of us: because he stuck with it and knew that if he tried, and time passed, he could make things better.

Yes I was carrying one of the heaviest burdens I have ever carried: the knowledge that all I had before was lost. I was having to rebuild a new life whether I liked it or not; and in that new life I would always have the knowledge that my husband had lied to me, laughed at me with someone else, lived three weeks in a different life. At the time I wrote this entry that burden seemed so great. Now I don't think of all those things because what I have is the new life I built, with all the new memories and I don't dwell on the past. Why would I?

I have said in this entry that I didn't know if I would stay; and I do think that it is quite normal to go through a period where things seem okay but you just don't know if it is right for you anymore. At the time of this journal entry I had fought so hard and for so long to survive that I was just tired of it. I started to wonder whether I would ever be able to control my thoughts, and be able to live happily with the knowledge of what had happened in my mind. I think it is just normal to start to wonder at that point of exhaustion, if you can keep doing it and if it would just be easier to move on.

I am not sure that it would be easier; all the things that are in your head will still be there and then the little demon will come out with the million dollar question: 'Do you think that you did the right thing leaving?'

I know now that it was just another phase of the recovery process. I had got stronger I was happy, but I was still unhappy and I questioned where I was. But Danny was contrite, he showed his remorse and regret over and over again; and that helped me to stay.

If Danny had been arrogant, condescending, refused to talk about it, had not showed how mortified he was by his actions; had not allowed me to talk about how I felt; hadn't tried to understand; then I wouldn't have stayed. I couldn't have stayed, because I had found me again and I was always going to protect me first.

After writing my journal that evening Danny played 'The perfect year' by Dina Carroll and we both danced and cried to it in the kitchen. We had made it through another year, and we both hoped that the more time passed the stronger our chances of survival. We had a long way to go but we just had to keep holding on, and that evening Danny asked me to renew our vows on out tenth wedding anniversary the following year.

Rosie

2009

A Marriage is an Achievement
A Wedding is an Event

CHAPTER 63

Stories to Tell - Wedding Planning - January 2009

Although I agreed to renew our vows I told Danny that he had to do all of the organising because I was now too busy at work. Danny agreed and a week later he rang me at work to say that he had booked the church. I was shocked; I really didn't think he would do it; and I was also touched because our first wedding had been in a registry office; so for Danny to find a church showed how much thought he was putting into it. In fact he had even booked for the bell's to be rung as we both arrived and left the church. Danny had remembered that I had always wanted bells at my wedding and never had the opportunity and it was just one of the small things that enabled me to fall back in love with my husband all over again.

The church was a pretty little medieval church in Bexhill; with an archway at the gate: mullioned windows and arches. Danny advised me that we had been asked to go back on the Saturday after he had visited so that the Vicar could meet us both and we could pay the deposit. So I found myself one cold freezing Saturday in January outside the church, and I can remember thinking to myself 'I don't know if I want to do this'; but I didn't have the heart to say that to Danny, because I knew it would break his heart, and I didn't feel the need to hurt him anymore.

When we arrived there was choir practice and we were invited to go into the church hall for tea and cake with the choir and the volunteers of the church. It still makes me smile today when I remember their reactions when Danny told them we were there to pay the deposit for our vowel renewal: they were all so pleased for us.

As I sat there with those people, most of whom had been married for forty years or more, they told us what they thought was important for a marriage and I listened. They all knew it was a journey, and that some of the terrain was rocky, and I took their comments with me after I left. It was as if they knew we had been through the mill and they were encouraging us to stick with it.

When we paid the deposit the admin lady for the church told us that she would make an appointment to meet the Vicar, and that we would have to attend 'marriage preparation days'. I couldn't believe it! We only wanted to renew our vows why the hell did we have to prepare for it? We could write a book on it! But the appointments were made, the deposit was paid, and I was on a ride that would show me so much.

I swear that so often someone somewhere was trying to tell me something.

CHAPTER 64

Stories to Tell - February 2009

The Vicar

We attended our first preparation evening, which was weird because it was full of all those embarking on marriage for the first time. Listening to the other couples was interesting: they talked about the dress, the cake, the day, whilst Danny and I sat there thinking 'It is so much more than a day: it is about life, not things.'

The second evening we attended we had to go to the Vicar 's house and he met with us together and individually, so that we could explain to him why we were renewing our vows and what it meant to us. For some reason I never told the Vicar what had happened; whether Danny did when he saw him on his own I don't know; but I can tell you that the Vicar knew, although he never actually confirmed that to me.

The Vicar explained that we should walk down the aisle together to celebrate what we had achieved; but Danny wanted Ethan and my sister to walk me down the aisle, and give me to him, even though he had broken my heart: to prove to him that they trusted him again. When Danny asked the Vicar if this was possible, the Vicar explained that it was not allowed because part of the vowel renewal ceremony was to be together as you walked down the aisle, because it showed unity after all the years of marriage. But when the Vicar looked at

Danny's face he relented and said "Oh why not! I won't tell the Bishop if you don't."

When the time came for the Vicar to talk to me alone he explained that he loved vowel renewal ceremonies because he thought that sometimes, where weddings were concerned, the day and the event become more important than the actual meaning of the ceremony; which was a stark contrast to when people renew their vows, because vowel renewal is all about the ceremony and commitment. The Vicar explained that people who renewed their vows knew exactly what they were committing to: that sometimes marriage can be hard work; and that it said so much about the relationship and the couple's love for each other: that despite all of the adversities that marriage can hold, the couple still wanted to re-commit.

I realised that he was telling me that when people renewed their vows they had faith in what they had; and he was right: I knew exactly what I was signing up to. But I know now that it was also about marking something new: our celebration was to celebrate that we had survived one of the worst things that could happen; but we still wanted to be together; and that in itself was something to celebrate.

At the next preparation day the Vicar announced to everyone that they should talk to Danny and I about what marriage was about; about what to expect.

Some came to talk to us, and it was interesting when the discussion turned to the worst things that can happen in a relationship; because it was about the partner having an affair!

I listened to the phrase I had heard so often, that I had said in a time long ago: "I could never have them back; I could never forgive them." And I thought 'You can never say what you will do until you are there. You will never know what you will do until you are in the moment.'

For me the most interesting thing was that these people were embarking on commitment to one another, and were already saying what would make them break that commitment. I understood then: marriage is a commitment with all the crap that may come with it.

Rosie

CHAPTER 65

Journal Entries - March 2009

A Thursday in March 2009

I always find it interesting to read what I have written in my journal. Tonight I read my first entry in this journal and it was interesting to see what I have put into place:

I have applied my plan with regard to my actions towards other people: making it clear that I am happy with the person I am, and that if they don't like me fine; it won't impact on my life because I don't care about them. It is liberating.

Danny asked me to marry him on New Year's Eve – to renew our vows on our tenth wedding anniversary; it means so much to Danny. I find myself saying that a lot and I know it sounds as if it means nothing to me; but it's not that, it's just that it means more to him. It's weird for me; because, although I want to do it, part of me is apprehensive. I do want to do it but sometimes I have no enthusiasm either way.

I am going to leave it there for me to read again. Perhaps I will understand it more if I do it that way!

Rosie

Reflections Here & Now

This entry shows that now I am starting to look at myself and what makes me the person that I am. Who would have known that what happened to us would take me on such a journey?

But the most important thing is that we were coming up to the second anniversary of the outbreak of 'The War' and I have not mentioned it. I have not brought up the past or what had happened in the March two years before; which is an important indication of just how much I had moved on.

Although I was unsure what was going to happen to Danny and I, the part of me that wanted to renew my vows had been bought to the fore by the Vicar. My enthusiasm began to grow; the doubts I had begun to wane, the Vicar's enthusiasm and belief had seen to that. To this day I have so much to thank that man for; his encouragement and his belief in love took me along with it, it truly was infectious.

Rosie

CHAPTER 66

Journal Entries - April 2009

A Friday in April 2009

When I started this journal I thought that it was all going to be about me; that I didn't want to bring what had happened to Danny and I into this journal.

But I now realise that I was wrong: I wanted to analyse me and understand the person that I am; but I cannot do that without acknowledging what happened because that is the main catalyst for what made me the person that I am today. By trying to exclude it meant that I was never going to achieve anything from this journal: which is mainly to get my head together and understand myself.

I find myself sometimes 'needing' to write in my journal but putting it off; and I realise that it was mainly because I have been running away from what happened and I can't. And now the writing is flowing out of me. ...

Two years ago today my world was turned upside down and the life I had died, and my heart was broken; but as always I got back up – I can't stay down for long.

I realised today when I had my appraisal at work, how significant what I have just written was: At my appraisal I was told that I had achieved everything, and some! Every key objective achieved with added extras. It was a brilliant appraisal and coming home in the car, I realised what a long way I had come, and it made me cry. Why?

I suppose some of it is that I have realised what a different person I am from that stupid fat lump that I was two years ago: I can always do it on my own; I am always on my own.

April is not a good month for me: My mum died, Danny left me. I know now that part of the reason I had Danny back was to enable me to move on. Although it has been bloody hard to have him back it has also made it easier because as I recovered and stood on my own two feet I could move on, on my own terms, not ones that someone else had laid down for me.

Danny and I were talking the other week about how some people stay together for what they have got, for the lifestyle they have. Danny looked mortified and asked me if that is why I stayed. I lied in part and said no; but it is the whole package that made me stay not just my love for Danny. I do love Danny, but not in that total all-consuming way that I did before. How can I? The crying over the past two years has been mourning for what we lost, because it is so very sad: I loved Danny totally. But I have stopped crying for that loss now; whilst I still feel sad my grieving has moved on.

I often go back to the words of James Blunt (from 'Goodbye my Lover') 'you can't break my spirit it's my dreams you take.' That is me: the all-consuming, never let you down love does not exist.

But I also realised that whoever said 'happiness is a state of mind' (it was Steve Maraboli) was right, there are no happy endings; and if you spend your life looking for them you will constantly be chasing the end of a rainbow, and trying to catch a ray of light.'

Rosie

Reflections Here & Now

I shared this entry on my blog, on what would have been the twelfth anniversary of 'The War'. I hadn't intended to share it, but twelve years later I realised the date as I sat in bed having a cup of tea. I reminded Danny of the date and we both laughed as we realised that neither of us ever remember now. For those first few years it was an 'anniversary', but as time has passed it is just another day now. I felt the need to share it with the people reading my blog to give them hope that one day they won't remember the date that is so significant at the beginning of this awful journey; but it is important to remember that can only happen if you let it.

In this journal entry I have clearly started to become my own person; and I am relishing it. We stayed at home that year; I can remember Danny asking if we should go away, but I didn't want to keep running away from it. I was stronger and I knew I had to face it to move on. I do remember for those three weeks every morning I woke I would think back to where I had been two years before. But the facts and the times were hazy, even then.

After I posted on my blog I read my entry to Danny, but as I read the post to him he looked so sad because I had said that I 'still don't have that 'all-consuming love'. I explained to him that what we have is real: it is not something that we have to strive to keep; we are people and we see each other for what we are and still love each other besides. People eat, they fart, they get angry, they get frustrated, don't listen to each other, are stupid in their actions sometimes; they hold each other's hands they laugh together and at each other, they think of each other and that is all real: that is true love. People are not perfect they are people: they snore in their sleep, grind their teeth, and sometimes they smell; and if your love is real you will still love them.

I finished my blog with this:

That one is for you Danny Joseph: I don't have an all-consuming love for you; I have real love; let us not forget I am following my dream, you didn't take them away from me; I just found the real ones and that is why I live here in France with you, now.

Rosie

CHAPTER 67

Journal Entries - May 2009

A Wednesday in May 2009

Here I am in London making my own way, being my own person. Life should never cease to amaze you.

The main reason that I have decided to write in my journal is that I read something in my book the other day (I am now an avid reader) but note the titles that I tend to go for: 'Wedding Tiers', 'How to lose a husband and gain a life.' - That one totally freaked Danny out as he thought it was a self-help manual!

But all joking aside I am not stupid – These titles are very telling, they say something about my sub conscious frame of mind: I relate to them because they relate to me. They are all about women moving on and recreating their lives; and although I may not care to admit it, sub-consciously that is what I am doing.

Yes, I am renewing my wedding vows; and at this present moment in time I could never see me leaving the Danny I have now: the Danny who is so sorry and so loving; but I note that as I am writing this and as I let the writing flow, I am never saying never because I know now, that there is more of a possibility of us growing apart than ever before. If I had written this a year ago I would have cried as I wrote it because of the grief, because I felt such immense sadness, because I knew the enormity of what Danny has lost.

As I write this I realise why I am keeping this journal: because this is what it is about: coming to terms, understanding, not being afraid.

I have had so many people say to me how 'lucky' I am, that they would swap places with me in an instant because Danny is so loving; yes he is, but he didn't make a fool of them, he didn't break their hearts. They would have no reason to have a plan B with him; they're not me!!!

Danny has re-joined one of his old marching bands. I felt threatened by that and I have had to ask myself why, when I know that it is the right thing to do. He is off work with a broken rib and wanted to go training tonight; part of me didn't want him to go, and I had to stop myself from asking him not to go because that would be wrong, for me as well. The reason, I believe, is because I know that the more and more we do things apart, the more I will break away and eventually I won't love Danny any more.

Even now his insecurities about his looks and the way he constantly puts himself down get on my nerves. I don't want to keep reassuring him; I begrudge reassuring him, why should I? He put me down so badly and I have had to pick myself back up; I don't owe him anything.

I told Danny to go training, because after thinking about it I wanted time to write this; to watch my programmes and have 'me' time. But what I also realised – and I went quiet last night because I felt like I was losing 'me' again – is that I need to get some interests or I will be back to where I was before; and that I should not be afraid of where gaining other interests will take me.

I suddenly felt as if all I do is go to work, clean and maintain this house and revolve my life around Danny. I won't start with Am Dram, but will start with yoga.

I could go on and on today but will leave it now.

To quote one of my 'lifestyle' books:

'I am solitary, but not lonely.'

Rosie

Reflections Here & Now

It is clear that when I wrote this I was afraid of giving myself to Danny, of letting my guard down. I was afraid because despite all my protestations, that is exactly what was happening to me, and I had no control over it. I thought I did, but looking back now I clearly didn't.

I did buy books because of the titles, because I could relate to them because most were chick lit books; and even now we laugh about the fact that Danny thought one of them 'How to lose a husband and gain a life.' was a self-help book. Although given what I have written in this entry, I can understand why he still felt that way and was still worried; even over two years later; even though we were in the process of renewing our vows.

I have learnt over the years that although it was important that I found myself again, and that did include getting my career back on track and earning enough to feel confident that I was not vulnerable, the mistake I made was that I then let my career define me.

I learnt that lesson the hard way. Here I am all these years later and I have completely given up that career that I felt was so important in this journal entry. It was not anywhere near what I thought it would be; and all I actually did was get lost in the same way I had got lost in Danny. My job became something to focus on to stop me focusing on 'The War'. In the same way that Danny became something to focus on after my mum died. By finding another focus it stopped me having to deal with the pain. When in fact that's what I had to do: process the pain and then really find myself.

I always say that you do have to find yourself and if, like me, you had lost all respect for yourself then yes you have to gain that back; but you also have to accept what has happened; and I found that I had to accept things about me that perhaps I was choosing to ignore.

I did learn important things from all of this: I was still here and I had survived; I was strong I was resilient, I had courage, I had humility; I also had empathy and understanding; and for all of those things I am truly grateful. That is what I have written in this entry: 'because this is what it is about – coming to terms, understanding, not being afraid.'

The reason for me agreeing to Danny re-joining the band for a commemorative tour was not because I thought it would help when I came to leave him; I know now I agreed because I knew that I had to trust him again, no matter how hard it was. If I didn't there was no point in renewing our vows; I had to allow myself to be vulnerable again in some aspects where Danny was concerned.

I still love my own company, I am not afraid of it, and I am not afraid of being on my own.

'I am solitary, but not lonely.'

Rosie

CHAPTER 68

Journal Entries - June 2009

A Sunday in June 2009 (Summer Solstice)

I couldn't decide whether to write in my journal or not; because I am able to reason a lot of things out in my head now. But something is niggling away and as always I re-read what I had written and found it very interesting and insightful.

Things have moved on at a pace over the last month: mainly that I have been offered another promotion and a company car!

I am so chuffed, so proud of myself. But I do feel that it is important to say here that I am under no illusion: work is not my life, and never will be. It is good to be successful in work, to give you some self-esteem; but at some point I will go off on my adventure and buy my house in France.

After my last entry Danny and I had a big chat about the band: it was a good chat. Danny said that he was afraid that I would see him as a 'saddo' because of throw away comment I had made when we first met: it was about how myself and my friends would ridicule the people who chose to be in marching bands.

I explained that I understand now how important this reunion tour was to Danny. It had been his life before he met me, he was in marching bands for many years, even going to the USA, and I understood now that they were part of Danny. I explained that I do not think Danny is a 'saddo', but I also explained that the marching band circuit was not my thing.

This has highlighted to me the difference between me and Danny; and although I am trying to be supportive I know that type of group set up is not my type of thing. I have never been someone who has got caught up in group activities where everyone has to follow. I find people who join groups to be people who need others around them, and I don't'.

One of the other things I have noticed about Danny is how manipulative he can be, small things like commenting when a close friend has not been in touch: 'Oh I notice so and so hasn't been on your back lately.' When he said that it was so clear that he was trying to undermine them and our friendship so I pointed out to him that they are not 'on my back' they are just looking out for me.

Also we had a mobile phone that had never been used; it wasn't even out of the box. To gain money for the band's tour they had all been asked to donate any old mobile phones because they could sell them. As well as all our old phones Danny wanted to take the phone that had never been used and I said no; so he went on and on about how we don't use it, will never use it. It just really pissed me off, I felt as if I was being manipulated into doing something by emotional blackmail and it made me dig my heels in and say no even more. But Danny just carried on so I turned to him and said 'get off my back. You're just trying to manipulate me and you're not having the phone.'

I could tell from the look on his face that it really stung, because I would never have been like that with him before 'The War'; but hey-ho I am now!

As you can see, and so can I now, things seem to be moving on at a pace. Don't get me wrong. I sit in my garden with Danny and I enjoy his company. I know I am not easy to live with, but he still loves me. What I am trying to say is that our friendship is based – see I meant to say our relationship is based more on friendship and I wrote friendship instead. How telling!

Rosie

Reflections Here & Now

When I read this entry I chatted to Danny about it. I realised just how hard it had been for Danny: he really did think that he was going to lose me every day.

When we renewed our vows Danny got so stressed about it, it was as if we were getting married for the first time; and it was only when I read this entry many years later that I realised why: Danny didn't think I was going to turn up to our vow renewal; that is how unsure he felt about me, even two years later, even planning a vow renewal he thought I was going to set him up and get my revenge.

I remembered how on the morning of our vow renewal the usher and I had been totally relaxed and watching TV; whilst Danny got so uptight and stressed that the usher pointed out to him that it was not as if I wasn't going to turn up; I was already married to him. I can remember laughing at the time, but now I understand.

In this entry it does show how the infidelity had changed me and our relationship because I picked Danny up on behaviour that made me feel manipulated and I challenged it. It was a small part of finding me and not getting 'lost' in our relationship again. At the time I wrote this entry I thought it indicated that I would not stay when in fact it was a new and healthy facet to our relationship.

Rosie

CHAPTER 69

Stories to Tell - Wedding
Vows - August 2009

Our wedding vowel renewal came around quickly. It was a small affair; we had invited all the people who had helped us get to where we were in the twenty-eight months since Dday. Danny was stressed to the max and there were many tears.

On the morning of our vowel renewal my brother in law, who was Danny's Best Man, came into our house and immediately went to the stereo; he played 'Hello Again' by Neil Diamond. It was pertinent because it was a song that we often played and cried to as we sang it to each other, especially the part where he sings 'We've been through it all and you love me just the same."

What made my brother in law pick that song I don't know, but for both of us it was a sign that life was telling us we were doing the right thing.

It was a beautiful sunny day, and so many people attended. They were all so happy that Danny and I had got to where we were; I know it was because we gave them hope.

At our reception we had speeches, and tears and we partied on into the night. But the most outstanding thing was the Vicar: he was so excited for us; he smiled throughout the ceremony, and got everyone to form an arch and clap Danny and I out of the church whilst the bells rang. As the ceremony went on he got more and more excited and at the end invited the congregation up to the nave for the final blessing; he explained this was not something that he often did, but he was so happy for Danny and I.

The enthusiasm of that man, the joy he felt because we were making that commitment again carried me forward. In January I hadn't been sure if I wanted to renew our vows at all, in fact I had only agreed to do it for Danny. But by the time the ceremony came round I was committed: If I was doing this I was going to do my best to make it work; I really felt as if I would be letting the Vicar down if I didn't.

We had readings in the church but there was one that I read. When I came up to the plinth to read it I looked out at all the people who had willed us to work; people who had given their support, and my eyes filled with tears; as I struggled to read the verse I looked at Danny, who had been crying all the way through the ceremony, and my voice cracked. Looking up at the congregation I could see their eyes were all glistening with tears.

I knew then that I had to make that commitment, I was renewing my vows and I had to take it seriously. Renewing our vows had a much bigger impact on me than I had ever realised that it would: with the friends and family who supported us, the Vicar and all the people we had met along the way. Life really was showing me the way.

Rosie

'We Have Lived and Loved Together
We have lived and loved together
Through many changing years;
We have shared each other's gladness
And wept each other's tears;......

Charles Jeffrey's

2010

CHAPTER 70

Journal Entries - January 2010

A Wednesday in January 2010

I am surprised at how long it has been since I wrote in my journal. Lots of things have happened and although there have been a few times I thought about writing in it I didn't, because somehow things seemed to right themselves.

Danny has been off with severe depression since September last year. (We did renew our vows in August and it was lovely.) He went to counselling and his counselling helped me: in that I do understand that I am in the acceptance phase: what happened has happened

It has made me feel and react a certain way and that is just the way it is. I understand why or what has happened is natural, and I don't beat myself up over it; in the same way I understand why some people are like they are. But I still make a choice (for example to step away from it) to protect myself; and I don't beat myself up over that either!

Rosie

Reflection Here & Now

We had a wonderful honeymoon in France and when we came home I collected my company car, and Danny marched on the reunion tour for his marching band with my support.

But when October came Danny had a breakdown. He was sent home from work because they couldn't trust him on the train tracks. It was as if he had been living on adrenalin for so long; and after we renewed our vows he felt safer in the knowledge that I would stay, so the adrenalin dropped and so did Danny.

Danny was absent from work for over six months. He had to see a psychiatrist twice a month and he couldn't return to work until the psychiatrist had signed him off as fit. Even then he was not allowed back on track for another four months after returning.

The psychiatrist asked that I attend one of the last appointments with Danny. I never asked Danny to tell me anything he had discussed at his appointments; I had come to realise that we cannot know everything about the person we love; even though we often think that we have that entitlement. None of us will ever know what is going on inside someone's head and through all of this I learnt that I didn't need to. We don't own those we love, we just share our lives with them.

However Danny wanted to tell me some of what had been discussed; and it was clear that a lot of the problems that he had been experiencing were because of 'The War'; and his own insecurities in keeping me: insecurities that I had played on so many times during our recovery. I look back even now at some of the things that I did and at how much Danny worked to keep me whilst constantly living in fear; and although I understand why I did some of the things I did at the time (because I had been driven insane) the sane me of here and now would change them if she could.

When I went to that appointment and listened to the psychiatrist whilst he explained to me that one of the things that played on Danny's mind was when I wrote in my journal I was shocked, because I didn't realise that Danny still felt that afraid; or that Danny always thought that I was writing about 'The War' and planning my escape.

I realised why the psychiatrist had asked meet me: to help me understand that I held Danny's mental health in my hands. It seems like a big responsibility to put onto someone who in fact had their own heart broken by the man who they now had responsibility for; but the biggest lesson I had learnt through all of this was how strong I was; and how that strength could impact on others. So I didn't begrudge that responsibility, I knew it was one of the lessons that life tends to throw your way. I love Danny: a big, gentle man; who had faced every fear to keep me and I respected him for that. I didn't want to destroy him.

My husband (and I am sure there are many others) cannot ever forgive himself for what he did; I wish he could. Although we can both see that it made us into better people, Danny let himself down and more than anything he cannot take away the pain he inflicted on me; and for that he still dislikes himself every day.

On the tenth anniversary of the 'The War' I pulled up outside our house in France only to hear a record that Danny would put on that made him cry (the Bee Gees 'Love Me Please'). Instantly I knew that he had been crying. When I entered the house Danny came down with a smile and I said "How long have you been crying darling?" He smiled, looked at me, and said "Ten years!"

I felt so sad, because I didn't want him to feel that way. Danny is one of those people who is truly sorry; he would do anything to make it right, but to him the only way to do that would be to go back in time and change it; which we all know is something that he cannot do. People make mistakes.

I got to a point, as you can see from what I had written, where I knew that I had to work with Danny, or lose him. But I also got to a point where I was not prepared to let the negativity of what happened destroy me, our relationship or our family. I had to make that choice and I used everything that I had learnt to help Danny and I, and so did Danny.

Rosie

CHAPTER 71

Journal Entries – May 2010

A Sunday in May 2010

Having read what I wrote in my journal entry in January, and given the time of year that it is, as I am writing this entry I understand that the main thing that has stopped me from being broken is my strength of personality. I am not prepared to give that up ever again. That is why I have learnt to be so independent, because I have to be. I am what I am (I understand where the song comes from now!) and everyone else tries to hang their problems on to me, but I don't think that it something I can mentally afford to carry anymore.

I think that I saw my job as my way out – to prove that I would always be able to stand on my own two feet, to make myself feel better. But I don't need to go any higher than I am already; I know now that I can always achieve whatever I want if I put my mind to it.

I would be lying if I didn't say that this time of year has got to me: I look at the blossom on my beautiful cherry tree and it will always remind me of that fucking BBQ. But Danny, over the past month, has been brilliant in supporting me; and he has not let me down during some really difficult times. But because the poor sod gave me one of the most momentous heartbreaks I have ever had in my life, things get turned on him; or is it because they say 'you always hurt the one you love the most'?

Danny just came up and I know that me writing in my journal worries him – he told the counsellor that – so I will stop for now.
Rosie

Reflections Here & Now

It is near to the anniversary of 'The War' (the 3rd anniversary) and yet my entry is not about what happened to us. It shows that I am now moving on to a different life: one that is not dominated by 'The War'.

It had been three years since the bomb went off and in this entry my tone is so different: almost philosophical. I can recognise that whilst it is a difficult time of year I also have something good with Danny.

What I have written about my personality is the crux of it all: I had started to realise just what an asset it was; but I had also realised just how destructive it could be if not managed, especially where Danny and I were concerned.

I can remember this time was challenging with work and I had at times been in tears with it; but Danny was there to support me all the way. I love the fact that I acknowledge Danny's fear where writing my journal was concerned, and stopped writing in it when Danny came up.

We were truly moving forward.
Rosie

CHAPTER 72

Journal Entries - October 2010

A Saturday October in 2010

I do know how important writing this journal is because you are honest with yourself and cannot run away from that honesty; but it is honesty without judgement. As I have written this I now realise why Danny cannot write a journal: because he is frightened to face the honesty it brings. Poor Danny, he is still running away. But I think that he will be like that all his life; it is too ingrained to change.

I have often asked myself over the past couple of months whether staying with Danny (interesting I meant to say that the other way around) Danny staying with me, is really the best thing for him. If Danny were being honest with himself and asked himself that question I wonder what he would say. I say this because I can see that he seems to be so desperate to keep me; so afraid of losing me, that I question whether this is really making him happy because sometimes I cannot see how it can be. But it is not just about me is it?

Danny does not want to go back to the person he was before; doesn't want to be the old Danny. But now I can see that if he was truly honest with himself he thinks that being the person he has become is all dependent on me keeping him where he is. But for me just lately, I can feel that pressure: I notice that I have been persuading him to do things on his own, when I am at work.

Small things: go for a motorbike ride, watch his programmes, go for a walk; even take a day of annual leave and go and watch his marching band. Subconsciously I have been trying to get Danny to gain some independence from me.

Now I thought about that and questioned how I have been feeling lately because the past has been coming back into my head. I have wondered whether it is because I am closing down.

But when I am with Danny I do love him, and I really enjoy his company; I just recognise that to keep me Danny must gain his own identity. But this is going to become more difficult over the next year because he is going to take his redundancy and will feel more dependent on me than ever. Ironically getting more time together will also enable us to follow our own hobbies without it infringing on our time together; writing this I know that Danny leaving his career is the right decision.

I know that I have a difficult few months ahead: puppy is on his last legs, my constant companion for the last fourteen years, he has never let me down (it was his birthday yesterday.)

Rosie

Reflections Here & Now

I was wrong: Danny adapted and evolved over and over again. But I was right that still to this day he would not be able to keep a journal; many people can't. They are afraid of the 'Pandora's Box' they may open; and I have come to understand and respect that.

I can understand my fears at the time I wrote this entry. One of the biggest fears of finding yourself and getting stronger is that you will leave the other person behind. I don't think that is necessarily just for those where infidelity has rocked the relationship, I think that it is the biggest risk to any relationship: that one person changes and moves in a different direction to the other.

The strange thing is the affair actually kept Danny and I together, because we both changed, but we changed together. As our vow renewal gift from our dear friend Toni says:

'A marriage is an achievement

A wedding is an event.'

Did we follow our own hobbies? No! We loved each other's company too much to do that. But I am not afraid of spending most of my time with Danny now; it's what I love to do, so I don't fight against it.

Rosie

2011

CHAPTER 73

Journal Entries - January 2011

A Monday in January 2011

I really don't remember (or didn't) feeling that way about Danny until I read my last journal entry from October last year. Some of it is true, but some of what I have gained from reading the books I read has rubbed off on Danny. Because of that I see a different Danny: a man who wants to learn, move forward, change, to be different. A big kind gentle man; I love him very much and I know that I am very lucky.

I achieved my promotion and Danny has put in for his redundancy; and we are moving in the right direction. Although it is frightening I am confident that we have made the right decisions. You have to change, life has to change or you will not move forward.

I was surprised when I realised just how little I had written in my journal over the last two and a half years; part of that is good: because I think I was a little bit mad when I first started keeping a journal. I do know though that I should write in it more to keep my head clear.

Rosie

Reflections Here & Now

I loved this entry: It is about a Danny and Rosie who have worked through the turmoil and are now working together. I had started read some of the psychology and spiritual books to Danny, what I love is that he took on board the philosophies. If you had told me when I first met Danny that he would embrace a new way of thinking I would have never believed it. It's true: life really does work in mysterious ways.

Danny left his job; it was a big step for him, and one night he told me that it made him afraid because he wondered if once he left I would tell him that I didn't want him anymore. He wondered if I would exact my revenge. In some ways I was shocked, but I had come to know this Danny more than the man that I married; so I reassured him that it was not the case, and I took on board how fragile he was.

Rosie

CHAPTER 74

Journal Entries - February 2011

A Saturday in February 2011

I am sitting on The Downs looking out to sea. It is a beautiful day: sunny and cold but beautiful. I have a lot to write.

Danny leaves his job officially on the 25th of February. I am still confident that it is the right thing to do. It will be strange, but lovely, having every weekend to ourselves. He has another job to start already: back to warehouse work and earning about £200 a week. It is a big drop in income but it's a job with no pressure and it will contribute enough to keep us afloat. I am confident that he will do well. I have felt a little more pressure because I will be the main wage earner but out of all the other things going on in my life I know that Danny leaving work is the right thing.

Danny is already looking at some extra activities he can undertake, and has been to visit the local coast volunteer centre because he is considering taking up volunteering. I am happy for him to get some hobbies because I am so conscious of how much Danny just focuses everything on us, and I don't need him to, or want him to.

After finding myself again I like to have time to myself without Danny. I do love his company: he makes me laugh every day, but I still need 'me' time, without Danny. I know sometimes that frightens him but it is what it is and we are where we are.

Rosie

Reflections Here & Now

How things can change! Danny now had to learn to trust me, and I was able to provide him with the support he needed for such a life changing event.

When we first got back together we talked a lot about how Danny's job and the commute impacted on his life: he had never felt part of our new life by the sea because he had always felt as if he was at work or commuting. As a result he had started to resent me and the fact that I worked part-time; despite the fact that this was actually something that he had wanted at the time.

As the years went by we realised that for us to work together Danny had to give up his career, or more importantly the commute. This was a very difficult thing to do because, as is often the case, Danny's career was one of the things that defined him. For Danny to leave his job, knowing that my career was in full flight was a brave thing to do. I also know that it was the right thing to do.

I learned that even though Danny was the person who had the affair, trust had to be gained on both sides.

But I also remember all of my insecurities coming back when Danny went out with his colleagues to celebrate leaving. The agreement was that he would only go to a pub with them; whilst I was more confident, when faced with Danny getting drunk and going to a nightclub, all of my insecurities came back. I stayed at Nel's house and Gus went with Danny to the pub; but when Gus came back from the pub without Danny and told me that Danny was going on to a nightclub I freaked. I called Danny and told him I was not comfortable with it and asked him to come back to Nel's. He did, within half an hour he was with me and worried that he had brought back all of the worries that I had before.

That simple act of listening to my insecurities and understanding them; not telling me I was stupid, but coming home, showed me so much.

Rosie.

CHAPTER 75

Journal Entries- August 2011

A Monday in August 2011

I wanted to write in my journal because this time in my life is marking the end of an era. My son is going to university next month and so is Adam.

In a way Danny and I cannot wait because we will have the house to ourselves and the freedom to do what we want. I haven't been like that in twenty two years! But I know we will miss them both and find that we have time on our hands. I plan to go to Zumba and yoga and Danny is going to look at some bands he may join. But it is sad, because we have had four years with both of them, and in some ways they were a large part of the cement that put us back together. or our responsibility for them was. I am not worried about cracks appearing between Danny and I, because I know it won't happen.

But for me, more than anything, it is the end of a major chapter in my life. I know that new ones are beginning; and that I have achieved my aim: my son is independent. I am so proud of him; he has so much talent and has got into such a fantastic university, but where did the time go? My baby, my little boy, the boy who was always in 'my team'; the son who slept with me, both of us reading Harry Potter so that I could get an hours sleep during 'The War'.

I am happy, but sad at the same time, because it is the closing of a chapter. And now, as always, because I have written this down, I feel better.

Rosie

Reflections Here & Now

This entry can still make me cry.

I included these entries to show how life was moving forward, and changing; and as it changed we went with it; and as we went with it the past got left behind more and more.

Some people may think that the boys leaving would have changed the dynamic between Danny and I because as I have said they were part of the cement that held us together. But we had rebuilt 'us' without them in the equation, with all the times that we had visited France and the stronger relationship that we had.

If Danny had been honest at that time I think that he was a little bit afraid that I would leave, because I was upset that the biggest chapter in my life was closing: looking after my child because he was making his own way in the world now. But he had nothing to fear and whilst I did find it hard in the house at first I also relished the space that Danny and I had.

Rosie

CHAPTER 76

Journal Entries - September 2011

A Friday in September 2011

I just read my last entry and it made me cry. I cried nearly all day on Monday!

But I came home, went for a walk by the sea, sat in front of the waves and looked out at the ocean and sky and I stopped crying. (Although I am crying as I write this!)

It is a weird feeling: when Ethan went and we came home after dropping him off the house felt different, as if there was something missing; just like it did during 'The War'.

Danny is putting on a brave face because I think he thinks that he needs to do that for me. But he has lived with Ethan for thirteen years now; and despite everything he has been his dad.

We are both so proud of Ethan; and if we were being honest proud of ourselves that we helped him and Adam. But we feel sad because it is the end of an era; although they will be back it will never be the same again; and it is only human to feel sad about that. But it is also important to look to the future. I am going to get my stepper back out and we may even go to ballroom dancing classes.

It seems poignant that it is autumn, a season that signifies the end of the summer, but with the promise of something new. My adventure begins…..

Rosie

Reflections Here & Now

I remember when Ethan went to university so clearly. I can remember walking around the university in a daze, putting on a brave face, because I just wanted to cry: my baby was flying the nest.

I have never been a mum whose child defines me and I gave Ethan a card when he left in which I had written that I had given birth to him, but never felt as if I owned him; that I wanted him to fly free and have the life he wants without worrying about me. But coming home to that house that felt so empty brought back memories of a time before when it had felt that way.

This time the tears were because things were changing, and although I have always embraced change it was still one of the most poignant times of my life.

Rosie

CHAPTER 77

Journal Entries - October 2011

A Thursday in October 2011

I was talking to Danny honestly on Saturday about why it upset me so much that the boys have gone; and also considering that Snowy may die soon. When my first marriage broke down and my mum and dad died I based my life on looking after my family: me, Ethan and the dog. Then Danny came into our life and I trusted him; and he let me down. When that happened my immediate focus was to look after me, Ethan and the dog again. They were my responsibility and in some ways because I could focus on them they helped me survive. Now Ethan has gone, and I know that Snowy will go soon; I will have lost my focus and my focus will have to be me; and that is scary!

Over the past week I have also started to think that I don't want to go any further with work. I don't want to give any more of my life to it than I am already. Again, as I am writing this I realise that I am moving towards my adventure…..

Rosie

Reflections Here & Now

I did find it hard; not because I was going to leave Danny, but because the things that had been my life, been the driving force during difficult times, were leaving. But I was afraid that with the change that had come, if things became difficult between Danny and I what would be my focus. Lack of focus made me feel vulnerable.

Over time I realised that I had nothing to fear because nothing was going to happen between Danny and I that would mean I would need something worth fighting for. What this entry does show is how change can make you feel so vulnerable; but is that about the infidelity or is that just life?

In the words of George Benson 'Everything must change'

Rosie

2012

CHAPTER 78

Journal Entries - January 2012

A Monday in January 2012

I have found it weird that I have written in my journal at exactly the same point in this New Year as I did last year.

I don't feel the same about work as I did this time last year, I have come to accept that it is work and that is it.

What I notice more than anything is that I have changed, especially when I look back over the last four years. I have become harder, or perhaps I just look at the world through different eyes. I have evolved, I have learnt and I am open and accepting of change; and as a result of that I have changed.

My perspective has changed in that I find I am leaving some people in my life behind: those who are resistant to change, those who are afraid of change because I understand, now, that you have to embrace change to be able to move forward in life.

Where Danny is concerned he does keep up. Since I last wrote in my journal Danny got a new job and then was made redundant three weeks after. But the company re-opened and they re-employed him which is a compliment to what a good worker Danny is; and he is adaptable now.

Due to the instability of employment in the current climate we have decided to try and accumulate some money as a cushion and on my birthday we are not, now, going away for the weekend; we have decided that we have the house to ourselves and to just spend some time together. I am content with that.

This year every day I am going to count my blessings by looking at three good things that have happened: small things like being able to see the crisp mornings, snuggling up every night, our health, our family. A reminder of the things that we all tend to take for granted.

Rosie

Reflections Here & Now

For me this entry shows a change: we were just moving forward in life and working together. I had started to realise that what I had used to define me (my work) whilst I found myself, was no-longer necessarily what I wanted.

We had started to make a new life together with just the two of us: looking forward to snuggling up on cold crisp mornings, a new 'normal'.

A Monday In January 2012

I am sitting here at 6.15am and I just thought I would reflect before I get ready for work. As always I have read what I have previously written and it is nice to see that I have started the year on such a positive note. I still feel chilled.

I have learnt over the years to be very careful of insecure people: Danny was insecure, 'she' was insecure, and the prats at work that I have to deal with are often insecure. I just cannot be doing with them anymore. I know that Danny is afraid that I will leave him behind; and over the past month he has been quite negative and huffy puffy. I did moan at him about it on Friday because that can really bring other people down too. It's January, we are in a really bad recession and it is tough, but you have to get on with it, and focusing on the negatives will not help. Bless him; he has gone off to work now all cheery since we had our 'chat'. 'The greatest thing you can ever learn is just to love and be loved in return.'

Snowy is struggling now. He was really bad at the weekend and it is getting more and more difficult to keep his skin condition under control. I know a decision is coming soon and that because I love him it is one I will have to make.

Rosie

Reflections Here & Now

When Ethan left and Adam went on his way to a new life I found that we actually pulled together more: we had nothing left to fight for only us and we actually started to work together as a tight unit more than we ever had before.

I love this entry: I can recognise Danny for who he is and love him for it. But as you will see, despite how I felt then, what happened continued to influence my thoughts. I suppose over time that is when I learnt that it cannot be undone, it just what it is.

Rosie

CHAPTER 79

Journal Entries – March 2012

A Thursday in March 2012

It has taken me some time to sit and write this because I had to have Snowy put to sleep on the 17th of February. I know that he was really suffering and that I had to make that choice but I still feel like I murdered him, my Dude.

I always knew this time would be hard. The family unit I had created after my mum died was Ethan and Snowy; now Ethan has gone his own way and Snowy, who was always with me, and always loved me unconditionally and supported me through my mum dying and Danny leaving has gone. My unit and focus has gone.

I know that I have to get a new focus, and that focus is me. I said all along after Danny came back that I wanted an adventure. I have given twenty seven years of my life to looking after people and now I want my adventure and to look after me.

I know that Danny was (and perhaps still is) worried that my adventure will not include him; but it will. Danny is my friend, he makes me laugh; we share so many things that my adventure would not be the same without him.

So I have re-evaluated, which is something that you should always do, and I don't want to stay where I am. I hate work now. So what do I do? Danny and I have always said that one day we will sell the house and use the equity to go on an adventure; it is just a fucking house!

Danny and I are both fifty next year; I think it is time for the adventure to begin.

I love you Snowy Dude.

Rosie

Reflections Here & Now

I believe that it is a very true saying that animals show us so much: to love unconditionally, but also to know that to do that your heart is likely to be broken. I believe that is their lesson: do not be afraid of a broken heart because then you will never love at all.

This was the start of the plan for the adventure, and I still miss that dog every day.

Rosie

CHAPTER 80

Journal Entries – May 2012

A Tuesday at the beginning of May 2012

I said that I should have written in my journal over the weekend, but I didn't. I should have.

April is not a good month for me, and at present I can't see that changing in my life. My mum's illness took off and she died in April and it was in April that Danny left me.

I know and accept that April is not good, but never the less at times it can bite me – still.

Danny always feels awful (afraid to be more exact); he brought me flowers for my mum's anniversary, but I still have demons in my head at this time of year.

I really fancied sex over the weekend, but somehow we never got our 'sync' together and it did not happen. I accept that it is not all Danny's responsibility. But when I wake up in the morning I imagine Danny kissing and caressing me, when he is actually lying in bed beside me, there is something wrong. As I am writing this I realise that I don't approach Danny for fear of a knock-back and Danny never approaches me. (Probably for the same reason)

But this morning Danny did his classic: the old Danny in his full glory! (But is it the old Danny? Or is it really Danny and he is just 'pretending' to keep me?)

I was my normal bubbly (probably too bubbly) self in the morning. When Danny came into the bedroom he was naked, and he stood with his back to me, so that I could not see him. I realise now that subconsciously I knew he was doing that so I approached him for a caress, something that I have done every day since we reconciled. But Danny did his classic cool and ignoring thing that he used to do before 'The War', and acted as if I was not even there. When I re-read this I will know what I am talking about: It made me feel like six years ago. Well he can fuck off, because I will not allow him to make me feel like that ever again! I have proved that I am better than him, and that I never have to put up with that shit anymore.

So why am I tearful? Anger I think. Memories of how I felt six years ago are lurking around my head and my defences have gone up.

I won't be approaching Danny again for a while. I know that Danny will now approach me, because his behaviour before he left indicates that he so knows what he did. He crawled around me afterwards. Too late!

I often say that if I find out (or when I find out, as my gut tells me Danny lied to me at the beginning about how long their relationship had been going on) I would leave. In some ways I cannot understand how I can be so happy in my life, but be that hard. But as I am writing this I understand it is because Danny will inherently always be the person that he was. We can all want to change, and change our ways, but inherently we will always be that 'base person'.

I often wonder: if I was not with Danny whether the awful memories in my head would fade and go. But I realised that they will never go: that feeling of humiliation will shape the person I am in the future, whether I am with Danny or not; they just won't matter as much is if I am not!

Rosie

Reflections Here & Now

Wow! A lot of my journal entries of 2012 are about work and not about 'The War', so I don't include them all, but I nearly missed this one out and it is so pertinent.

It is true that before 'The War' there was times when I would approach Danny for sex and he would act as if my hand was not even where it was. It made me feel like crap, but I did learn that it was not because of 'her' it was because of the pressure from work, and the worry about not being good enough for me. However, to not communicate that to me, to hide in his fears, and make me feel rejected, unattractive, and like shit at times was not the best way of dealing with it. So I do fully understand why the Rosie of then reacted in the way that she did: it took her back to a place in time when she had allowed Danny to make her feel like shit.

Before 'The War' we had talked about it often, and in fact Danny referred to it when we had one of our conversations whilst he was living with 'her', when he had told me I was 'too needy', and always 'looking for affection'. But I hadn't been, he had just turned his lack of communication skills back onto me and gas lighted me. Was it any wonder when five years later and he did it again that I reacted in the way that I did?

But...I can see from my tone in this entry that I was struggling with the time of year that it was; and I think Danny had picked up on that and, yes, reverted back to his 'base person' that I refer to here, and wanted to run away and hide.

I have learned over the years that I had to see the person that I was; it was not all Danny's responsibility to make us work, and five years in I sometimes reverted to my 'base person' and came out fighting when I felt vulnerable; and that was exactly what I had done here: I say how I am 'better than Danny'; really! Of course I wasn't better than him; I have a strong personality, he has a gentle personality and that is what makes us work. If we both had the same personality as me we would be killing each other!

But it took me time to learn this, yes even longer than five years.

Of course I had reverted back to believing that it would be so much easier if I was not with Danny as I wrote this entry; because I felt vulnerable and humiliated, and afraid (if I was honest) and all those things gave the Demon something to feed on.

Rosie

A Wednesday in May 2012

I have read my previous entry and I am okay now. I think it is important that I write that because I know the strength of emotion that I felt.

Danny and I have spoken about it. Danny said that he did not know that he was doing it; so I said that he needs to ask himself why he does it then, as it will always be one of the quickest things that will split us up. He needed to think about it to enable him to understand and get his 'base' person under control. He doesn't have to discuss it with me, in the same way that I don't discuss everything I write in here with him, but he does need to work it out for himself, otherwise he will just keep running away and making the same mistakes. But we are okay.

We picked up Tilly the Tiny Terror on Friday; in fact she now has her head stuck in my journal as I am writing this. She must be the tiniest kitten we have ever had. They said she was grey but she is chocolate brown and she is like a teeny tiny bear. We love cats, but we both miss 'Snowy 'The Dude' very much.

I am off on leave for the remainder of the week after the upcoming bank holiday; so that I can settle Tilly in and also to chill.

But what I did want to write about was a house that I visited last week with work, the people who lived in it had so little, and we have so much. It reminded me again that we should always look at how lucky we are; I should look at how lucky I am. I am able to go to work, able to get on if I want to; I have a man who loves me very much. Irrespective of what happened before I am blessed.

I sat in the bathroom of that house, with all the tiles peeling off the wall, and I felt ashamed. You could argue that it is because I am motivated, strive to move forward and make my life better; but I know that I am blessed to be able to think like that. Ethan thinks like me, because it is inherently in us and for that we are blessed.

I know that Danny strives to achieve because I drive him. He himself would tell you that. If I were not with him he would not strive to achieve what he has – if you asked him why he achieves things he would tell you that he was achieving them because it is what I would want him to do.

As I write this I am starting to understand that it is just in my make up to achieve, and that is why I manage people because I drive them to achieve. That is why I write lists of jobs, that is why I have what I have. It doesn't matter what I choose to do in the future (my adventure) I will be okay because I drive it.

When I had my Tarot cards read years ago I pulled out all the strong cards. The strongest card was in the middle and the reader told me that it did not matter what happened (to myself and my ex-husband at the time) that Ethan and I would always be alright as long as he was with me. In fact at that sitting the reader also saw my divorce in the future.

Rosie

Reflections Here & Now

This entry shows that we had learned that to talk was what we had to do: We had to learn to face our fears and talk about what happened between us.

Years before this entry I had spoken to my sister about something that was playing on my mind: how many times Danny had sex with 'her'. She told me that if I had something on my mind, then I should talk about it, calmly and constructively, because if I didn't it would fester and be blown out of all proportion. The same applied to Danny. It was good advice and it was something that we used often to face our fears: remind ourselves that if we didn't face what we were afraid of and talk about it then it would grow and become something that could undermine and destroy us.

To do this however it was essential that we both signed up to it. There was no point in one person wanting to talk about what was on their mind if the other would not engage with them. So we agreed to always talk about what was on our mind; and in fact if one of us notices (as you invariably do) that the other person appears distracted, or worried, or distant then we make them talk about it. Of course this is easier for me because my 'base' person is one who confronts things; but it was harder for Danny because his 'base' person is one who wants to run away from things. So sometimes when Danny gets hold of me and insists that I tell him what is on my mind I always do, because I respect the fact that he has faced his fears to do it.

Even now in France, I will remind Danny when he is running away from something, gently but I will say 'isn't that running away again?' I just leave it there because I know he will always go away and think about it and then come back and take the action that he needed to take.

I think it's important to highlight that it is this type of thing that has made us stronger than we were before; because we learned from what happened to us and we remind ourselves often of the lessons we learnt.

Rosie

A Friday in May 2012

I am writing this because of something that happened last night; but also because I said I would write in my journal every week. Perhaps what happened last night happened because it is just over a week since I last wrote in my journal and it is life showing me the way.

I have realised that I am high on the good old hormones, and when I came in I drank too much wine too quickly, and I know from past experience, that the two don't mix at this time of the month.

Danny was hungry, and we were having lamb chops. Danny did his usual and said that I had more than chops than him; and I don't know why but I lost it. I had weighed myself out six ounces of chops but when Danny said what he said I took his lamb chops and through them on the scales, and one fell onto the floor. Danny then lost it and said I was being stupid; I pointed out to him that he had over one pound of lamb chops. Danny said he couldn't understand why it had upset me; but then he realised that he had really upset me from my reaction.

Writing this it has made me giggle because it seems so stupid; but I need to know why it upset me, to learn from it, and also to know how to react next time.

Afterwards I told him I would not pick what was on the TV in case he thought I was nagging with that too. (thinking about it

I always pick what we watch.) Danny said I was being stupid and he was just going to leave me alone. I said 'go for it, it won't be the first time, you've done it before!' It was spiteful and a bit cruel and it really upset him and he left his dinner and went out into the garden. I realised how stupid it all seemed and went after him and persuaded him to come back and eat his dinner.

But it is still hanging in the air, and now I feel (as often happens) that I am the one who has to make amends; and I don't want to. Why?

As I am writing this the first thing that comes to mind is that in 'jest' Danny often says how I don't love Diddies anymore, because I love Daisy, and then he says to Daisy that I don't love her because I have Tilly. I love them all, so what is Danny's perception of me that he says things like that? It is a very true saying that 'many a true word is said in jest.'

It appears that Danny seems to think that I am selfish, and at times a heartless person; and that is why I reacted the other night.

I know that 'she' used to talk about me to Danny (in fact I think that most times I was the main topic of conversation), and part of what they talked about was how awful I was to Danny: how I would leave him for someone else, how I was selfish because I only worked part-time when he worked so hard, and how Danny earnt all the money and I just spent it.

Obviously the working and spending the money does not apply now because the boot is on the other foot. But Danny still thinks that I am shallow, selfish, greedy, doesn't he? Otherwise why would he say what he says 'in jest'? I don't, because I don't feel the need!

We are back to good old insecurity again: that Danny's insecurities are now my problem; but they are not! Now I understand why I threw them back at him yesterday: Danny left me and I am stronger because of it and in a roundabout way I was antagonising his insecurities because he was trying to put them onto my back.

I can remember a couple of months ago when I got upset because Danny was implying that I was planning to get rid of Diddies. I didn't address it at the time but now I know why I got upset, because he was trying to undermine me.

I now need to get a constructive plan together to address it next time it happens, constructively. This is Danny being his 'base person'; but I don't like his 'base person' and he needs to stop or I won't stay.

I got angry because in a surreptitious way Danny seeks constant reassurance because of something he did. Where does my reassurance come from? Inside me because I am the only person who can reassure me! I am happy to work with Danny to make our relationship work, but I don't 'owe' him anything; and it makes me angry when he acts as if I do.

My plan is to pick Danny up now every time he says something in 'jest', either directly or sarcastically back, 'in jest'! I may even suggest that he asks himself if he really likes me, or whether I make him feel too insecure.

Danny touched so many nerves and it has been a while now that he has made small innuendos: his and 'her' opinion of me!

I think that Danny needs to really think about what he wants; because I will not let him put me down ever again; I am vicious now whenever anyone tries. If you don't like me you can always 'fuck off'!

PS: Danny always says things 'in jest' when I have had a drink. The same old ploy he used to do with 'her' when they were making a fool of me and I need to be aware of that.

Reflections Here & Now

And wow again!

It is important that I highlight that although we were five years in, at this point and anyone reading this may be thinking 'oh my God, it will never get better!' it will. This was just part of the learning.

Before 'The War' Danny and I did not communicate as well as we were by this point; and part of this communication, for me, was understanding my reactions and Danny's; even though some of it was difficult to confront. If we had not done this, if I had not done this we could have very easily gone back to the same old same old that we had before; and if we had we would not be the people that we are today or here with each other today.

We both learned that to move forward we had to learn from things and the only way to do that was to confront them and analyse them.

Danny was being manipulative because that is what he had always learned to do: make a joke about a situation, hide from a situation, run away from a situation, and turn it around onto someone else. By writing in my journal and reflecting I was able to help him to do the same; and yes sometimes that was by being really blunt; sometimes it was by being sarcastic, or mimicking Danny's actions back at him, because then he would have to deal with them and not me.

But what is also important was that I was learning that we were two different people and I was questioning whether I could love Danny as he was. Over the years he has listened and learned and taken on board (of his own volition at times) things because he wanted to learn and evolve; and that was just another thing that made me love him all over again.

I have learned that I can be driven, and bossy and selfish at times; I have also learned that I did always choose the TV channels!

This was an argument over lamb chops! But it wasn't, it was much deeper than that and that is why I would always encourage people to keep a journal.

Rosie

CHAPTER 81

Journal entries – June 2012

A Monday in June 2012

So sticking with writing my journal every week – it never ceases to amaze me how much doing this can help you (me); the main reason being that if you lie in your journal you are only lying to yourself.

I have learnt, one of my main learnings in fact, is that things change; and you have to change with them, 'review and adapt your map' as M Scott Peck says in 'The Road Less Travelled.' Often what happens is that people do not want to do that: their map is set and they desperately try to stick with that plan; even though it is obviously not the right way for them and it makes them unhappy. Why?

When I look at the changes that I have made over the last five years, the adaptations I have had to make to my life's 'map': Danny and I, my relationship with Louise, Jackie dying, Ethan going to university, promotions at work, Snowy dying; I realise that my ability to adapt has enabled me to move forward and succeed: by writing journals and really being honest with myself has given me strength. By not believing I am always right, by working to adapt to change I have become stronger and more resilient.

Rosie

Reflections Here & Now

In the past few years I have reconnected with someone who I have known for a long time, and reading this entry made me realise just how little that person was able to change and adapt: they still do what they have always done, and they are still unhappy.

I live my life now with the understanding that everything changes, that we cannot hold on so tight to what we think we want because we don't know what is coming in the future; and I learnt all of that the hard way, from this experience.

Even now we are reconsidering our position in France and will probably move on again. We are older than when we moved here, the land is now too much, our lives have changed and in fact this book will change them again (the blog already has).

Do I regret what happened to us? The honest answer is no. I learned so much from this experience and now I am using what I learned and helping others; as the Tao says 'where there is good there is bad and where there is bad there is good.'

Rosie

A Monday in June 2012

I might write in my journal twice this week; I need to keep work clear in my head, but today I am not going to reflect on work; I just need to write something down: get it out in the open and reflect.

Over the past couple of weeks I have played the haunting tome from 'Four Weddings and a Funeral'. I even find myself humming it because I find it relaxing.

I have watched a fantastic series of half hour mini dramas called 'True Love', written by Dominic Savage. They were all set in the seaside town of Margate, and as I write that I realise that may be why they got to me more; because they were all about love, and the main theme was infidelity.

I knew that Danny would not be able to watch them; I knew that they would be too much like looking in a mirror for him – they would have been, some would have been.

The episodes turned from those committing infidelity to those involved in infidelity to those escaping infidelity, to those finding love and then the last one showed how easy it could be to lose true love because of implied infidelity.

The last episode showed how jealous people can be of other's happiness and how they can systematically set out to destroy it. The first episode showed a person who had not fully understood what he had (Danny); the second and third episode showed people who took what they had for granted (me) and in the fourth episode the person lost what they had.

In the fourth episode a lady whose husband was committing adultery was asked what she really wanted, and she said that she wanted to 'fly like a bird and be free.' I had answered the question out loud before she had answered it herself because I knew what the answer would be.

I have written many times that I want my adventure; I want to be free. What is that for me? I love my house, and I am happy in my life, but I still feel trapped sometimes.

I cried during those episodes, because I finally admitted that what Danny and I had is broken, for something so stupid. And when you break that thing you can never fully get it back. I found that so sad; sad for Danny, because he will never fully attain what he desires the most in life; because I can never give that to him again.

But then I have a lovely day like yesterday and I am so confused.

More to come no doubt.

Rosie

Reflections Here & Now

Of course there was more to come, there is always more to come, that's just life!

I was brave to watch that series but I still love it today. Perhaps it was a cathartic thing: to see how everyone messes up in something but life still goes on and you can put the pieces together and have something new but different.

I find it strange to read that although I had written so many times in my journal that I knew we had lost what we had; that I still cried for it five years later. But now I know that is just grief.

Rosie

CHAPTER 82

Journal Entries – July 2012

Thursday 18ᵗʰ July 2012

We are currently on holiday in Cornwall. I hardly feel 'the need' to write in my journal now. But I am today because yesterday I realised something:

Danny and I had decided to go and visit a pretty beach in Cornwall. It is a small 'surfers' beach and the waves are meant to come crashing in on the golden sands. But the weather in Cornwall has been awful so on the days it hasn't fully rained we have been surrounded by Cornish mizzle (a mixture of drizzle and mist). When we arrived in the seaside town you couldn't see the road in front of you, let alone the beach!

We parked on the steep hill that led down to the invisible beach and Danny said he would try and find us a coffee. As I sat in the car looking out at the fog I suddenly realised that I hadn't thought about 'The War' in the last few days!

For the first time in over five years I have had a few days where I have not thought about 'The War'!

Of course as soon as I realised this I then found myself feeling sad for Danny; but that is the thing now; I feel sad for Danny; I don't fear it anymore. I know at times it will come back to haunt me, of course it will; but this has also proved to me that it can go out of my mind now; and if there is one thing I know it won't beat me.

Rosie

> ...the greatest love of all
> Is easy to achieve
> Learning to love yourself
> It is the greatest love of all....

The Greatest Love of All
Linda Creed and Michael Masser

EPILOGUE

I will not say that there were not times in my journal over the years from 2012 until 2013 that I did not reflect on 'The War'; but I came to understand that what happened was a defining episode of my life and our relationship. So whenever the Demon popped into my head I was able to use my journal to shut him up! I learned that what I was feeling was just life.

In 2014 I had a breakdown brought on by the stress that I experienced in my career. Danny was caring and loving and understanding; but also terrified that it may trigger in me the urge to leave. Clearly it didn't!

In 2015 we moved to France and started our adventure; we needed all the strength that we had learned through 'The War' to work together: to move to a new country and start a new life takes courage and trust in each other.

Now as I write this we are considering another chapter in our adventure, and perhaps moving on to pastures new; but I know that life will show me the way.

I hope that this book has helped you, that when you have a bad hour, day, week or more that you can flick through and find something that I experienced and something that I did to help you get through.

I know you can do it. I did.

Rosie

THE THINGS THAT GOT ME HERE TODAY

I found myself and never let go.
I faced my fear of losing us to find myself
Music, music and more music kept me sane. (See our music list there may be some tracks there to help you.)
I used visualisations: The Demon, the Bath of Despair
I closed my eyes and breathed
I gave myself space from the situation
I listened to everyone including Danny.
I gave myself permission to do what I needed to do.
I didn't look to Danny to fix me, but he contributed to it without me realising it.
I never allowed myself to be a victim
I never let bitterness overwhelm me
I learnt about acceptance, and all that it entails.
I understood; That Danny was afraid.
I reflected on myself and my own actions.
I saw all the small things that life sent my way.
I wrote that journal and I still write a journal today.
I stopped believing in fairy tales and started living real life

BLOG POSTS

I have included in this section just some posts from my blog that I think some may find useful, they basically summarise the main things you will go through.

Questions, Questions, Questions but the questions I asked myself were the most important of all.

When Infidelity strikes then your life becomes a life full of questions:

Why? Why did they do it? Why did they not tell me? Why did they lie? Why are they still lying to me? Why don't they understand the pain I am in? Why, why. why why…..

Why did I do it? Why did I lie? Why did I risk everything I have? Why didn't I think? Why are they still bringing it up? Why are they still crying? Why are we still talking about this? Why won't it just go away?

How? How could they do this to me? How could they do this us, our family? How could they sleep with another person? How could they have been attracted to her/him? How long was the affair going on for? How could I have not seen it? How long will this pain go on for? How long before I get back to normal? In fact 'how Long' could have a section all of its own. Followed by the

How Will? How will I ever live with the knowledge of this? How will I live without them? How many times did they meet? How many times did they have sex? How many times did they call each other? How, how, how, how, how....

How could I have done it to her/him? How could I have thought that I was better there? How could I have lied to them so many times? How could I not think about my family? How could I have done that, when I loved my wife/husband so much?

What? What were they thinking? What were they doing when we were out with them? What did they talk about? What were they unhappy with? What if they contact them again? What if they are still lying to me? What if I cannot move on? What if they do it again? What, what, what, what ......

What was I thinking? What can I do to make it better? What can I do to stop them crying?

Will? Will they come back? Will they stop? Will they be sorry? Will it be alright? Will it get better? Will the pain go away? Will a day come when I stop thinking about it? Will, will, will, will, will ....

Will I be able to go back? Will they have me back? Will they forgive me? Will I be able to make it better? Will we recover?

How? Where? Why? What? Do? When? Are ....

The questions just go on and on.

From the betrayed's point of view we question ourselves about what we really saw, what we really knew, struggle to admit that we have in fact lied to ourselves. That is a hard one, because in most cases we have.

We ask ourselves if we ever really knew this person at all. Was it all just crap, just an illusion that we didn't see through? Was our life together just one big lie? God knows, whilst Danny was gone for those twenty one days I imagined that he was in fact gay, that he had illegitimate children, that he was having an affair with a man at work.

Even now I rarely look at our wedding photos, even though I know that in fact what we had at that moment in time was real. Because what happened destroyed it all and I couldn't believe that it was real for a long time; so once we made new memories I looked at those instead. In fact when I look at our wedding photos I feel pity for the woman standing there, because I know the heartbreak and pain that is going to come her way.

Then we move on to the **'should I stay? Or should I go?'** questions. Or if the betrayer has already left we ask 'could we have them back? Would we want them back? Did I really mean so little to them? Am I worthless?

I came out fighting, but not everyone can.

If they return there is **the interrogation stage:** trying to make sense of something that doesn't make sense (not then anyway, for some it never does). We ask them the same questions over and over again; and it doesn't matter what answer they give us we don't believe them. Eventually Danny told me what he thought I wanted to hear, and I still didn't believe him. It was only when I found myself and got stronger that I realised that I just didn't care anymore: what had happened had happened and all the answers in the world were not going to change it.

I am going to share with you now the questions that were the most important to me; they were the questions that I asked myself often. As you know I kept a journal, and that got me and us to where we are today. But when you write a journal it is different to even writing a blog, because you do not have to even consider in the back of your mind what your reader will think, because the reader is you; if you lie in your journal, or cut a corner, the only person that you are lying to is you. Here are the questions that I asked myself that helped me get to where I am today: **Have I lied to myself: Yes.**

When I look back I had a gut feeling for a long time that something was going on. I ALWAYS look back to the night that Danny brought me home from their house and then went back there; the night that I walked around the house talking to the dog and calling Danny a cunt.

Really I was calling myself it: because deep inside I knew that I was not confronting the reality of what was in front of my nose.

Have I admitted that to myself now? Yes. By doing that I knew that the anger that I felt was actually fifty per cent directed at me; and by recognising that I used it as a tool to find myself again and NEVER lied to myself again.

Did I listen to Danny in the past when he tried to tell me that he never thought he would keep me?

No. I thought that because I knew that I loved him that he must know that I loved him and he must feel secure; that if he didn't it was his problem.

Have I learnt from that? Yes.

I have learnt that just because I am a confident person not everyone is. I have also learnt that some people who are not confident turn on the confident people and set out to destroy them; and over the time I have learnt (even since moving here to France) to spot those people and steer away or confront them as is necessary.

Should I have listened to Danny then: Yes.

Do I really need to know how many times they had sex? No.

Is me knowing how many times they had sex, kissed, met, talked about me, going to make any difference to my decision making? No. Danny had sex, kissed, met with someone else, lived with someone else, and talked about me with someone else. Knowing how many times was not going to make any difference to my decision.

The way Danny behaved when he came back was the only thing that was going to affect my decision. I think that we get caught up in the semantics because we have been lied to before and now we have to know EVERYTHING! **How will we ever know everything?** All I need to really know was that he did it, & why he did it (and to be honest I never really found out why from Danny. I worked some of the reasons why on my own because even today Danny cannot answer that question. I also needed to know he was sorry and I needed him to show he was sorry in his actions because all of those things were so important in enabling me to stay.

What am I going to achieve?

A question I had to ask myself honestly often when I was thinking about going over phone records again, or being a bitch again, or considering walking away from it all. Going over the phone records was not going to make a difference to whether I stayed or went. I did go over the phone records, often, and then one day I asked myself this question: 'What am I going to achieve by doing this?' The answer was nothing! Only I could make the decision to stay or go based on the actions of the person there with me then.

Being a bitch always led me to ask myself why I was there and what I was doing –In truth being a bitch never made me feel better, it made me feel powerful at times, but only so that I could regain strength on the back of making Danny pay. Over time I had to ask whether that was something that I still wanted to do, and if that was how I wanted to live my life. The answer to that was no.

When I thought about walking away and asked myself this question the inevitable voice in my head told me I would be happier, but I had learnt early not to listen to that demon, and I would look at all the things I would lose, and all the things I would gain and I knew that I had a lot more to lose than to gain; because Danny was so contrite.

This is a question I still ask myself often today: Everything is cause and effect, everything we do is for a reason and everything we do has consequences. This might be a good one for people who are considering having an affair perhaps they should ask themselves: **What am I going to achieve?**

Am I happy? How often do I rate my happiness in my journal? I can only speak for me when I say if I was looking back to when we were two years in and if Danny was not contrite and I was not happy then this would have been a factor to whether I stayed or went. I do believe you only have one life.

What are the positives in my life? I list these often in my journal, it is so easy to just see the negatives.

So those are the questions that I ask myself to keep myself on track. Writing this blog I find now myself in a position where people ask me these questions:

How long does the pain last? I asked myself numerous times. The answer is as long as you let it.

If the person who betrayed has come back is truly contrite and wants to make it work then it is up to you whether you want to work with that or not. Perhaps you need to ask why you are there and what you are looking to achieve and then go with the answer....I did, I wanted to stay for the life we had built together, for the laughter we had with each other, for Ethan, to see if we could make it work, to make sure that if I walked away I would know that it was the right decision because I had tried.

If the person who has betrayed is not truly contrite, are the same person, don't seem to have learned, are putting it all back on you then if it were me I would be asking myself why I was there, what I was looking to achieve, did I love myself and was I happy. The answers to those questions would have given me the answer with regard to where my life needed to go. I wasn't in this position but I think that the posts I write would tell you what the outcome for me would have been. Only you can decide. All I would say is don't lie to yourself anymore. Don't lose yourself.

When do you stop thinking about it? This will depend on when do you want to? When do you stop picking? When do YOU decide that you are sick of the crap in your life and you are leaving it behind? In all honesty I finish my book with a journal entry from 2012. There are no time limits, the counsellor told me six months and I held on to that like a limpet. It will depend on whether things keep coming back to bite you on the arse, and so many other things beside. But what I do know is that you will stop thinking about it when you make the conscious decision not to let it dominate your life anymore. In whatever way you do it.

Should I trust them? My answer to that is that trust has to be earned; and I truly believe that takes years. In addition you have to trust yourself to listen to your gut because that tie in with whether you will allow yourself to be vulnerable again. So trust is not just about them.

It might help to just keep these questions in your mind:

Why am I here?
Have I lied to myself?
Am I lying to myself?
Am I listening?
What am I going to achieve from doing that?
Do I need to know?
What am I going to do with that information?
What can I do to change things?
Am I respecting myself right now?
Have I found myself again?
What are the positives in my life?
Am I happy?
Why am I here? (Again)
Rosie

Fear holds your hand, until one day …..

As I have been busy pulling my book together, and corresponding with other people who are in the painful place that I found myself all those years ago, I have been reading about my own fear then, and others have shared their fears with me from what they are going through now. I never really realised just how much a part fear plays in this whole infidelity sideshow; or how important it is to face that fear if you really want to survive. So I thought that it might help others if I shared my timeframe of fear with you. Because my fear is behind me now:

But before I start with my 'timeframe of fear' let's start with Danny and his fear; because let's be honest this is where it all started:

Danny was afraid that I was too good for him. He was afraid that one day I would wake up and wonder what the hell I was doing with him; he was afraid that he would come home from work one day and I would be gone. That voice in his head told him that he was not worthy, told him he was not good enough and every time he listened to it, his fear got bigger.

So all it took then was for a narc to arrive and play on all that fear and bingo! Danny went with the fear and the narc!

If you had asked me then I would not have realised at the start of our relationship that I had any fear. Where Danny and his love were concerned I was confident in that love. I was also a confident person who was confident in the love she had for her husband. (I was not wrong, Danny did love me then, as much as he loves me now. Often having an affair has nothing to do with love and everything to do with fear.)

But as the clouds started to form on the horizon of our happy life I started to fear that what I thought I had was perhaps at risk.

Then I was gaslighted, and my confidence in what I had diminished as the gaslighting took hold.

My fear then became very real and damaging to me: I was afraid that my marriage was under threat; I was afraid that I was imagining things; I was afraid of my image: I no longer felt confident in the way I looked. I was afraid that my husband did not love me anymore. I was afraid I was losing my mind. I can remember so clearly when I got a lamp from the side of my bed to inspect my bed for blond hairs. I can remember the fear that I was not listening to myself: because I wasn't.

In fact at that time I became really ill, looking back I had a series of chest infections and they thought, as 'The War' loomed on the horizon, that I had pneumonia at one point. I know now that this was the impact of the lying, and the gaslighting, and the fear.

When 'The War' broke out I was afraid of losing my house, not being able to put a roof over my son's head, and not being able to pay my bills. I know now they were things that could be resolved if you put your mind to them.

But more than that I thought at the time that the biggest fear was how I had made a fool of myself: I had let them lie to me, I had allowed them to make a fool of me; I had let them gaslight me and I had lost myself.

I was so afraid that I had lost the ability to see what was in front of me. I was afraid that everyone was laughing at me because (as I have said) 'how had he turned our life upside down for a woman who had made a play for nearly every other person's husband that we knew. Why did it have to be my husband who had fell for it?'

I feared other people's pity.

I feared being on my own and back out in the world of singletons. In fact that terrified me. I feared losing control: which was why I got on my stepper every day sometimes two or three times a day. That is why food would turn to cardboard in my mouth, because the thinner I got the more I felt that I had control over something; it was a dangerous place to be.

I feared that all the people who had thought that I should not marry Danny (they thought I was 'too good' for him whatever that fucking means!), who tried to persuade me not to; would now be able to say 'we told you so.'

But I got stronger in those twenty one days that Danny was away. I faced some of the fears: I used my anger and rage to do that and I turned the anger and rage back on the fear: I went back to work, got more hours at work, made myself do what I had to do: every day; I pulled on all the strength I had not to be defeated; I did not play the games they all played; I rose above it and I did not lose my integrity. ('No matter what they take from me they can't take away my dignity')

By doing this I knew that I could keep the house, put a roof over Ethan's head, make ends meet. By maintaining a dignified silence I knew that I was better than all the other players in the game; and that gave me confidence. So when the fear told me what a silly cow I had been I could tell it to 'fuck off', and let go of its hand.

As the time went on I cried because by the third week of Danny being with 'her', I knew that my off button was getting ready to switch. I was exhausted from it all and wanted to move forward. I had been engaged before, I had been married before, and in both cases as the time wore on, and their behaviour continued, I switched off. It was not what I wanted so I switched off. I can remember even today crying to the man I was engaged to: saying that I loved him so much, but that I knew that one day that love would just switch off because I was not happy. It did, and I was the one who eventually called time. I knew this was happening with Danny, and I was so afraid of that.

But then Danny came back, and as a result so did my fears: I feared that he would choose her over me. When he actually returned home I feared he would go back to her. When we went to the house to collect his stuff I feared he would not come back with me.

I feared that he was talking to 'her' again, laughing at me.

Then I feared that everyone was talking about the 'silly bitch that had her husband back.' When we went to that pub and Danny played the arsehole with the barmaids I feared losing myself again.

I was afraid about what Danny had told the counsellor. I was afraid that people pitied me: the poor cow whose husband went off with that old slapper.

I was afraid that they saw me as weak. In fact only this week my sister and I were talking about this blog and my book and she reminded me that I asked her if she thought any less of me for having Danny back. I had totally forgotten that conversation.

But that all made me angry: why should I feel this way because of something that Danny had done? I had proved in those days when he was away that I could survive without him, and that meant that I stopped fearing being on my own; so yet again I let that fear go.

Then it started to change: I started to accept that what we had was gone, and I feared that I would not stay. As I got stronger and stronger and achieved more and more promotions, got thinner, I got fitter, I found myself. I feared that I was closing the door on Danny and I; and at that time I did not even know if I liked what we had in the first place. In fact looking back now, and reading my journals right through until 2012, it was the biggest thing I feared: that one day I would walk away. I stayed, but it was Danny who kept me here.

I feared that Danny was lying to me; this was all led by the fact that he had lied to me before and thereby if he was lying to me again it meant that I would be letting him lie to me again: which meant I would be lying to myself again and then I would be lost.

That terrified me more than anything because as I have always and will always say: if you don't have yourself you have nothing. So I asked the never ending questions trying to catch him out on a lie and to prove to myself that I was not allowing him to lie to me again. I checked his phone, and phone records, where he had been, his texts, until in the end I was driving myself insane.

I was afraid to get in my car every night because I knew that the demon from my head would be waiting for me to tell me about all the things that I feared: Danny did make a fool of me; I let him; of how they laughed at me, how people pitied me. That is what the demon was: a manifestation of every fear I had.

As Danny worked harder and harder to keep me, I was afraid that I would leave him in the end. I was afraid that I could not live with the fact that he had an affair; afraid of having that knowledge all my life. As I asked myself often 'how could I live with that?' And in the end I was afraid (ironically) of throwing away something that I knew was real, and breaking Danny's heart.

Over time I learned that the only person that you truly have in life is you. No matter how much you love someone, no matter what you have, the only person you have from beginning to end is you. So many people are afraid of that, when in fact I believe they should embrace it.

Having this knowledge, and knowing that it was not something to fear, but in fact freedom, gave me the strength to 'tip people bollocks' with regard to what they thought. It was my life, it was my choices. I let that fear go.

I faced the fear of Danny lying to me again by knowing that if he did I would walk away. For me I was worth more than that, I had found myself and was never letting her go again. It was up to Danny to make the decision re any more lies, he was safe in the knowledge that I would leave. At that point it enabled me to put the fear of him lying behind me: it was his problem not mine, but as time wore on and Danny continued to work hard to keep me (he never gave up) I realised that the lies of the past were nothing to fear because actually all you have is the here and now.

So here is my advice: Write down (so you cannot lie to yourself) all the things you fear. Then look at how many of them are linked to what others think. Do other people live your life? As I said I am lucky I have the ability to 'tip people bollocks!'

Ask yourself how many of your fears are generated by your partner; honestly generated by your partner not by your own head; that way you can use that knowledge to tell the voice in your head to fuck off, and thereby letting another fear go.

If you fear so much, ask yourself why. If it is because of the actions of someone else (in the here and now) then ask yourself what you can do to stop those fears.

Rosie

Boundaries

When infidelity is discussed and people ask for advice the advice given is to set your boundaries and stick to them. But people are so often confused by that advice.

Firstly when you find out that the person who you have built a life with has had an affair, or had numerous encounters with others, and lied to you and gas lighted you and turned you whole world upside down you don't know your arse from your head. You don't know the person that you are, you don't know the person that you were, so how the hell can you set boundaries when you don't even know how to breathe at times?

Then there is the issue of why should you have to set boundaries? They have come back, they have said they are sorry; everything can just go back to normal; can't it? Not for me it couldn't; there was no normal, the normal I knew had gone and the normal I knew was just a lie anyway.

Often people are afraid to set boundaries, they don't want to drive the person away, they are afraid (back to good old fear again!)

So I thought that I would share with you the boundaries that I set at the beginning of our recovery; and then reset and re-evaluated as each year passed. Some changed, I changed them, and some still remain today. I can never tell anyone what to do, it is your relationship and whilst so many things are the same, when an affair takes place so many things are also different. I hope that by sharing with you what I did it will resonate and help others to understand their needs and set their own boundaries.

Firstly when Danny was gone, when he laughed at me, when he told me he didn't love me and so much more I realised that I was alone. The only person that I could ever rely on in life was me, because I was the only person who was always going to be with me all my life, and I used that to make myself stronger. I didn't realise it at the time but this was actually my first boundary: I became stronger and I never let that go. Despite Danny returning, despite him wanting everything to go back to 'normal' I was not the person that he left; I was stronger and that was a boundary: don't ask me go lose my strength because the answer will be no.

Then when Danny returned my two conditions were:

He had to get rid of his phone, this was an absolute deal breaker: keep the phone lose me, lose the phone and you may be in with a chance.

The other was that he had to step up to the plate: he had to stop being insecure (I know a really hard one given that he was in such a vulnerable place) and he had to have the balls to fight for me; irrespective of how I was towards him. He had broken our relationship and it was his responsibility to fix it at the beginning. This meant that I was not going to pussyfoot around him; if he did something that pissed me off I told him; if I was dying inside I told him; he had done this to me and he had to understand that and be brave enough to face the consequences.

No contact really goes without saying. If Danny had contacted 'her', spoken to 'her' out of his own volition then I was gone. When we left the house he had shared with 'her' and 'she' continually messaged him Danny had refused to tell her to 'fuck off'. I made him get out of the car and told him to walk back to her. I was not going to fight for him; he was the one who had to fight for me.

Total transparency in the here and now: there were some times that 'she' rang Danny's depot and he answered the phone; if he had not told me that 'she' had rung, even if he hadn't spoken to 'her' then I would have took that mortgage and bought him out of the house and left. If he hadn't told me when he had picked up the phone and had to speak to 'her' then I would have left.

I had started to find myself you see and I could not and would not feel as if I didn't like myself ever again. I would never allow myself to be weakened again.

When I looked at myself in the mirror at the pub we visited and I saw how vulnerable I was then I knew that I had to make it that I wasn't vulnerable any more. If Danny made me feel vulnerable then I told him and I did all the things I had to do to ensure that I was safe and that Ethan was safe: I went back to work full time, got on my stepper, lost weight, went for walks on my own. If at any time Danny commented on any of these things or commented that I had not discussed them with him, or intimated that I should have consulted him about my plans then I would tell him that he had put me in a vulnerable position and I didn't have to ask his permission to do things that would make me less vulnerable: he left me on my own and always had to feel safe on my own. That was a boundary: don't ever try and gas light me again into being in a vulnerable position.

Showing his allegiance to me with regard to the other people who had played games during 'The War' was also a boundary. If Danny's allegiance was not with me then why would I stay with him? He always did.

For me there would be no second chance. I can honestly tell you that I have such a strong personality that it virtually killed me to stay. Dealing with this was so much harder than anything I had ever dealt with in my life; including the death of my parents. I was never going to put myself through it again. If Danny cheated (yes I hate that word but seems appropriate here) again then I would have walked away. I just could not stay.

Allowing me access to his telephone records, and his phone: no passwords on the phone that I didn't know (we are still like that with each other today) was a boundary.

Understanding why I would check his phone records and not trying to emotionally blackmail me into shutting up was a boundary. Danny had created this situation and now he had to deal with it and make it better by understanding.

Not being defensive towards me was another boundary. If he was defensive about anything, or made me feel as if I was wrong then I would shut down and shut him out. My journal helped me with that and as a result Danny came to fear my journal.

And these were only the boundaries at the beginning. As the years wore on the boundaries would change and evolve; and in fairness to Danny he changed and evolved with them; and in fairness to me over time Danny set boundaries and I understood and respected them.

Rosie

If you don't have yourself you have nothing

Through my whole journey of recovery after Danny betrayed me, I held onto myself. I say often in this blog and also in my soon to be published book:

'If you don't have yourself you have nothing.'

I still live my life with that ringing in my ears today. I will always have myself. No matter how much I love Danny, no matter how much we have come through, I will hold onto myself and I will never let her go.

A lot of people ask me what I mean by that; they ask me how do they find themselves? I can only tell you what I did:

One of the first things that I did was be honest with myself in recognising that I had lost myself somewhere along the way.

When infidelity hit the fan in our relationship it hit home to me just how much I had lost myself: I was overweight, I no longer trained, I didn't want to pursue any career that would interfere with my time with Danny. So when he left I was in a very, very vulnerable position: on a low income, overweight, had to a degree lost my own identity. The Rosie of the past, before Danny, would never have allowed herself to be gas lighted or lied to in the way I had been. She would have confronted the situation head on. But because I had lost myself in our relationship I didn't do that, I allowed a web of lies to be spun around me.

Before I met Danny I had a good career and I also taught aerobics and keep fit six times a week. But somewhere along the line I lost that Rosie. Not all of it was as a result of my relationship with Danny: my mum had died and my dad had nine strokes and all of these incidents had happened over a six month period. So I gave up my career because I realised that I never seemed to spend any time with Ethan; and, as death tends to do, I recognised that life really was too short and things had to change.

Then I met Danny: this man who was so gentle and kind, this man who promised that he would take care of me; and I was vulnerable, and tired of fighting all the time, so I let him. I put all of myself into our relationship until eventually I gave up aerobics because it took me away from Danny too much. I worked part time and renovated our house and supported Danny in his career; I wanted to, I loved Danny; I believed that he was never going to hurt me. Here was a person who was always there to love, support and protect me. And then the crap hit the fan, and I found myself in a position where I didn't like my image, I didn't earn enough and I didn't even know who I was anymore.

I will tell you who I am: a person with an incredibly strong personality who listened to so many people who told her she was too loud, and too arsy, and too defensive. People who told her that other people didn't like her, so much so that I lost myself along the way. But as I say now at this moment I have learned that my personality is the essence of me and I learnt that as a result of this journey that I went through.

So the first thing I did when the infidelity circus came to town was I got angry; and I used that anger as a form of strength. I used my love for Ethan, and the fact that I had to make sure that he was alright and I was able to care for him, and I came out fighting.

I didn't just get angry I used that anger as a form of fuel for my inner power: I became quiet, I realised that I had more dignity in my little finger than all the other characters in the charade I had been caught up in, and I held on to it: I did not get sucked into their daytime soap opera, I rose above it.

I played the game: I knew that putting divorce proceedings into play would give Danny the kick up the arse that he needed to think about what he was doing.

When Danny came back I nearly (yes I nearly did) slip back into my old ways where he was concerned. Oh yes I pulled her partner off Danny when he was kicking shit out of him, and yes I would have gone to Social Services if he had not fucked off; and yes I am ashamed to say I took great enjoyment in punching shit out of 'her' when she attacked me. But afterwards I regretted it because it meant that 'she' had, for a moment, pulled me into the soap opera and I had already found myself enough to know that I was too good to be there.

But the biggest turning point for me was when I caught sight of the woman in the mirror, the woman who had been crying. At the time Danny, with his new found confidence, was lauding it up with the barmaids of the pub we were in. It was when that woman in the mirror looked at me that I knew that I was stronger than all of this. I knew that I would be strong enough to leave if I wanted to and I knew that I would survive. Yes I was afraid, and would be for a long time to come (but for different reasons) but I was more afraid of going backwards to the Rosie I had been before: the one who was dependent on Danny. Even at that early stage I knew that I could never go back to that again.

From that point on I set boundaries on what I wanted in my life and at the beginning my boundaries were the most important thing; I didn't care about Danny's. Not at the very beginning.

I ensured that I stayed fit; over the years as I became comfortable in my relationship, and my career was full on I stopped doing that sadly, and now age has caught up with me and arthritis. But at that time I needed to do that, I needed to be the fit person that I used to be before Danny.

I went back to work full-time, and anyone reading my story will know that my career took off. I made sure that I always looked good, for me. But it was the small things that I did that made all the difference: I would leave Danny indoors and go and sit on the beach, alone with my thoughts. I would get on my bike and go for bike rides along the seafront. I went to pubs on my own and sat in their gardens with a good book and a glass of wine. I didn't care if people were looking at me or questioning a that I was a woman on her own in the pub.

I spent time with friends, something I never did before 'The War'. I didn't engage again with the people who had not supported me, but I actively encouraged Danny to engage with them; if he chose not to I didn't pursue it because that was his decision and he was the one who had to live with it.

I abdicated the responsibility of keeping everyone happy for the sake of it.

I told people what had happened: that way it could never crawl out of the woodwork and bite me on the arse. I had nothing to be ashamed of and nothing to be pitied for either: I had found myself.

If I liked something or wanted to do something and Danny didn't I no longer 'went with the flow': I continued to do what I liked and like what I liked, and if Danny wanted to come along with it he could, and if he didn't then he didn't. I didn't ask him more than once.

Before 'The War' if Danny said he didn't want something or like something then I would change it, I would adapt. After 'The War' I would simply say 'don't you? I do'. I no longer needed to be in agreement with Danny all the time. I was my own person, and I still am today.

I no longer ran things past Danny (I probably do more today, not for his approval but out of courtesy); back then, if he didn't approve I would still do it anyway. I am me, not an extension of someone else; and Danny is Danny and I don't expect or want him to be an extension of me; I want him to be himself.

But more than anything I kept a journal; and in that journal I was honest with myself about myself. If you lie when you write in a journal the only person you are lying to is yourself. Many people fear what they will write and I understand why; especially when your life has been destroyed; and yet here you are trying to rebuild it with the person that destroyed it. (We are back to fear again.) I learnt to face that fear; to not be afraid that we may not survive, to understand that may be the best thing. But I also learnt to face the fear of staying, and to face the biggest fear of all: being vulnerable again.

Now all these years later I know that despite having myself I do have to allow a degree of vulnerability because I believe that goes hand in hand with being in love. Only this time I am vulnerable but I am not afraid. I have myself ....

Rosie

The songs that saved us:

Just Say Just Say	Diana Ross and Marvin Gaye
What goes around comes around.	Justin Timberlake
Hit em up style	Blu Cantrell
Heartlight	Neil Diamond
How Many Times How Many Lies	Pussycat Dolls
Back in God's Hands	Nelly Furtado
I don't need a Man	Pussycat Dolls
Out of Reach	Gabrielle
I will survive	Chantay Savage
Greatest Love of All	George Benson
Always A Woman	Billy Joel
Monster	Carlos Santana
Still	Commodores
Cuts both ways	Gloria Estefan
A House is Not a Home	Luther Vandross
You are everything	Diana Ross and Marvin Gaye
Sober	Pink
Love on the Rocks	Neil Diamond
I'd Rather	Luther Vandross
How Can You Mend a Broken Heart	Michael Buble
Stronger	Sugababes
You're a part of me	Diana Ross and Marvin Gaye
Shape of my Heart	Sugababes
In Your Eyes	George Benson
Crazy Love	Luther Vandross
Losing My Way	Justin Timberlake
Masquerade	George Benson
Body and Soul	Anita Baker
You Were Meant for Me	Donny Hathaway

Oh No	The Commodores
The Unreachable Star	Luther Vandross
Broken Wings	James Morrison and Nelly Furtado
Love Me	The Bee Gees
Wish I Didn't Miss You	Angie Stone
Goodbye My Lover	James Blunt
Always Tomorrow	Gloria Estefan
Lost	Michael Buble
Wishing On A Star	Rose Royce
The Perfect Year	Dina Carrolle
Another Song	Justin Timberlake
Coming Out of the Dark	Gloria Estafan
Stop Look Listen To Your Heart	Diana Ross & Marvin Gaye
Just To Be Close To You	The Commodores
Hurt	The Manhattans
The Closer I Get to You	Luther Vandross and Beyonce
Te Busque	Nelly Furtado
Hello again	Neil Diamond
September Morn	Neil Diamond
Somebody's Gotta Win	The Controllers
Need Somebody	Kings of Leon
Love me	The Bee Gees
Everything must change	George Benson
Cry Me A River	Justin Timberlake
Prayer for the dying	Seal
The Closer I get to you	Luther Vandross and Beyonce
Falling to pieces	The Script
Hey Girl	George Benson